the
wealthy
freelancer

Steve Slaunwhite, Pete Savage, and Ed Gandia

ALPHA

A member of Penguin Group (USA) Inc.

ALPHA BOOKS

Published by the Penguin Group

Penguin Group (USA) Inc., 375 Hudson Street, New York, New York 10014, USA

Penguin Group (Canada), 90 Eglinton Avenue East, Suite 700, Toronto, Ontario M4P 2Y3, Canada (a division of Pearson Penguin Canada Inc.)

Penguin Books Ltd., 80 Strand, London WC2R 0RL, England

Penguin Ireland, 25 St. Stephen's Green, Dublin 2, Ireland (a division of Penguin Books Ltd.)

Penguin Group (Australia), 250 Camberwell Road, Camberwell, Victoria 3124, Australia (a division of Pearson Australia Group Pty. Ltd.)

Penguin Books India Pvt. Ltd., 11 Community Centre, Panchsheel Park, New Delhi— 110 017, India

Penguin Group (NZ), 67 Apollo Drive, Rosedale, North Shore, Auckland 1311, New Zealand (a division of Pearson New Zealand Ltd.)

Penguin Books (South Africa) (Pty.) Ltd., 24 Sturdee Avenue, Rosebank, Johannesburg 2196, South Africa

Penguin Books Ltd., Registered Offices: 80 Strand, London WC2R 0RL, England

International Standard Book Number: 978-1-59257-967-9
Library of Congress Catalog Card Number: 2009934670

12   11   10   8   7   6   5   4   3   2   1

Interpretation of the printing code: The rightmost number of the first series of numbers is the year of the book's printing; the rightmost number of the second series of numbers is the number of the book's printing. For example, a printing code of 10-1 shows that the first printing occurred in 2010.

Printed in the United States of America

Note: This publication contains the opinions and ideas of its authors. It is intended to provide helpful and informative material on the subject matter covered. It is sold with the understanding that the authors and publisher are not engaged in rendering professional services in the book. If the reader requires personal assistance or advice, a competent professional should be consulted.

The authors and publisher specifically disclaim any responsibility for any liability, loss, or risk, personal or otherwise, which is incurred as a consequence, directly or indirectly, of the use and application of any of the contents of this book.

Trademarks: All terms mentioned in this book that are known to be or are suspected of being trademarks or service marks have been appropriately capitalized. Alpha Books and Penguin Group (USA) Inc. cannot attest to the accuracy of this information. Use of a term in this book should not be regarded as affecting the validity of any trademark or service mark.

Most Alpha books are available at special quantity discounts for bulk purchases for sales promotions, premiums, fund-raising, or educational use. Special books, or book excerpts, can also be created to fit specific needs.

For details, write: Special Markets, Alpha Books, 375 Hudson Street, New York, NY 10014.

*To my dad, a successfully self-employed professional
for more than 40 years. —Steve*

*To my wife Maggie, who always believed.
She just always believed. —Pete*

*To my son Andrew, whose love, kindness, enthusiasm,
and vivid imagination inspire me every day. I love you! —Ed*

Contents

Introduction

"Work," as we've come to understand it, is morphing before our very eyes. As we write this, the global economy is struggling to recover from the worst financial downturn in a generation. Layoffs are mounting at a rapid pace. And after cutting staff to the bone, businesses everywhere are scrambling to source talent for critical projects. Rather than reverting to the typical "hire and fire" cycle, many of these businesses are turning to freelance professionals.

The reason is simple: the freelance model works. Companies like it because it allows them to get work done without the salary, training, and benefits expenses that come with hiring. And it provides the flexibility to source specific talent for any project quickly, on an as-needed basis.

Meanwhile, as companies change their hiring strategies, employees' attitudes toward their careers are changing, too. There's a kind of widespread "awakening" afoot (maybe you're experiencing it yourself) as more and more people begin to question the *meaning* of work, its role in our lives, and whether or not the corporate grind is really worth it. Millions of professionals—whether they've been ousted from their jobs or finally grown tired of long commutes, 60-hour workweeks, childish office politics, and rationed vacation time—are scratching their heads and thinking, "There has *got* to be a better way!" In their quest for answers, thousands are discovering freelancing as a breath of fresh air and the beginning of a new, better way to make a living.

Not surprisingly, mainstream media is quickly catching on. Once a somewhat obscure career path, freelancing is now getting regular attention in or on *The Wall Street Journal, The New York Times, BusinessWeek,* CNN, Fox News, and many other media outlets.

As we enter what the three of us believe is a true renaissance in self-employment, what's missing is a practical guide for creating a freelance business that delivers a great income and a flexible, balanced, and fulfilling lifestyle. Lots of information already exists on the *mechanics* of launching a solo career, and plenty has been written about how to run the day-to-day aspects of a freelance business. But much of that advice follows a starving-artist mindset, with running themes of scarcity and day-to-day survival rather than positive expectations, continuous improvement in every area of your freelance business, and outright embracing of the possibilities that lie ahead.

That's where this book comes in.

If you've been freelancing a while and doing just "okay," the ideas we share with you in the following pages show you how to take things to the next level—for good—and create the kind of success you've only dreamt about. Or if you haven't yet launched your freelance business, this book helps you set out on the right path. Either way, you're about to discover dozens of *proven* ideas that can dramatically accelerate your progress and keep you from making costly mistakes.

Here's what you *won't* find in this book: hype. You won't find promises of afternoons spent napping on tropical beaches, working on the occasional project, and raking in enough dough each day to keep the margaritas coming endlessly. Achieving and sustaining freelance success, like any worthwhile endeavor, requires solid, honest effort. At times, it's hard work. But it doesn't have to be *grueling* work. And with this book as your guide, it won't be.

Each of us has built our own successful freelance business, completely from scratch. But we are not superheroes. We're people just like you. We each had a dream of creating a freelance business that would enable us to have the clients, projects, income, and lifestyle we wanted. Over time, we figured out how to make that happen, and now we're sharing our secrets.

As you read, keep an open mind. Many of the concepts you come across will be new to you. Resolve to take action on the tips, strategies, and ideas in this book. If you do, *you will create the wealthy life you are striving for.*

And when you're ready for more, join the exciting conversation already going on at TheWealthyFreelancer.com.

Steve Slaunwhite
Pete Savage
Ed Gandia
August 2009

Acknowledgments

No one ever writes a book like this without the support of many people. We owe a big thank you to our agent, Bob Diforio, and also to Mike Sanders, Randy Ladenheim-Gil, Christy Wagner, and the entire team at Alpha Books for working so hard to help make this book a winner.

To our families, for their loving support and encouragement as we embarked on yet *another* time-intensive (yet exciting!) project.

A special thanks to our coaching clients, seminar attendees, readers, listeners, viewers, and others in the freelancing community who follow us. (We have a confession to make: we often learn more from you guys than you do from us!) Thanks for all your support.

Finally, we owe a debt of gratitude to the many freelance professionals who share their stories in these pages. Your successes prove that being a wealthy freelancer isn't just a lofty dream. It's an imminently achievable goal.

What Being a Wealthy Freelancer *Really* Means

Steve Slaunwhite, Ed Gandia, and Pete Savage

In the movie *Jerry Maguire*, Tom Cruise plays a recently fired, now-freelance sports agent whose success mantra becomes "Show me the money!" As an audience, we watch in hopeful expectation as Tom's character struggles to rebuild his client base and his life while ever-so-slowly realizing that money isn't everything. He discovers there are other ingredients to success—relationships, lifestyle, family—that are just as important and, in some cases, fundamentally more so. As a result, and in a bold move, Tom's character revaluates his once hard-driving approach to his career. The final scene where he is walking through the park hand in hand with his new wife and her son on a sunny weekday afternoon says it all. Being wealthy isn't just about the dollars you earn; it's about the life you build—and the kind of person you become in the process.

Think of the dreams you had when you first became a freelance professional. Or the dreams you have now if you're just starting out in this special type of self-employment. Chances are, that vivid image of your ideal life includes a lot more than just money.

For example, you may be …

- A stay-at-home mom who wants a successful freelance business that provides a good income *and* the flexibility to spend all the quality time you want with your kids.
- A burnt-out corporate manager who wants to break free from the cubicle and work at home doing something that's just as financially rewarding and more enjoyable.

- A long-time freelancer who is stuck in the cycle of low-paying projects and clients and wants to finally break free and take her business to a higher and wealthier level of success.

- An ambitious professional who wants his freelance practice to generate an executive-class income so he can provide his family the lifestyle they deserve.

- An accidental freelancer, unexpectedly cast off by her employer, who is now determined to make this "freelance thing" work for her so she never has to get a "real" job again.

- A professional who sees freelancing as a stepping-stone to something greater, such as the establishment of a larger consulting practice or creative services firm.

- A freelancer who wants to earn an income but also make a contribution, such as someone with a passion for helping charitable organizations attract donations and grants.

Most freelancers begin their self-employment journey with a dream. And in this book, you'll read about freelancers who are living theirs. We hope their stories inspire *you* to go after—and achieve—your own unique vision of a wealthy life.

However, we'd be remiss if we didn't prepare you for the journey ahead by mentioning a harsh reality that can trip you up. That is, as a freelancer, it's easy to lose sight of your dreams. Over the years, we've known hundreds of freelancers who started their businesses with the best of intentions and with a driving determination to manifest the rewarding, successful future they had envisioned for themselves. But somewhere along the way—in the midst of struggling to land clients, earn decent fees, achieve a sane work-life balance, create a steady cash flow, deal with tight deadlines, and more—their dreams faded and they began to wonder whether this "freelance thing" was really for them.

"One day I sat in front of the computer to work on a client project and just started to cry," one very successful freelancer told us. "I just didn't want to do it anymore." After taking a couple weeks off to revaluate things, she realized that she had lost focus on what her original vision was for her business. So she made some serious changes. And today she is one of the wealthiest freelancers we know, with a reputation that consistently attracts great clients to her doorstep and a flexible schedule that enables her to do what she hadn't been able to do before: spend more time with her son. She had forgotten her freelance dream. Her business and life changed when she re-acquired it and began to really *live* it!

Her definition of being a wealthy freelancer may not be the same as yours. But that's the point. Whether you're a writer, designer, copywriter, marketer, PR pro, illustrator, trainer, or any one of the dozens of other freelance professions, you have your own unique vision of what being a "wealthy freelancer" means. You have a dream. Hold on to it!

And never, *never* doubt that if you have the skills, talent, and knowledge that are valuable to potential clients—for example, if you're a fantastic web designer, a savvy copywriter, a dynamic corporate trainer, or a skilled publicity consultant—you can create a freelance business that provides you with the projects, clients, income, and lifestyle you want. You really can! You just need some simple strategies and good ideas to help turn your dream into reality. And that's what this book is all about.

Getting Good at the "Big Four"

People who are new to freelancing or struggling to build a successful freelance practice often make the false assumption that there's some mysterious secret or magic formula to really making it big. So before you go down that road, let's do a little dream analysis. No, not in the Freudian sense of the term. Instead, we're talking here about breaking your dream into four key areas so you can clearly see what you should be aiming for:

1. The *projects* you want

2. The *clients* you want

3. The *income* you want

4. The *lifestyle* you want

We call these the "big four" because each plays an incredibly important role in the success of a freelance business. In fact, this is how we sum up what it means to be a wealthy freelancer:

A wealthy freelancer is someone who consistently gets the projects, clients, income, and lifestyle he or she wants.

Simple, right? Now let's take a look at each of the big four in more detail.

The Projects You Want

Projects, of course, refer to the type of work you want to do as a freelance professional. For example, you may want to work on major marketing campaigns for gargantuan corporations … or grant proposals for small, striving charities … or cutting-edge logo designs for ambitious start-ups … or book ghostwriting for big-name celebrities. It's important to be as clear as you can about the projects you want to apply your skills and talents to each day. If you're not clear, you risk attracting projects just because they pay well or just because a client wants you to do them.

"I don't know how I fell into writing opt-in articles for business owners," a freelancer told us recently, "but I wish I could get out of it." The problem is, he's booked solid with that type of work, and it pays reasonably well. He has unintentionally created his own golden handcuffs, and now he can't find the key!

That's why having a clear definition of the kind of projects you want to handle is a good starting point on your journey.

The Clients You Want

Hand in hand with being choosy about projects is deciding what type of clients you want to work with.

If you want a rewarding freelance business, choose your clients wisely. Just two or three great clients you really enjoy working with can make each day of freelance work seem like an adventurous vacation. Conversely, just a couple difficult clients, or clients who just aren't a good fit for you, can make your life miserable. Every time their number flashes on your telephone, your heart will sink! Who needs that?

We know there's someone out there who's thinking, "Be choosy? Are you kidding me? Clients are tough to find. If I need the work, and their check is good, I'm taking the project!" Of course, good clients are a challenge to find. And there's no doubt you're going to have to take on a less-than-ideal client from time to time. But your goal should be to set things up so you can attract the right type of clients consistently, so you don't have to compromise. How do you do that? By following the client-attracting strategies in this book.

The Income You Want

How much money do you need or want to earn from your freelance activities? This is an area where many freelancers settle for far less than they deserve. We've seen professionals with exceptional track records in their fields accepting projects that pay, in some cases, little more than minimum wage. Not necessary! Let's set the record straight once and for all:

> As an accomplished freelancer, or even as a newly self-employed professional with solid training and experience, you can and should be earning at least as much, and even more, than your employed counterparts.

Here's a daring exercise: write down how much you think you can realistically make as a freelance professional, either per hour or per project. Then add 50 percent. Without even knowing what figures you wrote down, we can say confidently that the *higher* number is probably achievable.

Think of it this way: you have skills, talents, and knowledge that are vital to helping your clients solve their problems and achieve their goals. You deserve to be paid accordingly. That's why there are two secrets in this book devoted to pricing your services for success and being smart about how you manage that income (Secrets 7 and 12, respectively).

The Lifestyle You Want

Lifestyle. Isn't that the most important marker of a successfully self-employed professional? Yet strangely, it is often the first thing freelancers put on the back burner when things get tough or busy. Don't *you* make that mistake. Lifestyle is just as important an ingredient to being a wealthy freelancer as projects, clients, and income.

Freelance marketing coach Charlie Cook certainly understands this. As he frequently writes about on his website, MarketingForSuccess.com, being able to indulge in his passions for skiing, biking, and kayaking is just as important for his business as attracting clients and customers and making money.

So go ahead and schedule lunch with friends on Wednesdays, or adventurous vacations with your family, or walks around a lake on Thursday afternoons, or fun times with the kids every day of the week. Make those things as integral to your business as clients, projects, and money. Your success depends on it. And you'll find plenty of help in this book on making the lifestyle elements of your wealthy freelancer dreams a reality.

$ Success Story

Make Your Business Fit Your Lifestyle

One of the many benefits of freelancing is the ability to create a working environment better suited to your current or desired lifestyle. For Marina Martin, a freelance efficiency consultant (www. TheTypeAWay.com) who helps low-tech businesses use technology in order to save time and money, that's precisely what attracted her to strike out on her own. "I love to travel and enjoy living out of a suitcase," says Marina. "So I set up my business in a way that would allow me to travel as often as possible and do much of my work remotely. That meant pursuing clients in other states, something many professionals in my field aren't willing to do."

Marina not only goes out of her way to find out-of-town clients, she also does much of her work while taking extended trips. In 2008, she spent a total of 185 days away from home, including a two-month stint in Germany. According to Marina, this flexibility is possible because much of her work involves brainstorming and coming up with implementation plans for clients—activities that can be performed any time and from anywhere in the world. She is also diligent about grouping projects and tasks. "I can group four or five meetings back to back one week and then take off for Germany the following week. That pace works great for me!"

Write It Down; Make It Happen

We don't know where you're reading this book right now. It could be at your desk or on a plane or standing in a bookstore. But wherever you are, take a few moments now to write down what being a "wealthy freelancer" means to you. Don't be afraid to be ambitious here. Dream big! Fill your description with inspiring details.

One freelancer we know, a specialist in crafting product success stories for companies, actually wrote down, "I start each day by driving my kids to school. Then I drop by a favorite café with my laptop and work on a client project for a couple of hours. Then I go to my comfy home office and ...." She went on and on in wonderful detail, describing the type of projects she handles and the money she earns. She wrote that description several weeks *before* she actually hung her shingle as a freelancer.

That was four years ago. Can you guess what her life is like today? With just a few exceptions, her freelance life has unfolded exactly as she originally envisioned. As Henriette Anne Klauser says in her excellent book, *Write It Down, Make It Happen: Knowing What You Want and Getting It* (Touchstone, 2001), "Once you write down your goal, your brain will be working overtime to see you get it, and will alert you to the signs and signals that ... were there all along."

So really have fun with this writing exercise. (Actually, it's first and foremost a daydreaming assignment.) Using the following "Wealthy Freelancer Worksheet," describe your own unique vision of *you* as a wealthy freelancer. There's room for you to lay out your vision for each of the big four categories we just covered: *projects, clients, income,* and *lifestyle*.

Wealthy Freelancer Worksheet

The type of *projects* I want:

_____

_____

_____

_____

_____

_____

_____

The type of *clients* I want:

_____

_____

_____

_____

_____

_____

_____

The *income* I want to earn for my project work:

_____

_____

_____

_____

_____

_____

_____

The *lifestyle* I want for my freelance business:

_____

_____

_____

_____

_____

_____

_____

We can't stress enough how important it is to dream big. Don't hold back and try to rationalize or settle. Don't assume that a certain amount of money is too much to expect for the project work you do or that lofty lifestyle goals just aren't attainable. Like a child with crayons who draws pictures of sunny days and adventure and fun, create an optimistic vision that inspires you. When the going gets tough in your freelance practice, as it's bound to, the answers you wrote down on this worksheet will help motivate you to press on.

We suggest you keep your completed worksheet handy as you go through this book. When you come across a great idea, tip, or strategy you suspect will propel you closer to your freelance dream, make a note of that section. Then create a plan for putting that idea, tip, or strategy into action.

We don't, of course, know your answers to the "big four" questions. But we do know one thing for sure: having worked with hundreds of freelance professionals through our books, blog (TheWealthyFreelancer.com), articles, seminars, and coaching programs—and being working freelancers ourselves—we know that whatever you wrote down on that worksheet is probably achievable. And this book will show you how.

Take advantage of the great ideas in these pages and, in the not-too-distant future, you just might look back on that worksheet and smile, real-izing you've actually achieved the wealthy freelancing dream you originally envisioned.

How This Book Works

This is *not* a "how to start a freelance business" book. Although these pages are packed with great information to help you build a successful practice, this is really a "great ideas" book—*proven* ideas that will efficiently and predictably lead you down the road to freelance success! It's packed with tips, strategies, step-by-step instructions, advice, best practices, and inspiration for landing great clients, high-paying projects, the income you want, and an optimal work-life balance.

In fact, within the 12 secrets featured on the following pages, there are more than 50 great ideas and dozens of plans for putting them into action. Some of these will give you a quantum leap toward the success you want to achieve right away. For example, you'll learn how adding one short paragraph into your project proposals can double your chances of winning the work.

Imagine the immediate impact that will have on your business! Other great ideas in this book act like minor course corrections; you won't notice much of a change right away, but after a few weeks or months, your business will arrive at a completely different and more desirable destination.

Even if you have some experience freelancing, lots of the ideas you'll discover in these 12 secrets will be completely contrary to what you've been taught about freelancing. For example, did you know that going after fewer prospects may actually net you more and better-quality clients? Or that following up systematically with prospects who aren't ready to hire you today could help *double* your income while reducing your prospecting efforts by 30 to 50 percent? Or that striving to be the "best" freelancer in your field is almost always a losing strategy? Or that setting an hourly rate for your services may be the worst thing you could do? These are just some of the ideas and insights we'll be sharing with you in the following pages.

More Than 50 Great Ideas

This is a book you can refer to again and again throughout your freelance career because it covers all aspects of freelancing:

- Secrets 1, 4, 8, and 9 feature breakthrough strategies for setting goals, positioning your business for success, and increasing productivity.

- Secret 11 explains how to boost your income by taking advantage of alternate income streams.

- Secrets 2, 3, 4, 5, and 6 give you insights into attracting great clients and projects, more consistently and with less time and effort.

- Secrets 7 and 12 show you how to set the right price for your services, win more quotations and proposals, and establish a solid financial foundation for your freelance business.

- Secret 10 provides you with tips on how to achieve the perfect work-life balance so you can enjoy your life as much as you do your work.

- And at the back of the book, the appendix gives you "been there, done that" wisdom for dealing with the obstacles and opportunities you're bound to encounter on the road to wealthy freelancing.

Review the following chapters carefully. You can read them in order or jump back and forth throughout the book, letting your needs and interest guide you. Each chapter is self-contained and doesn't require you to have read the one before. Just be sure you read them all! You don't want to miss a thing.

As Einstein is famous for saying, "Nothing happens until something moves." So as we suggested earlier, make notes on those tips and strategies you want to use and then get moving!

Create Your Own Action Plan

Reading this book is a little like being in a chocolate shop. You'll want to try everything you see right away! But you'll get a lot more out of these tips and strategies if you take your time and implement them one by one. Start with what you think is the best idea that leaps off the page at you. Give it a chance to work and become part of your freelance business and life. Watch how it improves your ability to get the projects you want, from the clients you want, for the prices you want, with lots of time left over to enjoy the life you want. Then move on to the next idea.

Say, for example, that you identify nine ideas in this book that you're itching to put into action. If you try to do all nine at once, you'll quickly get overwhelmed and frustrated. Instead, create a simple "wealthy freelancer action plan" that strategically and realistically maps out your moves. Here's an example:

Wealthy Freelancer Action Plan

Jim Smith

Freelance Blog Designer and Consultant

Week 1: Revisit my goals and set new, bigger, and better ones!

Week 2: Develop my master fee schedule.

> *Weeks 3 to 6:* Assemble a list of 100 high-probability prospects.
>
> *Week 7:* Rework my quoting process.
>
> *Weeks 8 and 9:* Brainstorm a list of 5 alternative income-stream ideas.
>
> *Week 10:* Try the "50-Minute Focus" technique for getting more work done each day.

Notice that Jim played it smart. He didn't try to do everything at once. He looked at his schedule and planned accordingly so he could get one great idea implemented and working well for him before he moved on to the next. Notice, too, how he allotted enough time for each of the tips and strategies he selected. That's because, while some of the ideas in this book can be put into action fairly quickly, others require a few weeks.

Ten weeks to implement six solid business-building ideas isn't a long time. And can you imagine how much more successful Jim's business will be within just a few months? In every way we've discussed so far—projects, clients, income, lifestyle—he will have taken a Goliath-size step toward fulfilling his vision of living life as a wealthy freelancer.

And if you do the same, you will, too.

You're Part of a Very Special Group

Without even knowing who you are, we know you're a special person because not everyone would be drawn to pick up and read a book like this. But do you actually realize just *how* special you are? It's true. As a freelance professional, you are one of the most important contributors to the workforce of the new economy. In fact, there are millions of freelance professionals throughout North America and around the world in categories as diverse as writing, graphic design, programming, virtual assistance, illustration, consulting, public relations, marketing, business communications, training, and more. Even those in credentialed occupations such as accounting, law, and architecture have joined—and continue to join—the freelance ranks. So if you're an aspiring or established freelancer yourself, you're in very good company! And your destiny is truly in your hands.

This is all good news because freelancing used to have a somewhat negative connotation to the masses. Ten or so years ago, if you were a freelancer, that meant you were a beginner, or not qualified to get a "real" job, or lazy, or just dabbling in your occupation, or were between jobs, or were not a serious player in your field. Today, things have changed dramatically. Being a successful freelance professional—a *wealthy freelancer*—is something many corporate professionals (including some of your friends and family) envy. A few years ago, it wasn't uncommon to hear something like, "So you're a freelance copywriter. Oh." Now it's, "So you're a freelance copywriter. Wow!"

In fact, according to a recent CNNMoney.com article titled "The Rise of Freelance Nation," fully 31 percent of the U.S. workforce—roughly 42 million workers—is currently made up of independent contractors, part-time or temporary staffers, and the self-employed. *30 percent!* And if you think that's a staggering figure, wait until 2019. By then, experts predict 40 percent of the workforce will be made up of independent workers—freelancers like you and us!

Adam Sorensen, a compensation and benefits expert at WorldatWork, is quoted in the article as saying, "We're in the early stages of what will be a really different era in the workplace, and a growing segment of workers will need to structure their career around this model." So congratulations, because you're doing that right now.

There's never been a better time to be a freelancer! Rewarding, well-paying projects are everywhere, more plentiful than ever before. Using the Internet, you can work with clients around the globe and never leave your home! As of this writing, Elance.com, a large online job site for freelancers, lists thousands of clients posting more than 25,000 available projects. A competing online job site, Guru.com, reached an all-time high in 2008 for freelance projects posted. It also saw a 27 percent increase from the previous year in freelance projects transacted. And that's just the tip of the iceberg. Most freelance projects, at least 95 percent, are never advertised!

Freelancers have become so important to corporate America that even best-selling marketing author Seth Godin is recommending that companies create a position called "manager of freelancers."

Welcome to the age of the freelance professional. Our time has finally arrived! And now that you have this book, you really are just a handful of ideas away from becoming one of the truly successful freelancers—the ones who really do enjoy a great income and an enviable lifestyle.

Never underestimate the power of just one great idea. A few years ago, Steve was struggling to teach his five-year-old daughter, Erin, how to ride a bike. Things weren't going well. Erin just couldn't seem to get the hang of it, and she was becoming increasingly nervous about falling over. Then his neighbor happened by and said, "Hey, Steve, I have a great idea that worked well for my son." He explained that if Erin simply practiced on a short, gently sloping, grassy hill—rather than the sidewalk—the momentum would teach her to peddle and ride more quickly. And the soft grass would give her the confidence not to give up. A little skeptical, Steve tried the idea with his daughter. Literally five minutes later, she was riding her bike as if she had being doing it for months!

And that's exactly what this book will do for you. It will give you the great ideas you need to explode out of the starting blocks or, if you're already an established freelancer, take your business to exactly—and we mean *exactly*—where you want it to be.

So let's get going in that direction right now with the 12 secrets.

Secret 1: Master the Mental Game

Pete Savage

As a freelancer, on those days when life is filled with roses and sunshine, it's easy to stay confident and upbeat. It's when the storms roll in—and they *will* roll in—that your mental toughness will be put to the test.

Some freelancing storms you're sure to go through (if you haven't already) might look like this:

- That long and lucrative streak of work, the one that seemed as though it would just never end … ends.
- That favorite client of yours who thinks you're the best thing since TiVo suddenly begins to send less and less work your way.
- Your bank account takes a nosedive.
- Your friends or, much worse, your *spouse* begins looking at you with unmasked nervousness, as if to say, "Hmmm. This freelance thing of yours isn't going as well as planned, is it?"

In the face of all these things, what does a wealthy freelancer do? In this chapter, you learn how to exercise and strengthen your mental muscles, so you'll be ready to take on these and other challenges that come your way.

Your Goals Will Guide You Through the Storm

In his book *The Success Principles: How to Get from Where You Are to Where You Want to Be* (HarperPaperbacks, 2006), Jack Canfield tells a compelling story about the power of goal-setting. As the story goes, Bruce Jenner, famed U.S. decathlete and Olympic gold medalist, was speaking to a roomful of Olympic hopefuls. He asked the group if they had made a list of their goals, and all hands went up. This isn't surprising, really, when you consider that aspiring Olympians are intensely focused, dedicated, and ambitious overachievers.

Then came Jenner's follow-up question: "How many of you have your list of goals with you right now?" Only one hand went up. Of all the premier athletes in that room, the only one who carried his goals with him, so he could remain focused on them always, was Dan O'Brien. Not surprisingly, O'Brien went on to achieve a huge goal when he won gold in the decathlon at the 1996 Olympics.

O'Brien's story is just one of millions that illustrate what we humans can achieve when we set goals and stay focused on them. You may not be training for the Olympics, but if you want to accomplish extraordinary things in life, you must set goals. There's a reason why virtually every self-help book, personal achievement guru, and success coach loudly extols the virtues of goal-setting: *because setting goals works!*

And yet, time and again, research continues to tell us that most people simply do not take the time to set goals and put them in writing. Do you? Suppose Bruce Jenner walked up to you today and asked to see your goals list! What would you say?

If goal-setting is so effective, why on earth do so few people do it? I suspect most people aren't in the habit of setting goals for themselves because most people work in organizations where their goals are set *for* them, by their superiors. Another factor at play is plain old human laziness. When something looks like it might be too daunting a task, we tend to put it off, and many perceive goal-setting as a chore.

But who says it has to be?

The most difficult part of goal-setting is to actually decide what you want. T. Harv Ecker, author of *Secrets of the Millionaire Mind: Mastering the Inner Game of Wealth* (HarperBusiness, 2005), puts it best when he says, "The reason people don't get what they want is because they don't know what they want."

I agree, but I think people *do* know what they want, on some level, even if they aren't aware of it fully enough to articulate it. For instance, some people reading this book right now are doing so not because they have a crystal-clear vision of their future life as a freelancer, but because they know there's *something* about the freelancer's life that strikes them as more appealing than their current work situation.

Goal-Setting Made (Very) Easy

So how do you go from having a general sense of what appeals to you to setting specific goals you can strive for? You're going to like the answer: *use your imagination!*

Think about it. All goal-setting is, really, is the use of your imagination to create a vision for your future. That's it!

Wealthy Words

Most freelancers I know do not have a business vision. That's unfortunate because your business vision defines the business life you want to live. Your business plan includes the concrete objectives and marketing tasks that support your vision, but it all starts with your business vision.

—Paul Lima, freelancer writer, trainer, and author

Here's a practical (meaning you'll actually *do* it) goal-setting exercise you can do to get clear on what you want out of life. This is one of the easiest techniques I know for getting your goals down on paper, in part because it's only three steps:

1. Envision your ideal day.

2. Compare and create your ideal and current days.

3. Prioritize and execute.

This exercise is especially enjoyable for freelancers. You'll see why.

Envision Your Ideal Day

Freelancers have a whale of a time with this first step because we revel in the idea of doing what we want, when we want. So have fun with this exercise! Ask yourself, if you could create the perfect workday for yourself, what would it look like? What sort of work do you want to be doing? For what sort of clients? At what times during the day? Does your ideal day include a 60-minute workout at the gym or a 30-minute jog in the park? If so, schedule it in!

Picture every component of your ideal day in vivid detail, describing what you would do from the moment you wake up until your head hits the pillow. Outline your day in half-hour or hour increments.

When you've mapped out your ideal day, have a look at it and realize this, your ideal day, is really a one-day snapshot of your ideal *life!* And this is a visual representation of your goals manifest. From this visual of your ideal day, you can extract a list of goals and keep them on a separate piece of paper.

Optional: Don't stifle your own creative energies. Don't stop at imagining just one day if you don't want to. Heck, go ahead and create the ideal year if you want to. You don't have to map out all 365 days, but you can certainly ask yourself what kind of vacations you'd like to take, how much time you'd like off, what your weekends would look like, etc. Get as carried away as you like with this exercise, but stop when it starts to feel like a chore.

Compare and Create

When you have your ideal day mapped out, compare it to how you currently spend your days and note the differences. Now create a list of all the things you can do to bridge those differences. What do you need to do, starting right now, to make your ideal day—that is, your ideal life—a reality?

Write down anything and everything that comes to mind. I bet you'll fill a page, if not an entire notebook, with creative ideas. These ideas will become more refined if you break up this step over a few days.

Prioritize and Execute

If you placed no limits on your thinking during step 2, you'll end up with a giant list of ideas, notes, tasks, projects, plans, and even new goals to strive for. In all, you could have 20, or 120, different items on this giant list. Now you need to prioritize these items into a manageable list of "Things to Do." As you prioritize, you can discard any items that turn out to be of little use.

Decide on a deadline for achieving your ideal day. Three years from now? Ten years from now? Knowing this helps you set mini-timelines for executing your list of Things to Do. For example, which tasks can you accomplish by the end of this month? This calendar year? Which can you accomplish next year? And so on.

Because Dan O'Brien always carried around his list of goals, he could review them regularly and stay focused on what was important to him. You can apply the same principle. Carry an index card around with you in your purse or wallet if you're so inclined. Write your ideal day on one side and the extracted goals on the other. Or at the very least, print out your ideal day and your goals list and hang them in your office so you glance at them for a motivational boost several times throughout the day. It will help keep you on track.

And if your idea of the ideal day changes as time goes by, that's terrific. It means you're developing a clearer vision of how you truly want to spend your time. Simply modify the details of your ideal day when you need to and create new "to dos" to get you there.

Your Goals Should Never Be Etched in Stone

Even if you already consider yourself a gold medal goal-setter, this goal-setting exercise is worthwhile because it gives you a fresh perspective on your current goals, and it may lead you to make some modifications.

Having established goals to shoot for is critical to becoming a wealthy freelancer. While the achievement of your goals will no doubt be rewarding, the pursuit of those goals can—and should—be enjoyable. The next section on setting standards shows you how to get more enjoyment out of your freelance work.

Set Standards and Prosper

My first-ever freelance copywriting job was for a tiny little marketing agency in town owned by a guy we'll call Carl. Carl needed a freelance copywriter on a full-time basis for a few weeks to help him with a backlog of work.

The first few projects Carl sent my way were pure copywriting jobs writing brochures, scripts for radio commercials, copy for websites, and the like. But things changed fast.

Unknown to me at the time, Carl was in the habit of taking on any kind of work he could get his hands on. By week two of working for him, the assignments he offered me were as far from copywriting as you could imagine. The absurdity peaked in week three, when Carl asked if I'd be willing to spend a few days walking around the city's downtown core with Cher on my arm.

Well, not Cher *exactly*.

You see, Carl had won a bid to be the event planner for the grand opening of the city's brand-new arena. Cher was to be the headline act on opening weekend, and Carl's idea for promoting the event was to turn loose a Cher *look-alike* on the streets of downtown.

I accepted Carl's assignment, which was to follow the phony Cher around for hours on end and hand out free concert tickets to any member of the public who approached her and said, "Hey, you look like Cher."

This went on for five days. Often in the rain. This was not exactly the lifestyle I had envisioned for myself when I set out to become a freelance copywriter.

So why did I accept this ridiculous job? I had bills to pay—lots of bills. And my experience as the sole member of the faux Cher's entourage provided me with plenty of much-needed cash. But more importantly, it gave me an appreciation for the fact that, as a freelancer, I needed to put some *standards* in place!

Wealthy Words

Without standards, you end up accepting any morsel of paying work that comes your way, like a hungry mouse devours a crumb. You remain stuck in that gut-tightening, demoralizing position of doing work you despise, for clients you don't like, just because you need the money.

—Pete Savage

After my Cher days, I knew that if I didn't outline the criteria under which I was willing to work, I would never rise to the level where I could be selective about the projects I took on.

So I set about defining my standards.

All this means is that I began to envision and then list conditions under which I would accept work, as well as the type of work I was willing to do and not do.

A Sample Set of Standards for Freelancers

What sort of standards should you set? Here are some example standards for a freelance business that may appeal to you. Some of these statements are from my actual list of standards; some aren't.

Business Standards for John Smith's Freelance Copywriting Business

I do not provide free or "spec" work for any reason.

I charge a 25 percent premium for all rush jobs.

I do not begin work without 50 percent of the project fees paid up front.

I don't write white papers or annual reports.

I don't work for ad agencies.

I don't answer the phone every time it rings. To speak with me, clients or prospects must first book an appointment.

I don't do work that requires me to sacrifice my weekends.

I only do work that is within my target industry and/or niche.

I only accept projects where my average hourly earnings will equate to $150/hour or higher.

Let me tell you, when I was preparing my list of standards, I took great delight in coming up with a long list of statements like "I won't do this" and "I don't do that"! Just creating my list filled me with a great sense of control. And it's crucial for every aspiring wealthy freelancer to get comfortable with the idea—and the feeling—of *being in control*. Why? *Because most freelancers are completely out of control.*

By that I mean they let *other* people (clients) set the terms and conditions under which they work. To me, that's like working for an employer but without the dental plan. No thanks.

Wealthy freelancers, however, are in control. They really do call the shots. They really do have the freedom to decide what work they take on and what work they reject.

Start as You Mean to Go On

Immediately after my faux-Cher experience, I wasn't so naive or arrogant to expect that all my freelance work would conform to my new lofty standards right off the bat. But that's not the point. The point is, I was ambitious enough to know that I would *one day* have a set of standards like the ones I shared earlier.

What's important is that you set your standards *right now* and that you make them lofty and ambitious. In other words, aspire to them *now* and adhere to them *later*. Then from this moment on, you can begin to compare *every* project that comes your way to your new standards.

Realize, especially if you're just starting out, that hardly any—or perhaps none—of the projects you take on will conform to your full list of standards. But that's fine. There's no shame in taking on work that's less than perfect if you have bills to pay, mouths to feed, or credibility to build. It's one thing to *choose* to accept work that falls below your standards as a stop-gap measure, and another thing to be completely oblivious to the notion of standards in the first place.

When you take the time to think about and write down your ideal standards, you take a gigantic mental leap forward in your freelance business. The freelancer with a set of established standards is on her way to becoming wealthy! Standards put you in the right frame of mind to receive the right kind of work. They help you focus on the kind of work you ultimately want to do and give you the motivation to keep seeking out high-quality clients who will send this work your way.

Imagine the sense of accomplishment you'll feel when you actually land the project that, for the first time, conforms to *every single* criterion on your list of standards! I can tell you, it's a euphoric delight! Do not rob yourself of this experience. Set your standards now.

$ Success Story

The Power of Bold Action

Taking the plunge into full-time freelancing can be scary—especially when it involves leaving a secure job and a steady paycheck. That's where Jennifer Remling, a freelance corporate recruiter and author of *Carve Your Own Road: Do What You Love and Live the Life You Envision* (Career Press, 2009; www.CarveYourOwnRoad.com), found herself a few years ago. At the time, Jennifer was a highly successful corporate recruiting executive. Although successful by all traditional standards, she longed to chart her own course, write a book, and pursue other fulfilling projects. So rather than quitting her day job and starting a solo business from scratch, Jennifer decided to do some consulting on the side, trusting that her path would unfold perfectly.

And it did. Within a few months, a prospect offered Jennifer a sizeable 1-year consulting contract. "It wasn't enough to replace my full-time income, but it did give me the confidence I needed to go out and find additional business," she recalls. "So I quit my job three days later and sure enough—within 30 days—I had landed a second long-term client that helped me far exceed my income expectations."

Author Dorothea Brande wrote, "Act boldly and unseen forces will come to your aid." Jennifer agrees wholeheartedly with that advice. And although leaving the security of her paycheck was somewhat frightening, because she was clear about her goal and took bold action when presented with a good opportunity, she was able to make her decision with a great sense of peace and confidence.

The Four Tenets of Mindset Mastery

My brother Paul is a highly educated, well-paid, corporate financial guy with more letters behind his name than I care to keep track of. The illusion is that he would be the type of person who would have it made in the shade out there in the corporate jungle.

And yet, after 15 years in the corporate world, Paul had had enough. He recently decided to escape the daily grind and launch his own freelance consulting business. Over the past 18 months, we've had many long phone conversations about his frustrations with corporate life and his growing interest in "life as a freelancer." So when he called me one day to say "That's it! I'm out!" I was very excited for him.

I sat down to write him a short e-mail, with a list of important things to keep in mind as he prepared for this transition, focused primarily on the *mindset* he would need to develop in order to thrive as a freelance consultant. As I began writing, however, I realized that my advice to him would also serve all freelancers—as a refresher for those of us who have been at it a while, and as a heads-up for those about to take their first step of the journey.

And so that short e-mail to my brother Paul, fledgling freelancer, eventually evolved into what you see here: the Four Tenets of Mindset Mastery, followed by the IDEA Matrix for Mindset Mastery™, which helps you effortlessly integrate the four tenets into your life.

[C] Wealthy Words

Kyle Tully is an Australian freelance copywriter, Internet marketer, and business coach. One of his students, a freelancer, posed the question, "Which usually comes first, the money or the mindset? Must you believe before you can receive, or is it the receiving that creates belief?" Tully's answer: "Personally I've seen it work both ways ... but every *significant* increase in income has come from *mindset* changes first."

Tenet 1: Invest in Your Success

Subscribe to relevant publications in your industry so you can stay current with what your clients are reading. Also, be prepared to invest in tools that will help you better market your services. A plethora of articles, books, e-books, teleseminars, and coaching services on how to market your freelance/consulting/small business are available. Some are great; others, not so great. Seek out these materials, buy the ones that appeal to you, and *try* the techniques you discover.

Equally important is investing in books and audio programs that help you specifically manage the mental side of things, which directly support the second tenet ....

Tenet 2: Develop Unshakable Belief in Yourself

You have to believe you will succeed. I know, this sounds cliché, but recognize that this alone is the number-one determining factor in whether or not you will achieve your goals and realize your true potential. The best way is to continue to impregnate your subconscious with positive thoughts and imagery. Ed Gandia has a great recommendation on how to do this:

> To nurture unshakable belief, you should read as many legitimate rags-to-riches stories as you can find. I'm talking Napoleon Hill, Earl Nightingale, Warren Buffett, Mother Teresa, Oprah Winfrey, Stephen Spielberg, J.K. Rowling. These are people who came from nothing, and went on to overcome tremendous (almost unbelievable) obstacles to achieve what others thought was impossible.
>
> Immerse yourselves in these books. Read them and re-read them. Buy them used if money is an issue. Check them out from the library if you have to. But whatever you do, don't dismiss the need to believe in yourself as an overly simplistic, hollow or cliché piece of advice. It will happen for you. But you have to believe first.

That's great advice from Ed. And if you take his words to heart, you'll be well prepared for tenet 3 ....

Tenet 3: Expect That This Belief in Yourself Will Be Tested

You will experience self-doubt. You will encounter moments, days, maybe even weeks when you're not sure if you can do what you set out to do. When these dark moments come, realize that they are temporary. They will pass, but don't be in a hurry to escape them, for trying times often present you with the gift of self-discovery. Remember what Winston Churchill said: "If you're going through hell, keep going." It's usually when we feel the most challenged, discouraged, or downright beaten that we suddenly find out what we're made of and emerge stronger, with a clearer sense of purpose. That's the perfect set up for tenet number four ....

Tenet 4: Absorb the Feelings of Success When They Come

When you enjoy small successes in your freelance business, acknowledge and appreciate them. When your schedule is packed full of projects you truly enjoy, when you're fully expressing your creativity through your work, and when money is steadily flowing your way, take the time to *enjoy* it!

Notice how you feel during those days when everything is going according to plan. Notice how your performance level is high and yet your stress is low! It's because you're loving your work and the financial rewards it brings. *That* is the feeling you want more and more of. *That* is what being a wealthy freelancer is all about. Once you really get a taste for, savor, and enjoy the feelings of success, you'll be more motivated to build a freelance business where these feelings are the norm and not fleeting moments.

So how do you practically apply the four *Invest, Develop, Expect,* and *Absorb* tenets? Should you schedule these things, so on Monday you *Invest,* on Tuesday you *Develop,* and so on? No, don't worry; it's much easier than that. Putting these four tenets into practice is simply a matter of becoming familiar with the IDEA Matrix for Mindset Mastery™, which I designed to help you apply all four tenets *intuitively.* In other words, once you understand the simple matrix, you can master your mindset by going with your gut! Let's take a look.

The IDEA Matrix for Mindset Mastery™

The IDEA Matrix for Mindset Mastery™ is a tool you can use throughout your freelance career, to *continuously* develop the winning mental edge wealthy freelancers possess. To use the IDEA Matrix for Mindset Mastery™, all you need to do is be aware of two things in any given moment: your *performance level* and your *stress level*. These two things are, of course, completely subjective and quite easy to observe. In fact, you're likely already quite good at knowing when your stress level rises and falls.

To monitor your own performance level, simply look at how well you're executing the work you're doing. Are you being productive and efficient and busily producing high-quality work as you go about your day? These are all indicators that your performance level is high. (Note that it's possible for you to work at a high performance level during periods of both high stress and low stress.)

Don't overthink it when it comes to observing your own stress and performance levels. Just go with your gut. The point is to be able to *quickly* observe within yourself where you are with respect to these two levels, so you can look at the IDEA Matrix for Mindset Mastery™ and instantly place yourself in one of these four quadrants:

Quadrant 4 **Absorb**	Quadrant 3 **Expect**
Quadrant 1 **Invest**	Quadrant 2 **Develop**

Performance Level (vertical axis)

Stress Level (horizontal axis)

When you've identified which quadrant you're in, all you have to do next is refer to the corresponding tenet shown. That's it!

The beauty of the IDEA Matrix for Mindset Mastery™ is that it enables you to "self-medicate," so to speak. All you have to do is become good at assessing your own stress level and performance level, and the matrix will help you identify the right tenet to follow—the right "prescription," if you will—for continual improvement every time! To prove this to you, let's quickly look at each of the "prescriptions" shown in each of the four quadrants.

Quadrant 1: Low Performance, Low Stress

If you're not performing at a high level but you're not particularly stressed about it, that's a good indication you're not busy enough. You might be spending your days chipping away at some work here and there, floating around the Internet. The low stress level also indicates that you're comfortable with your bank account level. It's rare to be in dire straits financially and maintain a consistently low stress level.

Therefore, in quadrant 1, your instructions are to *Invest.* You can spare a little time and the money, so invest in one or more of the kind books or programs described in tenet 1, *Invest in Your Success.* (For ease of reference, quadrant 1 in the matrix corresponds to tenet 1, quadrant 2 corresponds to tenet 2, and so on.) You need to get these materials on hand so you can begin to get familiar with them.

Quadrant 2: Low Performance, High Stress

Okay, your performance is low but your stress is surging high. Uh-oh. Maybe there's not enough work on your plate to keep you in the rhythm of performing focused work. Or maybe you have work, but you just can't get motivated to churn through it. Your mind is wandering, and you're worrying about the future. You're in a rut, and it's stressing you out. How do you shake it? The instructions in quadrant 2 tell you to *Develop.*

It's time to pick up the ongoing work of *developing unshakable belief in yourself.* You need to read and hear inspiring stories and uplifting messages. You need to be reminded of the awesome power of the human spirit, and you need to start applying proven strategies for peak performance. All these things can be found in the self-help books, coaching programs, etc. you've investigated and purchased because you followed tenet 1. (You did follow tenet 1, didn't you?)

Quadrant 3: High Performance, High Stress

Wow, things are really moving now. You're faced with a busy workload, maybe even a little backlog, and *man*, are you ever stressed! So stressed, in fact, you're beginning to doubt your ability to execute. Everything you've been hoping for is falling into place lately, and you've got great clients and lots of challenging, meaningful work. It's showtime!

But ... do you *really* have what it takes to execute? Are you really as knowledgeable and capable as you've led your clients to believe? It's pretty stressful when you're the sole person responsible for delivering results for your clients on a project, isn't it? How do you shake off all this stress and self-doubt? Just follow the instructions! Quadrant 3 tells you to *Expect*.

Remember, you should *expect* that the belief in yourself—that belief you work on developing when you're in quadrant 2—will be tested. The truth is, as a freelancer, you continually go through periods of high stress where you question your ability to execute. If you're always surprised when this stress shows up, you'll always be thrown off your game. It's as simple as that.

However, you can count on quadrant 3 to always remind you to *expect* stress to show up and shake your belief in yourself. This way, you won't be knocked off your feet with shock each time it happens. Instead, you'll know, "Oh, here comes the stress; gee, it's been a while. Okay, it's normal ...," and suddenly you'll be able to ride it out.

Quadrant 4: High Performance, Low Stress

Did you notice something? The instructions in all the other quadrants are designed to *move you out* of that quadrant by either lowering your stress or increasing your performance. Quadrant 4 is the place to be. When you're here, you want to *stay* here! You want to *absorb the feelings of success when they come*. (Go back and read tenet 4 again so you really understand why this is so important.)

If you adhere to tenet 4 each and every time you're fortunate enough to be in quadrant 4, you'll develop a hunger that will keep you wanting to go there again and again. Keep this in mind: getting into quadrant 4 is always the goal, but you will always be moving from quadrant to quadrant through-out your freelance career. And when you suddenly find yourself outside of quadrant 4 again, either because your performance slipped or your stress spiked, remember, all you have to do is observe two things. Take a moment to assess your *stress level* and *performance level*, pinpoint where that puts you on the matrix, and follow the tenet that corresponds with the quadrant you're in.

Flex Those Mental Muscles!

By now you've seen see how crucial it is to spend time setting goals, estab-lishing standards, and mastering the mindset of a wealthy freelancer. It's quite a workout, isn't it! And like any workout program, it's designed to make you stronger and stronger.

The freelancer's life can be a rocky road, and most of us who decide to go it alone do encounter our fair share of setbacks, rejection, and disappoint-ment. So when the storms roll in, those seemingly insurmountable obstacles you encounter on your path to success, what do you do?

Identifying and Overcoming Obstacles

When you find yourself worrying about a certain obstacle, pay close atten-tion to what's really going on there: you're worrying because you haven't fully *decided* in your own mind that you're going to overcome it.

To illustrate this, think of something in your freelance business that's causing you anxiety, stress, or worry. Maybe you're worried about a proposal you submitted but didn't hear back on. Or perhaps you're anxious about how to go about finding new clients. Something will likely spring to mind, but if it doesn't, put down the book and think for a minute. (And if you're really in an "everything's roses and sunshine" period right now, bookmark this page so you can come back to it when the storm clouds roll in!)

Now, back to that thing that's bugging you. That thing is the *obstacle*. How long has it been since this obstacle first reared its ugly head? A day or two? A week? A year?

If something's been bugging you for a while, that means you're still focusing on the obstacle rather than the path to overcome it. In other words, you haven't decided, *really decided*, that you're ready to overcome it. And that's why it's still bugging you one day, week, month, or year later. This is not a slight! It's just a result of the fact that your mind can only focus on one thing at a time. You're either focused on the obstacle or the way around it.

Focus on the Way Around It

Imagine you're driving down the highway when suddenly a transport truck 100 yards ahead of you drops its load—of two dozen logs! To avoid a crash, you'd have to very quickly forget about the logs and focus on a way around them. Can you quickly switch lanes? No, other cars are there. Drive onto the soft shoulder? No, there's no shoulder. Aha! Accelerate and head for the off-ramp exit!

You can't focus on the logs forever. At first you might be mesmerized by them as they come flying toward your windshield in all their majestic beauty, but pretty soon you'd have to take your focus off the logs and get your car over to that off-ramp.

Wealthy freelancers minimize the amount of time they spend worrying about obstacles. Let's look at how you can, too.

Refuse to Let Obstacles Stop You

You have a lot of very compelling reasons to want to enjoy the dream life of a wealthy freelancer, so don't waste any precious time sabotaging your own success. Instead, begin the practice of consciously *deciding* to overcome any obstacle that temporarily blocks your path. For example, let's say you want to get new work as a freelance copywriter in the financial industry, but you've never done any financial copywriting before.

Is this an obstacle? Sure it is. So first of all, *acknowledge* it, which is easy to do. Simply say something like this to yourself: "Okay, I don't have any samples of work in the financial industry to show prospects."

Next, *decide* it's not going to stop you. Say, "This is an obstacle, but it's not going to stop me." The simple act of saying these words—out loud and with passion—can snap you out of the worst funk and get you moving toward, rather than away from, your goals.

In the face of obstacles, *acknowledge and decide*. Take time to *acknowledge* the obstacles in your path and consciously *decide* that they won't stop you. When you do, you'll be able to take them on with less anxiety and greater confidence.

Vanquish *"Easier Said Than Done"*–itis Once and for All

Some readers of this book, upon first learning of the work habits and rituals of wealthy freelancers, may suffer from a momentary onset of what I call *"Easier Said Than Done"*–itis, or *ESTD-itis* for short.

> **ESTD-itis** [noun; "est-*die*-itis"]   The momentary mental muttering of the phrase "easier said than done" when presented with a new idea, concept, tool, or technique for achieving success.

ESTD-itis is brought on by the sudden realization that a certain level of success involves a certain amount of honest effort. It's a common disease for which there is only one known antidote—fortunately, when administered properly, it is 100 percent effective in every case:

> Hold in your mind the *expectation* that a certain level of success requires a certain amount of honest effort.

If you do this, the phrase "easier said than done" will disappear from your language when you come upon ideas, concepts, tools, or techniques that have the power to lead you toward success. You'll be infallible in the face of opposition. Your confidence may waver, but it will be replenished. You may be discouraged, but you will press on. You'll be motivated to take action. You'll be less afraid of failure. And you'll be free to tenaciously pursue the life of your dreams, the life of the wealthy freelancer.

Perception Is Reality: How Do You View Your Business?

The final but critical component of mastering the mental game as a freelancer is *not* to view yourself as a freelancer.

Huh!? Didn't we just spend the entire chapter on developing the mindset of a wealthy freelancer? Yes, but the truth is that wealthy freelancers actually see themselves as more than freelancers. They see themselves as *entrepreneurs, business owners,* and *businessmen* and *businesswomen.* All this means is that they view their freelance practice as a full-fledged business, complete with all the functional areas of a business. What are these functional areas?

- Sales
- Marketing
- Operations
- Human Resources
- Customer Service
- Production
- Finance and Accounting
- Research and Development

Each of these functional areas topics is quite broad, but they're easy to understand, and they'll be explained in full detail throughout the remainder of this book. For now, let's just take a quick look at short descriptions of each area.

(Don't worry—viewing your freelance practice as a business is not as daunting as it sounds! To become a wealthy freelancer, you need to know how each of these functional areas work, but you don't need any sort of business background in order to understand any one of them. We promise!)

Sales is what you do to earn money. It involves reaching out to, and having conversations with, prospects and customers. Secret 2 shows you how to pursue and close sales.

Marketing is how you make yourself known to prospects who want to hire you. Secret 4 explains the most effective marketing tactics used by wealthy freelancers today and gives you a proven tool for determining your own marketing efforts.

Operations are the actions you go through each day to support your craft. This includes the systems you have in place that enable you to perform your craft more easily, including scheduling your time, writing quotes for clients, and managing workflow that you outsource to staff or, more likely, assistants. Throughout the secrets, we outline proven systems in detail so you can put them in place right now.

Human Resources is the department responsible for training and developing employee skills. Secret 1 tells you precisely when you should invest in developing your skills. And what about other HR issues like office hours, vacation time, and maintaining work/life balance? You'll see how wealthy freelancers manage all of these things in Secret 10.

Customer Service means ensuring you're treating your customers well. How can you "go the extra mile" for customers and reap the rewards? It's all explained in Secret 5. How do you deal with clients who don't like your work? You'll find instructions for handling this delicate situation in the appendix.

Production is the factory floor. Think of your freelance business as a factory with a "capacity of one." Wait … isn't this a rather demeaning way to look at things? To take all your creative, inspirational freelance work and say that it came out of a factory? Not really. Even the most beautifully crafted and artistic products in the world (think of Rolls Royce cars, diamond rings, and fine wines) leverage *production efficiencies*. Improving your productivity lets you create in a more efficient and stress-free environment, which actually increases the quality of your output and the enjoyment you derive from practicing your *craft* (whether your craft is illustrating, graphic design, photography, or something else). Secret 9 is all about productivity.

Finance and Accounting involve money. Wealthy freelancers do not work for free, and money plays an important role in the life of a wealthy freelancer. Secret 12 shows you how to lay a solid financial foundation that supports your wealthy lifestyle.

Wealthy freelancers know their business is in a constant state of change. *Research and Development* is about embracing change in your business and using it to your advantage. Research involves looking for and finding new ways to enhance your business, and Development is bringing those enhancements to life. If this sounds exciting to you, it is! In Secrets 8 and 11, you'll see what R&D can look like for freelancers.

Wealthy Takeaways

- As a freelancer, you'll encounter your fair share of challenges and setbacks. But remember, they needn't stop you from achieving the lifestyle of your dreams. And they won't, if you practice and implement strategies for staying focused, developing a winning mindset, and overcoming obstacles.

- Use your imagination to set goals so you have a clear direction to pursue. Have fun with your goal-setting and remember that your goals aren't etched in stone, and you can modify them as you see fit.

- Create your own set of business standards that describe the conditions under which you take on and perform work. Make them ambitious so you have a high standard to aim for.

- Master the right mindset by regularly assessing your own stress and productivity levels. Then use the IDEA Matrix for Mindset Mastery™ to see which of the four tenets will help you improve your mindset, ultimately moving you back to a state of high performance, low stress.

- When you encounter obstacles, take a moment to acknowledge them and then consciously decide that they won't stop you.

- Avoid the tendency to say "Easier said than done" by holding in your mind the *expectation* that a certain level of success requires a certain amount of honest effort.

- View your freelance practice as a *business*, with distinct functional areas, each of which you can focus on and optimize.

Secret 2: Simplify the Process of Getting Clients

Ed Gandia

Attracting and landing clients is, without a doubt, one of the toughest challenges for freelance professionals, regardless of their level of experience. For newbies, getting that first client can seem overwhelming. Where do you start? Whom do you target? How do you contact them? What do you say?

Similarly, seasoned pros who have grown their businesses organically (via word of mouth, referrals, or personal and professional contacts) tend to struggle when they have to go outside their comfort zone to actively promote their services.

The Master Marketing Formula

Wealthy freelancers understand that landing clients is a process—a simple process anyone can follow to attract more and better clients with less effort. This process, developed by Steve Slaunwhite, is called the Master Marketing Formula and comprises the following steps:

1. Find high-probability prospects.

2. Generate leads.

3. Get opportunities.

4. Close the sale (land the client).

5. Nurture "not today" prospects.

Think of the Master Marketing Formula as a funnel. You start with anywhere from a few dozen to a few hundred prospects. As you move down the funnel, or from one step of the formula to the next, you have progressively fewer prospects to work with until you end up with the handful of clients who are right for you. Here's how it looks:

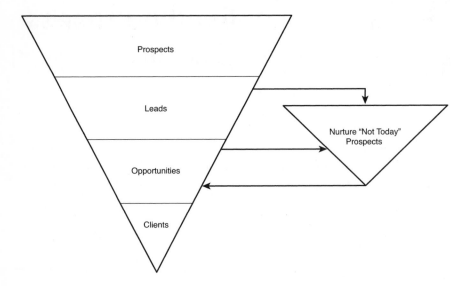

The rules of the Master Marketing Formula are simple, but you must follow all of them for the process to work:

- *Each step in the formula has a definite beginning and end, and you must complete one step before moving to the next.* Depending on your profession and the nature of the prospect or lead, some of these steps may last as little as a few minutes or as long as a few months.

- *Your objective is to continually move prospects down the funnel, one step at a time.* If your prospects aren't flowing downstream, there's a problem. Think of yourself as a traffic cop. You need to keep traffic moving, even if it moves slowly at times.

- *You must continually feed your funnel.* If you don't, it will eventually dry up and you'll have to start all over. And because it can take weeks or months to get prospects to move from the top of the funnel to the bottom, you may find yourself scrambling for work (that's no fun!).

Beyond its usefulness in helping you find and land clients efficiently, the Master Marketing Formula also acts as a highly effective troubleshooting tool. If you're ever stuck or just not getting the results you need from your marketing efforts, taking a closer look at each step of the formula and asking yourself the right questions (which I give you later in this chapter) helps you identify the source of the problem.

Let's explore each step of the Master Marketing Formula in more detail.

Wealthy Tip

There are many ways to define prospects and the various stages they go through as they enter your funnel. However, to avoid confusion, here's how some key terms are defined throughout this book:

prospect: Individuals you've determined would be good targets for your specific services based on a set of criteria you've established.

lead: Prospects who have somehow indicated a certain level of interest in what you have to offer.

opportunity: A lead who has given you a chance to present your services, discuss a project, or quote a job.

Don't confuse *prospects* with *leads*. Prospects are individuals you believe *may* be interested in your services. Leads, on the other hand, are prospects who have *already* indicated a certain level of interest in what you have to offer.

Find High-Probability Prospects

The first step in getting clients is to compile a list of high-probability prospects. Take your time assembling the best prospect list possible. To a large extent, the success of your prospecting efforts hinges on your ability to start with a quality targeted list. Focus on the job titles of people who tend to hire freelancers in your field or who, with the right message, would consider doing so.

Also, focus on organizations and industries where you would have the highest probability of success—either because of your background, experience, skills, client roster, specialized knowledge, and location, or because of current changes or growth in that industry.

In my case, the best prospects are marketing managers in high-performing midsize software companies that market in-demand software systems for hot or growing industries. Notice how specific I am with my criteria. I've identified the most receptive job title for my services (marketing managers). I've also named the industry I prefer to focus on (software), the fact that the company must be doing well financially, the type of software they must market (systems that are in high demand), and the type of customers they're after (organizations in hot or growing industries).

You don't have to get that specific, and you don't have to create just one list. You can, in fact, create a few different lists, each based on a set of specific criteria. For instance, you can create a general list of midsize businesses in your area only (location-based), another of companies in an industry you have significant experience in (experience-based), and one that's made up of companies in a number of industries that market products to a target market you know a lot about (knowledge-based). (By the way, if you need help identifying or narrowing down your ideal target market, see Secret 4.)

How many prospects do you need on your list? It depends. The more aggressive your goals are in terms of income level, the larger the list you'll need. However, a good number to shoot for is 150 to 200 total names. Start there and concentrate on quality and repeated effort over the course of a year or two, rather than assembling a larger list and contacting those individuals only once or twice. In other words, go deeper with a smaller list before you expand your list size.

🔧 Wealthy Tip

The most practical method for assembling a prospect list is to use a simple spreadsheet. Include column labels for first name, last name, job title, company, street address, city, state, zip (postal) code, country, phone number, and e-mail address (if you have it). Also include a "source" column so you know where you got the name. This can help you identify where your responses are coming from and what sources are worth mining further.

Where do you find prospects for your list? Although you may be tempted to rent or buy a list from a list provider such as InfoUSA, Hoovers, or OneSource, the objective here is not efficiency and volume; rather, it's to create the most responsive list possible. That's tough to do if you're grabbing names blindly or trying to quickly assemble a huge list. Instead, compile your list manually, using a variety of high-quality sources. Let's look at some great places to start.

Industry Associations

If you've decided to specialize in an industry or if a specific industry is part of your target market, start by looking at industry associations. If you're already a member of an association, consider using its member directory. If you're not a member, find out what its membership rates are and ask if you can receive a membership directory (one that includes actual names, titles, and contact information) when you join.

Industry associations can be a great resource for your list because in many cases, membership in a specific association can tell you a lot about a prospect. For instance, if a company belongs to the Direct Marketing Association, chances are it's a direct marketer. So if you're a freelance advertising production manager in the direct marketing industry, this would probably be a great association to join and get involved with.

Company Rankings in Industry and Trade Publications

Every year, hundreds of industry magazines and journals publish a list of the top companies in their field. *Med Ad News* magazine, for example, ranks the top 100 biotechnology companies every year. If you're targeting biotechnology companies, this could be a good list to start with. Most of these lists don't provide you with names and addresses, but when you have a company name, you can go to that company's website (or use other tools I discuss shortly) and find the right contact and his or her mailing address.

It's not uncommon for an industry to have one or two publications that publish these annual rankings. Google terms like "top U.S. insurance companies" (if your chosen niche is insurance) or "top Chicago law firms" (if that's your target). You'll be surprised at what turns up.

Your Local Business Chronicle

If you're targeting local businesses, and if your metropolitan area has one, consider subscribing to the local business chronicle. Keeping up with what's going on in your local business community is a great way to identify potential prospects. Companies that are growing, expanding, changing strategy, or acquiring competitors can often be good targets because such events tend to create needs that can't be fulfilled completely with internal staff.

Also, many of these publications put together an annual "book of lists," a ranking of local companies by industry and sector. Along with the company name, address, and website, many of these lists include names of key decision-makers within each organization.

Your Local Library

Large public libraries are another great resource for prospect names. Once you have a better idea of what kinds of prospects you're looking for, consult with the reference desk librarian. Dozens of industries publish annual company directories, and even if you can't get the names of your ideal contacts, having a good list of company names and addresses is a great start.

Early in my freelance career, I found a directory titled *Direct Marketing Marketplace: The Networking Source of the Direct Marketing Industry*. Published annually by National Register Publishing, this meaty directory lists the names of key marketing executives at companies that use direct marketing as part of their mix. Because I was positioning myself as a freelance direct-mail copywriter, this was a target-rich resource.

Google

If you have company names and addresses but are struggling to find the right individuals within those organizations, you might want to try using the site-specific search function in Google. This handy little feature enables you to search for specific terms within a specific website. The command is:

> *Keyword* site:*domain*.com

So if you were trying to get the names of some of the marketing managers at *National Geographic* magazine, you'd type this in the Google search area:

> "marketing manager" site:NationalGeographic.com

If the job title you're looking for is made of more than one word, placing quotes around it tells Google to search for only that specific term within the *National Geographic* website. That way, you won't have to sort through results where the words *marketing* and *manager* do not appear together. Go ahead and try this or a similar search. I bet your search results are promising.

Jigsaw

Another valuable resource for hard-to-find names deep within an organization is an online tool called Jigsaw (www.Jigsaw.com). Jigsaw is a member-maintained online exchange of downloadable company information and more than 12 million business contacts.

So let's say you've identified 100 companies you'd like to target, but you don't have the names of operations managers (the specific job title you're targeting) on that list. All you have are company names and addresses. You can go to Jigsaw and have it check its database for operations managers in those specific companies. If any turn up (and they often do), you can buy those names with points, which you can earn either by uploading some of your own personal or professional contacts or buying them outright.

I've assembled some very targeted lists using Jigsaw, and I continue to be amazed at the depth and accuracy of the contact information it contains.

LinkedIn

LinkedIn (www.LinkedIn.com) is a business-oriented social networking site used mainly for professional networking. As of May 2009, it had more than 40 million registered users spanning 170 industries. The best way to use LinkedIn to find specific individuals is to join the site (it's free) and use its search feature.

If you're looking for, say, an engineering manager at Acme Corporation, simply search for "engineering manager Acme Corporation" and see what comes up. You'll not only often find the right individual, you may also find people who held that role at Acme in the past and are now with competing firms—a nice bonus!

Investor's Business Daily's SmartSelect Composite Rating

If one of your prospect-selection criteria is the company's financial performance, pick up a copy of *Investor's Business Daily* (IBD). IBD is a U.S.

newspaper that covers international business and finance. Besides stock quotes, IBD also publishes its own "SmartSelect Composite Rating" for thousands of publicly traded companies. This rating combines five key stock-performance measures of each company into one number. Results are then compared to all other companies in that industry, and each company is assigned a rating from 1 to 99, with 99 being the best. For instance, a rating of 95 means the stock is outperforming 95 percent of all other stocks in that industry.

Stock price is not always an indicator of a company's ability to hire freelancers in your field. It's also not a surefire indicator of how the company will perform in the future. And this method focuses only on publicly traded companies, many of which are large or midsize—a problem if you want to go after smaller local businesses. However, stock performance is closely tied to financial performance, so if a client's financial health is important to you, or if companies in your field tend to spend more on freelancers when they're doing well, this selection criterion can help you narrow down your choices.

Generate Leads

Once you've compiled a strong list of high-probability prospects, the next step in the Master Marketing Formula is to turn as many of those prospects as possible into leads. As I mentioned earlier, a lead is a prospect who has indicated a certain level of interest in what you have to offer. Essentially, it's someone who has raised his or her hand and said, "I'm interested. Tell me more about what you do."

Lead generation (or prospecting) is the one step of the Master Marketing Formula where most freelancers stumble. That's why we've dedicated a whole chapter to the topic (Secret 4). For now, just remember that prospecting is merely one step in the process of turning prospects into clients. Just because you have a lead doesn't mean the lead will become a client. To do that, you must first convert the lead into an opportunity.

Get Opportunities

If you go back and reference the funnel diagram, you'll see that the opportunity stage is the bridge between the lead stage and the client stage. A prospect must become a lead before it can turn into an opportunity. And a lead can become an opportunity only when you get a chance to present your services, discuss a project, or quote a job. Here are some examples of opportunities:

- You send out a sales letter to 100 prospects. One of them calls you and asks, "How much do you charge to write a _____?" That individual has gone from prospect to lead to opportunity in a matter of minutes. (I love it when that happens!)

- You have a conversation with a prospect at a networking event about a potential project, and you agree to call her later that afternoon to get more information on the project.

- A lead you've been staying in touch with suddenly asks you to submit a quotation or proposal.

- You're a designer, writer, or illustrator and you get invited to show your portfolio to a marketing manager or creative director in an ad agency.

How do you get these opportunities? Simple. You follow up with your leads! And you follow up consistently and methodically, using a series of focused questions that help you accomplish three very important objectives:

1. Move leads farther down your funnel.

2. Give you clues that help you decide if a lead has a high-enough probability of becoming a client.

3. Provide the information you'll need to quote the project (if applicable).

Wealthy Tip

Don't underestimate the power of effective follow-up. According to a recent article in *Selling Power* magazine, a lead is four times more likely to become an opportunity if you follow up effectively. Or to put it another way, the right follow-up process could potentially help quadruple your income without having to raise your fees or generate more leads!

Now let's go over the wealthy freelancer four-step process to following up with leads to turn more of them into opportunities.

Identify a Project and Learn More About It

The first thing you must do is thank the lead for her interest in your services. If the lead came to you via one of your direct-mail campaigns, sending a handwritten card thanking her for downloading your buzz piece (more on buzz pieces in Secret 3) is a very nice touch that makes you stand out. If the lead came via a referral, social media site, Google search, or other means, make it a point to thank the person for her interest during your initial phone call. It's the classy thing to do, and it will set the tone for your conversation.

Your next objective is to try to uncover a specific opportunity you can focus on, quote, and pursue. For most freelancers, that opportunity is a project. Without some sort of potential project—or, at a minimum, a defined challenge she's trying to solve—you don't have something tangible to hold on to, something on which to focus your conversation and follow-up. To help you identify an appropriate project, ask the lead some questions:

- What's the actual challenge you're trying to overcome? (if applicable)
- What are the consequences of this/these challenge(s)?
- What are you looking to accomplish?
- Can you tell me more about the project? (if the lead has already identified one)

Based on the answers you get, try to determine the following:

- Is the project well defined?
- Is this a project you can do well?
- Are the prospect's expectations realistic?
- Is the prospect approaching the challenge in a logical manner?

Basically, you're trying to determine if this lead (and the project you've identified) is a good fit for you. You want to know if she and her project are worth pursuing. These questions help you make that determination, helping you focus only on opportunities where you can add value and get the fees you deserve.

Determine the Project's Budget

When you've identified a project to quote and pursue, it's time to go deeper and ask the "money" question. Okay, I admit it. Money questions can be tough to ask. But if you're going to spend time putting together a quote or proposal, you have the right to know if your lead has a budget set aside for the project and what that budget might be.

And don't worry—if you don't feel comfortable asking for the project's budget, you can instead provide her with a ballpark price range for the project she's inquiring about and see if that fits within her budget. Doing so helps you screen out leads who can't afford anything remotely close to your fees, saving you a great deal of time and frustration.

Here are some great budget-related questions to ask:

- Has a budget already been set aside for this project? If so, what's your budget range?

- My fee for this type of work is between $1,000 and $1,500. Is that within your budget?

Sample responses that would concern me include the following:

> "Well, we don't really have a budget now, but I'm trying to make one available."

This tells me that the lead is either unprepared, shopping around, or just not very serious about the project.

> "We can't pay much now, but we have a *ton* of work in the pipeline. So if you work with us on your fees, we'll give you all our future work in this area."

That's a huge red flag. Even if your lead is sincere, these arrangements hardly *ever* work out for the freelancer. So as tempting as it may be to accept such an offer, don't do it! Stick to your standard fee ranges instead.

Find Out More About the Decision-Making *Process*

Next, it's very useful to know (and not out of line to ask) how the lead will make a decision. These questions can yield important clues as to whether or not this project is worth pursuing:

- Who will be involved in making a decision on this project?
- Are you considering other freelancers or firms?
- How will you make a decision? What will it be based on?

Here again, these questions may come across as a bit aggressive to some people, but don't let that worry you. The last thing you want to do is waste one or two hours quoting a project for which 10 other competitors will be submitting proposals or a 14-person committee will be making a joint decision. So be wary of answers such as …

> "My boss's boss will be making the decision. I'm just collecting information for her."
>
> "We're also getting quotes from six other freelancers."
>
> "It's really going to boil down to price. We have a very limited budget and are looking for someone who will be flexible in that regard."

Determine the *Timing* of the Decision

Finally, you should ask a few questions about the timing of a decision:

- Do you need a quote for budgeting purposes, or are you looking to hire someone soon?
- When will you make a decision, and when can I expect to hear back?
- Once I send you my proposal, when should I follow up with you?

Pay attention to the answers you get. Noncommittal answers to "When will you make a decision?" could be a sign that the prospect either is not that serious or is shopping around for the lowest quote. Or maybe the person inquiring is not the decision-maker.

To make this follow-up process easier and to ensure that you don't miss any questions, draft a one-page document with all the questions you need to ask, and keep it handy. When you call to follow up, or when a lead calls you, pull out your document and ask away!

Dealing With Voicemail Hell

This follow-up process is very effective. But you can't move leads down the funnel if you can't get in touch with them. So what do you do if you get her voicemail every time you call? As frustrating as voicemail can be, understanding how to use it to your advantage helps ensure that you get the most value from your prospecting efforts.

First, come to grips with today's corporate reality. Your prospects are working longer hours than ever before and probably even doing the work of two or three people. With the increased workload come more meetings, e-mail messages, and calls. So when these people are at their desks (which is happening less frequently), they let most of their calls (not just yours) roll to voicemail. When I started prospecting for freelance clients a few years ago, I was getting voicemail about 80 percent of the time. Today, it's closer to 90 percent. That's the current reality. Accept it.

Next, because you're going to get voicemail most of the time, instead of hanging up, take advantage of the opportunity and leave a brief, value-oriented message. Think of it as a 20- or 30-second opportunity to deliver a clear and value-laden message without being interrupted. It's your (brief) chance to shine! Make it powerful, but get to the point right away. Your entire voicemail message may run for 30 seconds, but your true value better come through in the first 5 to 10 seconds. So craft a message script that keeps your prospects from hitting the delete button. Here's how:

1. Remind the prospect why you're calling.

2. Immediately reference the person who suggested you call her (if applicable).

3. Ask if she ever uses freelancers.

4. Explain in two or three sentences who you are and why you're different.

5. Practice your script until it sounds natural and professional.

If, after leaving three voicemail messages and sending one or two follow-up e-mails over the course of three or four weeks, you haven't received a return call, move on. But stay in touch with your lead from time to time by adding her to your nurturing list (see Secret 6).

Close the Sale

Once your lead becomes an opportunity, your job is to close the sale. So assuming you already have a project identified, your next objective is to quote and land that project. The process of closing the sale—which includes asking the "expected results" question, writing a persuasive proposal, and following up—is covered in detail in Secret 7.

Take some time to go over and practice that material. Freelancers often lose valuable projects at this last stage, and knowing how to manage the quoting and final follow-up process like a pro will dramatically increase your chances of getting the work at the right price.

Nurture "Not Today" Prospects

Even the best and most experienced wealthy freelancers don't land every client and project they go after. Some leads decide to go with other freelancers. Others stay in a holding pattern for a long time. That's life.

But don't give up on these prospects or forget all about them. As you'll learn in Secret 6, the difference between truly successful freelancers and those who constantly struggle to get work often lies in what they do with prospects who aren't ready to hire them today. That's because most qualified prospects end up hiring freelancers within a few months of making their initial inquiry. And the freelancer who stays in touch is often the first one they think of when they're ready to move forward.

Troubleshooting Guide

Besides providing you with a simple and proven client-attracting system, the Master Marketing Formula can also act as a troubleshooting guide. By compartmentalizing each step in the process of getting clients, it enables you to more easily identify the root of the problem should you find yourself in a rut. Let's review how you can use the Master Marketing Formula to better diagnose your situation.

If you find yourself in any of the following situations, work on *finding high-probability prospects:*

- You don't have a prospect list.

- You're open for business and your website is live but your phone isn't ringing.

- You're wondering why, if everyone is a prospect for you, you should try to narrow it down to a small list.

- You don't have a lot of industry contacts, and your prospect list consists of fewer than 50 individuals.

- You assembled your prospect list without putting much thought into the types of companies and job titles that would have the highest probability of hiring you.

- You find yourself spending a lot of time and effort trying to "sell" leads on the value of your services or on outsourcing the work to a freelancer.

- You don't have the actual names of individuals, only company names.

If you find yourself in any of the following situations, work on *generating leads:*

- Your workload tends to be very volatile. You're very busy for a while and then have nothing at all for several weeks.

- You know what types of prospects to go after, but you're not sure how to approach them.

- You tend to do prospecting only when you have few or no projects in the queue.

- Your prospecting efforts are usually haphazard and based on whatever feels right at the time.

- You don't have a "buzz piece."

- The phone isn't ringing, and you're not getting e-mail inquiries.

- Your closest friends and relatives have no idea what you do for a living (and therefore wouldn't know how to refer you to people they know).

If you find yourself in any of the following situations, work on *getting opportunities:*

- You don't always follow up (or follow up promptly) with leads who call or e-mail you to inquire about your services.

- You don't always contact referrals given to you by clients, friends, or relatives.

- You follow up with most leads, but you give up after one or two attempts.

- Following up with leads makes you nervous.

- You don't have a set of follow-up questions written down.

- You haven't accurately defined what makes a good opportunity.

- Your leads often have trouble defining a project or deliverable you can quote.

- You spend a lot of time putting together proposals for prospects who turn out not to be that interested in your services.

If you find yourself in any of the following situations, work on *closing sales:*

- You're not sure how to best follow up on your proposals. (You don't have a process in place.)

- You spend a lot of time putting together proposals that don't turn into work.

- You come across many enthusiastic leads, but after sending a proposal, you have a hard time turning them into clients.

- Prospects don't return your calls and e-mails after getting your proposal.

- You don't have a master fee schedule.

- You don't have a pricing strategy.

- You don't have a negotiation strategy.

- You have a difficult time overcoming pricing objections from prospects.

If you find yourself in any of the following situations, work on *nurturing "not today" prospects:*

- Many of your leads are qualified but aren't ready to hire you today.
- In your field, timing is everything.
- Developing a high degree of trust and credibility with prospects is critical before they feel comfortable hiring you.
- The total lifetime value of a client in your field is significant.

Wealthy Takeaways

- Wealthy freelancers are able to land more and better clients with less effort by using a simplified yet very effective model called the Master Marketing Formula.
- Think of the Master Marketing Formula as a funnel with five specific stages: finding high-probability prospects, generating leads, getting opportunities, closing the sale, and nurturing "not today" prospects. Your job is to continually move prospects down the funnel.
- The best prospect list is the one you assemble on your own. Focus on the job titles of people who tend to hire freelancers in your field or who, with the right message, would consider doing so. And limit your search to organizations and industries where you would have the highest probability of success.
- A lead becomes an opportunity when you get a chance to present your services, discuss a project, or quote a job. You get opportunities by following up with leads, which in turn enables you to be sure there's a good fit between their needs and your services.
- Besides providing you with a simple and proven client-attracting system, the Master Marketing Formula can also act as a troubleshooting guide. By compartmentalizing each step in the process of getting clients, it enables you to more easily identify the root of the problem should you find yourself in a rut.

Secret 3: Create Your Amazing Buzz Piece

Steve Slaunwhite

When the dot-com boom crashed and burned in 2002, freelancer Michael Stelzner was in trouble. He had been working for an impressive range of high-tech clients as a creative strategist and copywriter, but "When the downturn in the industry hit, my business just dried up, virtually overnight," says Michael. Clients who didn't go out of business altogether drastically cut their spending. "I quickly went from being very busy to having next to no project work."

Worried about how he was going to support his young family, Michael decided to create a buzz piece to promote his most profitable specialty: white paper writing. In fact, his buzz piece, which took the form of a short special report, was called, appropriately, *A White Paper on White Papers.* Just one month after making it available as a free download on his website, he attracted more than 400 businesspeople hungry for that information, many of whom were good prospects for his freelance services. His project schedule began to fill again with lucrative work, and today Michael is arguably the most sought-after white paper expert in the business.

Copywriter Nicky Jameson experienced similar results. Just starting out as a freelancer, she had no clients, no contacts, and no track record. She considered cold calling to try to get her first paying client but knew that was going to be an uphill battle. Then, acting on the suggestion of her marketing coach, she decided to create a buzz piece. It was in the form of a 7-page list of tips called *The 19 New Rules of Social Media Copywriting.*

She posted the report on her website and announced its availability by issuing a press release and sending out letters to local marketing managers (her target market). "Things happened very quickly after that," Nicky reports. Hundreds of people—several of them potential clients for her services— requested the tips, and several notable blogs and industry publications picked up the story. Cape Peninsula University even added the document to the required reading list of its undergraduate advertising program!

Today, Nicky is on the cusp of becoming an internationally recognized social media copywriting guru. And she's currently fielding several copywriting, consulting, and even speaking offers. "I couldn't have got my freelance business off the ground so quickly if I hadn't created that buzz piece," Nicky reports. "Thank goodness I did!"

What is this amazing buzz piece that did wonders for Michael's and Nicky's freelance business—and could very well do the same for yours? That's what you're going to learn in this chapter. As you'll discover, a buzz piece can help you attract a lot more clients, position you as a go-to expert, and … well … create a buzz that brings opportunities to your doorstep. Next to an effective website, creating a buzz piece is the best investment you can make in your business. And considering how relatively easy it is to create, you'd be a fool not to have one!

What a Buzz Piece Is and Why You Need One

A *buzz piece* is simply an information piece of some kind. It's usually in the form of a special report but can be created in a variety of other formats as well, such as the following:

- Workbook
- Checklist
- Overview of survey results
- Toolkit
- Bundle of similar articles
- How-to guide
- Topic overview
- Chapter or section of a book

- List of tips
- Explanation of a best practice
- Great ideas guide

It's typically 5 to 10 pages in length, and most freelancers publish it electronically, as a PDF (Portable Document Format) so it can be easily downloaded from a website or sent by e-mail. However, some freelancers also have a nice-looking print version done.

For example, freelance marketing communications strategist Dianna Huff specializes in helping companies market their business on the Internet. To gain the attention of potential clients, she offers a free buzz piece called *The Web Marketing Toolkit*. It's published as a PDF and packed with useful ideas, tips, and checklists. "That toolkit attracts all the leads and enquiries I can handle," Dianna reports.

Whatever form it takes, if done right and promoted effectively, a buzz piece can draw new clients to your business like a high-powered magnet.

I was recently one of those clients who felt its pull. I was looking for a plumber to do some work in my home. I Googled plumbers in my area and visited several websites. Many of them just pitched their services—"Call us for quality service!" Nothing wrong with that! But then I came across a plumbing company that did more than just pitch—they also offered a free guide on their website called *How to Find Leaks BEFORE Water Damage Is Done*. I found myself filling out the online form right away to get it. A couple days later, I received a thank you e-mail from that company asking if I had found the guide helpful and offering me a 20 percent discount coupon on their after-hours emergency service. They got me! I didn't even consider the other plumbing companies. I called them, and they got the work.

That's the key benefit of a buzz piece. It *attracts* people. It also makes just about every aspect of the marketing and promotion of your freelance services easier and significantly more effective. For example ...

- Want to become known as the go-to corporate photographer in your city? Publish a special report called 7 *Strategies for Scheduling Busy Executives for a Photo Shoot*. You'll be seen as the expert. After all, you "wrote the book"!

- Want to make cold calling a lot less chilly? Don't call strangers and pitch your services. Instead, call contacts in your industry and offer them a complimentary copy of your buzz piece. You'll get a lot more "yes"s.

- Want to develop more opportunities from networking events? When you meet someone, don't just exchange business cards. Offer that person a free copy of your special report. You'll make an impact.

- Want to double the response to the pitch letters you send to potential clients? In that letter, offer a free copy of your buzz piece.

- Want to win more project proposals? Send a copy of your buzz piece along with your quotation. It will add a lot of credibility and distinguish you from others going after the same job.

A buzz piece sure is handy!

Selecting the Right Topic for Your Buzz Piece

Can you break into freelancing, or take your current freelance business to the next level, without a buzz piece? Sure you can. But why would you want to try it? A buzz piece is relatively simple to create, and the career-building benefits are significant, to say the least. But before you rush to your computer and start banging out your masterpiece, it's vital to ensure you select the right topic because if you select the wrong one, you're going to waste a lot of time.

I've worked with many freelance professionals who have complained that the buzz piece they worked so hard to create just isn't working. After asking some questions and reviewing the piece, I usually discover the problem lies in the topic they've chosen. It's either of no interest to their target market or not related closely enough to the type of freelancing they do—or both. The sad thing is, these professionals have often invested days or even weeks creating their buzz piece. That's a lot of wasted energy.

How do you select the right topic? Let's take a look at the two conditions *every* buzz piece must meet.

It Must Be Related to What You Do

If you're a freelance photographer specializing in corporate work, you could write a special report on how to get cheap vacations in the Bahamas and offer it for free on your website. But would that be an effective buzz piece for your business? No. Why? Because that report would only be of interest to those looking for low-cost holidays in the sun, not corporate PR directors seeking a top-notch photographer!

Your buzz piece must be related in some way to what you do. You want potential clients to be impressed that you're such a knowledgeable, skilled professional that you publish in your field. You want to be positioned in their minds as the go-to corporate photographer (or whatever your freelance expertise may be), not the go-to guy for Caribbean getaways!

Say, for example, you are indeed a freelance photographer. What kind of buzz piece would work best in attracting just the right kind of prospects to your doorstep? The best way to figure that out is to think about the top challenges, needs, and interests your potential clients have and your freelance services can address. Then create a buzz piece around one of those topics.

If your photography services target PR directors of major corporations, possible buzz piece titles could be something like these:

5 Elements Editors Want to See in a Press Release Photo

Grooming Your Executives for a Photography Shoot

Simple Instructions for Adding Photography on a Corporate Website

How to Create an Online Virtual Product Tour That Will Wow the Press

7 Inside Secrets to Making So-So Corporate Photos Look Great

As a photographer, all these topics would be related to what you do— *and* be of high interest to your target prospects. A PR director who is looking for a first-rate professional to take portraits of the executive management team is going to be impressed by your helpful report on how to schedule such an event. She's going to immediately position you in her mind as a helpful, knowledgeable expert. And as a result, the likelihood that she'll hire your freelance services—and spread the word about you to her colleagues—increases significantly.

Prospects Must Want the Information

I once worked with a graphic designer who was creating a special report on how to design an effective logo. He was going to offer this buzz piece in a direct-mail letter to a list of 350 marketing managers of companies in his city. He assumed that a report on this topic would position him as the obvious choice for logo design and other corporate branding materials.

His plan was good, but I was worried about the topic he'd chosen. I challenged him, "Dave, who would be interested in a special report on how to create a logo?"

Dave thought about it for a moment and then answered sheepishly, "I guess other designers!"

"Not the people you're mailing the letter to?" I said.

Dave immediately realized his mistake. He was creating a buzz piece that was certainly related to what he did but would be of no particular interest to corporate marketing managers, his potential clients.

"What do you know about logo design that would be really helpful to marketing managers?" I asked.

We discussed it for a while and came up with a new topic: how to review logo concepts and select the best candidate—a task with which marketing managers often struggle. Dave changed his buzz piece topic accordingly and came up with the title *A 5-Step Strategy for Selecting the Perfect Logo Design*. It was a winner. When he offered the free report in a mailing to local marketing managers, a whopping 7 percent responded, and of those, several eventually became new clients.

When you're brainstorming topics, think carefully about the potential clients you want to attract. Be sure your special report, guide, tip list, or other type of buzz piece is on a topic that's of high interest to that group so they'll be motivated to request it.

Creating Your Buzz Piece

Writing your buzz piece is comparable to crafting a website that your current freelance promotes your business. It's going to take a lot of work, but it's worth it.

It took me more than three weeks to create my first buzz piece, a special report called *101 Writing Tips for Successful Email Marketing.* It was written at a time (the late 1990s) when e-mail was just emerging as a viable marketing channel. The best practices had yet to be established. I had to do a lot of thinking and research to come up with those 101 tips! But my efforts paid off big time. Once I started using that report to market my services, I quickly became known as an e-mail copywriting expert and attracted several F-500 clients. Some companies even hired me to teach their in-house writers how to craft effective marketing e-mails!

So prepare yourself for a little work. Like your website, your buzz piece is going to represent you. It's going to showcase your knowledge and skills to potential clients and others who can help your business grow. It may very well become your number-one calling card.

Let's take a look at some tips for getting your buzz piece created. These are in no particular order. What I've done here is give you the best ideas and strategies I've discovered while creating buzz pieces for my business and coaching other freelancers in doing the same.

Start with a Compelling Title

The title of your buzz piece is like the headline of an advertisement. It has to gain attention. If it doesn't, then no matter how interesting the topic is, there's a risk that many people are not going to notice and request it. So take the time necessary to brainstorm several options. Ideally, you want the title to motivate a prospect to think, "Hmm, this is interesting. I could really use this information. How do I request this free guide?"

Don't worry about being clever. Your title doesn't have to be particularly creative to be compelling. In fact, the best buzz piece titles are often simple. For example, the special report by copywriter Nicky Jameson, the one I told you about earlier in this chapter, is called *The 19 New Rules of Social Media Copywriting.* A title doesn't get much more straightforward than that! Yet its appeal is undeniable. Marketing managers struggling with how to leverage social media sites in their own campaigns want to know what those 19 new rules are!

In fact, buzz piece titles that begin with "How to ..." or contain a number—*17 Tips to Selecting the Right Wedding Photographer*—are often winners. So start your brainstorming there.

Sometimes you'll develop a title that's intriguing but doesn't clearly describe what the buzz piece is about. If that happens, add an explanatory subtitle. I once worked with a freelance copywriter who wrote a buzz piece called *The SOS Technique*, a curious title, but not one that gives you any idea of the content. I suggested adding the subtitle *A Simple 3-Step Strategy for Getting a Higher Response to Your Google Ads*. He did, and as a result, the buzz piece became much more successful for him.

Break It Down into Sections

A nonfiction book, like this one, is broken down into chapters, sections, subsections, and in some cases, sub-subsections! This helps the reader access the information more quickly and easily and helps the writer write it! Do the same thing with your buzz piece. Divide it into sections and subsections. Then simply fill in each area.

When my friend, graphic designer Michael Huggins, sat down to write his buzz piece, *The 5 Keys to Creating a Lead-Generating Brochure*, he simply divided the work into those five sections and then divided each section into the two or three main points he wanted to address. That made the writing process a lot easier.

Try the Question-Answer Technique

Regardless of how the content is organized, most buzz pieces are essentially answers to a series of questions about a particular topic. And that's a great way to approach the writing process. Simply think of each section as a question and then answer it!

For example, if your buzz piece features some instruction on how to select the right color schemes for a corporate logo, turn that into a question: *What are three tips for selecting the best logo color schemes?* You can answer a question, can't you? (Assuming you're a logo designer, of course!)

Interview an Expert

Some of the freelance professionals I coach ask, "I want to create a buzz piece on *[insert topic]*, but I don't have a lot of experience in that area yet. How can I write about it in any authoritative way?" That's a common challenge, especially if you want to use a buzz piece to break into a new market.

I once worked with a freelance copywriter who wanted to attract white paper writing assignments. But the only portfolio sample he had was one he did for a fictional company during a course. How could he write a buzz piece on that topic with any real credibility? I suggested that he find an expert to interview and turn that into a buzz piece. He did, and the resultant special report he created helped him become very successful in that specialized market. The expertise of the white paper guru he interviewed rubbed off on him!

In my experience, most experts are more than willing to participate by being interviewed for a buzz piece. For them, it's free publicity.

Keep It Focused

Remember, you're writing a short special report, how-to guide, or other type of buzz piece that should be no more than 10 pages. That gives you room to do justice to a few good tips or ideas. That's why so many buzz pieces feature a number: *5 Keys to Creating* …, *3 Steps to Organizing* …, *7 Ways to Accomplish* …, and so forth.

If there's more information on the topic you think is important, add a list of helpful resources where readers can learn more.

Take a Stand

Don't be afraid to have a strong opinion on the topic you're writing about. Do you feel a two-column e-mail newsletter layout is more effective than a single-column design? Then say so! Readers will respect your definitive opinion, even if some disagree with it. You'll get no respect, however, for being wishy-washy or sitting on the fence.

One final tip: write your buzz piece in a style that's informative and conversational. This isn't the place for stiff formality. (Is there such a place?) This is your conversation with the readers, many of whom will hopefully be potential clients for your services. Let them hear your voice!

Blow Your Own Horn with a Persuasive Bio Page

Your buzz piece is a gift to potential clients and others who can influence the success of your business. Ideally, it contains highly valuable information readers can put into action. In a real way, you're giving away a big slice of your expertise—perhaps even some of your inside secrets. So what do you get in return?

That's where your bio page comes in. The bio page is the place where you get to tell the reader who you are, the freelance services you provide, and how they can benefit from your skills and knowledge. While the majority of your buzz piece contains solid information that's relatively nonpromotional, the bio page contains a persuasive pitch of your services. And why not? After delivering all that great content, you've earned the right!

Most readers won't mind this at all. In fact, the valuable content of your buzz piece will likely whet their appetite for the kind of services you provide. They'll want to learn more about who you are and what you do. So don't be afraid to "go for the business" on the bio page. You can ...

- Invite the reader to visit your website and sign up for your e-newsletter.
- Ask the reader to call to discuss a potential project with you and receive a prompt quotation.
- Make another offer, such as a discount on one of your most popular services.
- Encourage the reader to ask for portfolio samples of your work that closely match his needs.

Following is a good example of a bio page of a buzz piece created by freelancing team Karen Zapp and John Withers.

Do you find this bio page in any way sales-y or overly promotional? My guess is not. However, it is very persuasive, informing the reader of the beneficial services available and encouraging him or her to get in touch. If you're a marketing manager who has read this buzz piece—which features a great series of tips on how to boost Google advertising results—wouldn't you want to learn more about the authors and their services? Of course you would! And the bio page is the first place you'd look.

Karen Zapp, PE

Since the turn of the century I've been exclusively involved in sales, marketing, and direct response copywriting. Yup; I'm a licensed professional engineer (PE) who loves marketing.

For 22 years I worked in engineering related positions in oil and gas, facilities maintenance, and construction. Then when I entered the field of marketing and copywriting, and found I could combine this creative passion with the technical side of my brain . . . I was thrilled.

Plus I have a special knack for translating the complex into copy anyone can understand; copy that gets results for you.

John Withers

I've been a "writer for hire" since 1993, drafting everything from instruction manuals and test reports to web pages and white papers. I'm also a magazine columnist.

My background is aviation (helicopter, glider & airplane pilot) and engineering. A Navy veteran, I was also a flight instructor and taught helicopter aerodynamics.

As a writer and speaker I found I had a talent for explaining a technical subject to a non-technical audience. My diverse experiences and engineering background – including a physics degree – allow me to relate to a wide range of business audiences and craft results-driven copy for each.

Who we are and what we do

When you work with us you've got a team. And we thoroughly enjoy working with B2B marketing managers eager to improve marketing results; **online or offline**.

Perhaps you want help with lead generation – we'll use the latest **copywriting** strategies to strengthen your PPC ads, landing pages, emails, confirmation pages, autoresponders . . . and on it goes.

Or perhaps you're seeking help with copy on your website, crafting white papers, special reports, case studies, sales copy, or online press releases. Just give us a call or drop us a line. We'll be happy to discuss ideas and get a prompt quotation to you on a project whether it's print or online.

Quite simply our passion is working with any industry that sells **complex products and services** to a business audience. **Examples include** aviation, audio and video, construction, energy, and software. Another example of who we enjoy working with is **professional associations**.

Our offer to you

Remember on page six when John Caples said the appeal was the most important part of an ad? Knowing *why* the prospect takes your desired action? Well, there are a multitude of Internet-based tools that give you insight into your prospects and web visitors. Many of them are free. They're designed to be used on web pages to reveal "why" people do what they do.

Just give us a call or send us an email and we'll send you a free list with at least 10 of these tools.

Karen Zapp & John Withers

Copywriters & Marketing Advisors

scribe@B2Bscribe.com

240.556.0637   http://www.B2Bscribe.com

"But I'm Not a Writer!"

If your freelance specialty has something to do with writing—copywriting, corporate writing, speechwriting, etc.—then you're in pretty good shape. You can craft your own buzz piece. And you should. After all, it's not just a few pages of good information but also a showcase of your effective wordsmithing.

But what if you're not a writer? Instead, you're a designer, photographer, web programmer, or other nonscribing freelancer. The benefits of a buzz piece are so significant that you're definitely going to want one. But how are you going to get the darned thing written?

I have some tips to share with you that will help. But first, let me challenge you: are you *sure* you're not a writer? Why not give it a try? You might be surprised by how well you do. You might, in fact, be able to churn out a pretty decent rough draft you can send to a good freelance editor to polish. I've worked with many nonwriting freelancers who have written their own buzz pieces and did very well.

However, if you're still hesitant about writing it yourself, here are some alternate strategies:

- Write a very rough draft, no matter how awful the result. Just get your information and great ideas down on paper (or on screen). Then hire a good freelance writer to take that raw material and organize, rewrite, and polish it into a completed piece.

- Speak your buzz piece into a tape recorder and get it transcribed. I know many freelancers who have done this, ultimately surprised by how close the transcript is to a decent version of a written draft. There's not a huge difference between good writing and good speaking. Hire a freelance assistant (commonly called a *virtual assistant*) to do the transcribing for you. The cost ranges from $50 to $75 per recorded hour.

- Get a freelance writer to interview you. This is an effective technique if you're struggling to flesh out the information in your buzz piece and organize it. A good freelancer can probe by asking the right questions and get the great ideas out of your head and on paper.

The most expensive option, of course, is to hire a freelance writer to do the entire job, from interviewing you on the topic; conducting research to fill in the gaps; to handling all the writing, polishing, and editing. You can expect to pay $1,500 to $4,500 for this soup-to-nuts service. Sure, that's a bit of an investment, but considering the business-building benefits of a well-written buzz piece, it may be worth every penny.

Getting It Published

As I mentioned earlier, most freelancers publish a buzz piece as an electronic PDF file. This makes it easy to post on a website, send in an e-mail, and distribute in other ways online. It's also the cheapest way to publish a document—in fact, it's virtually free. You can, however, get your buzz piece published as a printed piece. Check out FedEx Office (formerly Kinko's), The UPS Store, or another print shop for the options available. You should be able to get your document printed with a color cover and a simple comb or coil binding for just a couple dollars each.

If it's within your budget, consider publishing it in both formats, electronic and print. You'll find that having a printed version comes in handy when you're at a meeting, networking event, tradeshow, or other situation where you want to put your buzz piece directly into the hands of someone who could influence the success of your business.

That brings us to the topic of design. You don't need to get too fancy here. In fact, for the inside pages of your buzz piece, you can probably do a decent job of laying out the text and images using your computer's word processing program. Microsoft Word has a variety of easy-to-use templates you can use for this purpose.

I do suggest, however, that you invest in a good cover design. It's said that books are sold by the cover, and special reports, how-to guides, tip lists, and other types of buzz pieces are no different. If you're not a graphic designer yourself, spend a few bucks to hire a good freelancer to create an eye-catching cover for you. It really makes a big difference. People will take your buzz piece more seriously. It will look more professional. And tactically, you'll be able to use a thumbnail of the cover on your website and in your other promotional materials.

A decent, professional-looking cover design for your buzz piece will run you $50 to $200—well worth the money.

Using Your Buzz Piece to Build Your Business

You've created a knockout buzz piece to help build your business. Now how are you going to use it?

A big mistake I see freelancers make is just posting their buzz piece on their website and then forgetting about it, or just sending it out to a few contacts. You need to do much more than that. Hey, you've got a terrific buzz piece in your hands, so let the world know about it! You must be constantly on the lookout for ways to leverage your buzz piece to attract more clients and win more projects. The good news is, there are several ways your buzz piece can dramatically improve the success of just about every aspect of your business. Let me share a few ideas.

Make Your Website More "Sticky"

Place your buzz piece on your website home page along with an invitation to visitors to request a free copy. Be sure to include a sign-up form so you can capture names and e-mail addresses.

Not only will this tactic increase the amount of inquiries you get into your freelance services, but you'll build a list of prospects you can follow up on later to get even more clients and work.

Offer It in Your Sales Letters, E-Mails, and Ads

If you use sales letters, e-mails, or advertising to promote your business, you know how hit-and-miss these strategies can be. But offering your buzz piece as a free giveaway in your marketing piece will dramatically improve results.

Bob Bly, a renowned freelance copywriter who has worked with hundreds of clients on their advertising campaigns says, "There's absolutely no doubt about it. A free report or other valuable information giveaway will substantially increase the success of your direct mail letters, emails, ads and other direct-response marketing campaigns."

Use It to Improve Your Cold Calls

No one likes doing cold calls. But sometimes they're necessary for making new contacts and building your business. If you want to make your cold calling more effective, offer your buzz piece. Consider these two examples:

Cold call without a buzz piece:

> Hi Mr. Johnston. This is John Smith calling. I'm a freelance web designer specializing in e-mail newsletters. I'm just calling to introduce my services to you and to offer you a free review of your current e-mail marketing template.

Cold call with a buzz piece:

> Hi Mr. Johnston. This is John Smith calling. I'm a freelance web designer and the author of the special report called 7 *Ways to Get More Clicks and Sales Off Your Email Newsletter.* In fact, that's why I'm calling you today, to ask if you'd like me to send you a free copy.

Both of these scripts are good. But if you were Mr. Johnston, which cold call would you respond to more favorably? My guess is the second one.

Give It Away at Networking Events and Speaking Engagements

When you meet a potential new client at a networking event, offer him a free copy of your buzz piece. You'll make a much greater impression on him than if you just exchanged business cards.

If you talk before groups to promote your business (a great strategy, by the way), tell the audience about your buzz piece and offer a free copy to anyone who gives you his business card. In fact, your presentation can be built around the topic of your buzz piece!

Announce It to the Press

Publication editors are always interested in good information on hot topics. The availability of your buzz piece could be picked up as news, or its content could be quoted in related stories.

Freelancer Nicky Jameson sent out a press release announcing her special report, and the story was subsequently picked up by several industry blogs and two major publications.

Clip It to Quotations and Proposals

When you're quoting on a project, a buzz piece can add credibility that distinguishes you from the other freelance professionals going after the same job. Every time my friend, graphic designer Michael Huggins, clipped his buzz piece on creating effective brochures to his proposals, he won the work—even when his price was the highest bid!

Send It to Past Clients and Other Contacts

A buzz piece is an excellent way to stay in touch—or reestablish contact— with past clients, prospects, and other contacts. You can send an e-mail that says something like, "Just getting in touch to say my new special report on how to create winning direct-mail pieces has just been published. May I send you a free copy?"

This is a particularly effective technique to get back on the radar screens of contacts who may have forgotten you. A few months ago, I was working with a freelancer who offered her new buzz piece to every prospect she had any contact with over the past four years but who had *never* used her services. Within a week, two of those presumably dead-end leads contacted her to request project quotes. She won one of those projects, worth $7,800!

A buzz piece? No freelancer should be without one.

Wealthy Takeaways

- A buzz piece is a document you create to position you as an expert in what you do. It's usually published in the form of a special report, 5 to 10 pages in length.

- The topic of your buzz piece must be related to what you do and of keen interest to your target prospects.

- Using a buzz piece in your marketing and other self-promotion activities can double the results you get.

- A buzz piece can help you win more quotations and proposals, as well as attract more referrals and publicity.

- You don't have to write your buzz piece yourself. You can get a good freelance editor or writer to help you.

Secret 4: Employ High-Impact Prospecting Tactics

Ed Gandia

One of the most disappointing moments of my freelance career occurred during my first month in business. I had just completed an extensive copywriting course and was anxious to land some work. So I set up a simple website and mailed 600 sales letters promoting my services to potential clients.

The result: a whopping zero response.

I couldn't believe it! Why wasn't the phone ringing? Why weren't potential clients contacting me to quote projects? After all, I had gone about this in what seemed to be a very logical fashion. To compile my list, I had used a directory I found in my local library—a resource that listed the names of marketing executives at companies that use direct marketing to promote their products. I was positioning myself as a direct marketing copywriter, so I thought for sure these marketers would be happy to hear from me.

That was my first mistake: confusing *prospects* with *leads*. As discussed briefly in an earlier chapter, prospects are people you've determined would be good targets for your specific services. That determination is based on the industry they're in, the titles they hold, the work they do, and other important qualifiers. Leads, on the other hand, are prospects who have indicated a certain level of interest in what you have to offer.

The people on my list were merely prospects. They were good targets because they were in my target market. But until they responded to my mailer, they couldn't be considered leads. This may seem like a trivial distinction, but had I realized the difference between a prospect and a lead, I would have reset my expectations and given my prospecting plan a little more thought.

My second mistake (I made a few more; I tell you about them later in this chapter) was to go about my prospecting in a haphazard fashion. Direct mail is an excellent tactic for generating leads, but I had no real plan behind my campaign. I had picked direct mail just because it sounded like a good idea and because I thought my letters would generate a ton of leads.

However, for wealthy freelancers, prospecting is not necessarily about generating the most leads possible. It's about generating *quality* leads—leads that have a high chance of turning into clients. Rather than picking prospecting tactics based on what sounds good at the moment (which is tempting to do when so many options are available), wealthy freelancers concentrate their time, effort, and budgets on the prospecting tactics and approaches that produce the best results for the time and money invested.

That's high-impact prospecting. And in this chapter, I show you how to turn your limited time and budget into a customized prospecting strategy that produces a steady and predictable flow of high-quality leads. We have a lot to cover, so fasten your seat belt and hang on to your hat!

The Marketing Effectiveness Matrix™

The first step in developing your own high-impact prospecting plan is to narrow down your prospecting options to only those that will work best for your particular situation. To help you do that, you need a framework that takes into account your goals, available time, and preferences and tempers those factors against the effectiveness of the many different marketing vehicles available.

That's where the Marketing Effectiveness Matrix™ (MEM) comes in. The MEM is a powerful decision-making tool that takes much of the emotion and guesswork out of prospecting decisions. It helps you determine which prospecting efforts you should focus on and which ones you should steer clear of.

As you can see, the MEM is divided into four quadrants. *Quadrant 1* contains prospecting tactics that tend to be both highly effective and time-efficient.

Quadrant 2 represents tactics that are also very effective but require more time to develop and execute. Regardless of your goals, most of your efforts should revolve around these first two quadrants.

Quadrant 3 contains tactics that could work well, but you have to be very selective here, as the effectiveness of these tactics is often much lower than for the tactics in the first two quadrants.

Finally, *quadrant 4* represents tactics that are mostly wasteful because they take too long to carry out *and* they deliver questionable (or very little) value—a double whammy! (Amazingly, many freelancers spend an inordinate amount of time in this quadrant. The reason: when you don't have a sound prospecting plan, it's easy to confuse activity with effectiveness.)

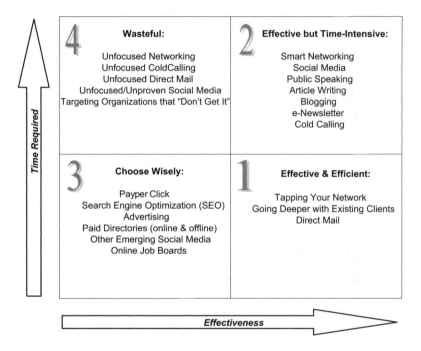

The Wealthy Freelancer's Prospecting Mix

Although there's no *one* combination of prospecting tactics ideal for all freelance professionals, virtually every wealthy freelancer employs one or more of the following five tactics, each of which resides in either quadrant 1 or quadrant 2:

- Tapping your network
- Getting more out of existing clients
- Investing in smart local networking

- Leveraging social media as a networking tool
- Employing direct mail

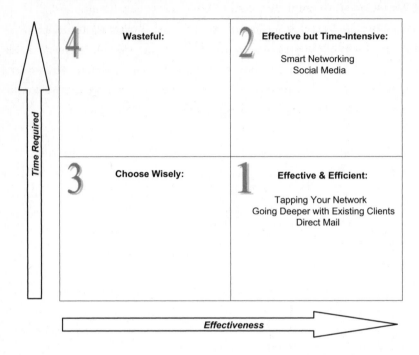

Tapping Your Network

Whether you're new to freelancing or already a seasoned pro, approaching people you already know—personally or professionally—about your freelance business is always the best place to start prospecting.

First, people who know you already trust you to some degree (hopefully!). Second, it's often easier and less stressful to approach people you know than it is to contact complete strangers. And finally, if you're just getting your freelance career started, talking to friends, colleagues, and relatives about what you do allows you to develop and refine your message in a less threatening environment.

Relatives, Friends, Colleagues, and Potential Partners

Start with the people who know you best. Even if your closest friends can't take advantage of your expertise, they may know someone who can. For instance, when I was launching my business, I made sure to tell as many friends, colleagues, and relatives as possible. I also got in the habit of taking friends out to lunch or coffee a couple times a month. I would explain my plans and ask them if they could think of anyone who might need the services of a freelance copywriter. Most of these conversations didn't pay off in terms of landing new business, but a few did.

I remember one in particular where I took a good friend (a freelance marketing professional) out to lunch. After running through my plans, she told me she might know a couple businesses that could use my services. I thanked her for her offer to make some calls on my behalf, but frankly I wasn't expecting much. Well, a couple months later, she hired me to work on a project for one of her clients. A few weeks after that, she referred me to one of her previous clients, who ended up hiring me on the spot. Four years (and tens of thousands of dollars) later, this company is still a good client of mine!

Current or Previous Employer

Another great—and often overlooked—source of potential work is your current or previous employer. I'm not suggesting you approach your employer while you're working for them, but they may be worth keeping in mind once you go out on your own. So whenever possible, try to leave on good terms.

Also, when you're out on your own, you may want to contact other previous employers. Let them know what you're doing, and ask your contacts there if they can put you in touch with the right individual.

Previous Employer's Competitors

If your previous employer is not interested or able to hire you as a freelancer, you might want to consider pursuing some of the their competitors—especially if your knowledge and experience in your field make you a very attractive service provider. When pitching your services, be sure to let prospects know right away about your experience and background. Don't bury this information in your e-mail, letter, or call.

One caveat: be careful that you're not violating any nondisclosure or noncompete agreements with your previous employer. Consult with an attorney if you have any doubts about this.

Going Deeper with Existing Clients

If you already have an existing freelance business, don't overlook your exist-ing clients as sources of leads. Referrals from happy clients can be one of the most effective ways to market your freelance business. We look at referrals and how to cultivate them in Secret 5, but for now, try to get in the habit of asking your clients for the names of peers and colleagues who could also benefit from your services.

Besides being excellent sources of referrals, existing clients can also be great sources of additional work. In fact, too often, freelancers lose projects to competitors because clients are unaware of the many additional services their freelancers offer. You also miss out on fantastic project opportunities when other key decision-makers within a client organization don't know about you. This is another valuable strategy we cover in more detail in Secret 5.

Smart Local Networking

Wait! Before you skip over this section because you think you're not cut out for schmoozing at cocktail parties, I have a confession to make: I'm not a fan of networking functions. In fact, although I spent a great part of my career in sales and consider myself a fairly social person, I prefer more intimate settings and more one-on-one interaction rather than large meet-and-greet events.

If you're a master networker and can work a room like a pro, by all means, do your thing. But if you're *not* a natural at this, I have a few ideas that will make networking a very valuable prospecting tactic.

Focus Your Efforts

First off, it's essential to focus your efforts. Going to every networking breakfast and joining every leads club in town is counterproductive—and completely insane! You'll be spreading yourself too thin. Instead, stick to a couple organizations and get involved as much as possible in each one. Begin your search by selecting no more than six organizations. Attend a few of their events and meetings, and see which ones you truly like.

Focus on organizations loaded with potential prospects in your chosen specialty or target market. At a minimum, concentrate on organizations whose members *truly understand the value of your services and could potentially hire you*. When you have a really good feel for each of these organizations and the type of people who attend its meetings and events, narrow your list to no more than two or three (sometimes one organization is all you need) and become a member.

For me, the Technology Association of Georgia (TAG) has been a wonderful group to get involved in. Because my target market is software and technology companies, this is a prospect-rich audience. Plus, TAG gives me exposure in my local market.

Go Deep

In addition to focusing your networking efforts on only a couple organizations, I've also learned that it pays to go deep within each one. By "deep" I mean getting truly involved. Don't just attend the meetings. Join the board. Get involved in some of the committees. Volunteer and help out in any way possible. Frankly, you can't expect to get to know prospects over coffee and doughnuts at the occasional meet-and-greet. If you truly want to develop meaningful relationships—and if you want prospects to get to know you— you need to serve on a committee or a board with them. Giving generously of your time is the best way I've found to do that.

For instance, I'm a member of the TAG Marketing Society's board, where I've also served as the chairman for, and adviser to, the annual "TAMY Awards"—Georgia's technology marketing awards—for a number of years. This volunteer position has enabled me to get to know potential clients and partners. It has also given me name recognition, and it has helped me—both directly and indirectly—land a significant amount of work.

Truthfully, the work I've landed as a result of my involvement with TAG has come from a genuine desire to help out and make a difference first—from putting together great meetings for the members and memorable awards ceremonies for the local technology community. I've discovered that when your efforts are motivated by sheer joy, people recognize that you're not just doing this to promote your business. You're doing it because you want to make a difference.

Think Long Term

Finally, think of networking as a long-term investment in your business. Most of the benefits won't come overnight. They'll take time and often come when you least expect them—and surprisingly, when you need them most!

So don't expect a miracle from attending one meeting. Focus, go deep, put in the time and effort, and you'll see results in due time.

Networking with Social Media

When it comes to new trends and technologies, I consider myself a bit of a laggard. In fact, in some cases I can be downright cynical about the latest and greatest fad. Social media is a perfect example. When Facebook and Twitter got really popular, it seemed as if everyone lived for this stuff. No longer did you need to chat on the phone or have a meaningful face-to-face conversation over lunch. You had Twitter! You had Facebook! Why do anything else? Why even leave the house?

Well, in late 2008, I could no longer ignore the Twitter and Facebook freight trains. So I joined both sites. And frankly, I've been blown away by the possibilities of these social media tools—especially for freelance professionals looking for new clients. Through Twitter alone, I've been able to connect with high-profile individuals I would never have reached had I tried to contact them via phone or e-mail. I've had interesting private and public exchanges with best-selling authors. And I've been contacted by several potential clients and joint venture partners—all while I sat at my desk wearing pajamas!

$ Success Story

Build a Very Focused Prospect List

A few years ago, freelance marketing professionals Noelle Abarelli and Carey Kauffman (www.SoleadoMarketing.com) started taking a much more focused approach to prospecting. Rather than promoting their services to everyone who was targetable, they decided to manually compile a list of 100 high-probability prospects.

Because of their technology marketing backgrounds, Noelle and Carey began their search by focusing on only U.S. technology companies. Next, they pared their list to include only small and midsize companies located in their region. Finally, they strategically analyzed each of those companies, looking for businesses that sold technologies Noelle and Carey had experience marketing, seemed exciting, or showed big promise. When they had their finalists, they reached out to their industry contacts to see if anyone had relationships in these companies. "If we found someone who knew a key marketing contact in one of these companies, we would try to get a personal introduction, which would help us bypass a lot of barriers," explains Noelle. "Other times we would just get insights into the culture or marketing philosophies of some of these companies, which was great, too. That kind of insider information would often help us decide if a company should even be on our list."

Noelle and Carey's success with this approach has been phenomenal. It has not only focused their efforts but has also cut their marketing expenses and allowed them to spend less time screening prospects. Most importantly, it has enabled them to maintain a steady flow of work.

What Exactly Is Social Media?

Social media is nothing more than content created by its own audience and the publishing technology used to share that content. But more importantly, social media marketing is an engagement with online communities to generate exposure, opportunity, and sales, according to Michael A. Stelzner, founder of WhitePaperSource and author of *Social Media Marketing Industry Report*. Says Stelzner: "The real shocker is that experienced folks are investing more than 20 hours each week in social media."

For most freelancers and solo professionals, social media marketing is a fresh, new phenomenon. And contrary to popular belief, this type of marketing is not just for twentysomethings. In fact, Stelzner's report revealed that 72 percent of the 880 surveyed professionals (most of whom were small-business owners and solo professionals) had been using social media for only a few months and their median age was 40 to 49.

That's all fascinating stuff. But as a freelancer, is it worth adding social media to your prospecting mix? The answer is a resounding "Yes!"

Thousands of freelancers are already harnessing the power of social media to generate leads, opportunities, and clients. The time has come to join the party!

Popular Social Media Sites for Freelancers

What are some of the most popular types of social media (and some specific sites) wealthy freelancers are using to generate leads?

Online discussion forums. Online forums enable you to showcase your expertise by contributing ideas and responses to forum members' questions. They may not be as sexy as some of the newer forms of social media, but there are tens of thousands of popular forums out there, and based on the traffic most of them generate, I don't see them going away anytime soon.

Blogs. The key to prospecting successfully with blogs is to focus on blogs rich with authors and commenters who could be potential prospects for you. Once you find these blogs, make it a point to contribute your comments, opinions, and insights weekly. It won't be long before you get noticed.

LinkedIn (LinkedIn.com) is a business-oriented social networking site used mainly for professional networking. As of May 2009, it had more than 40 million registered users spanning 170 industries. When used strategically, LinkedIn can become a powerful networking and business development tool.

Twitter (Twitter.com) is a social networking and "microblogging" service that enables you to send instant short messages (up to 140 characters in length) to people who want to receive them. Your tweets (what these short messages are called on Twitter) can be about anything, including what you're working on, what you're thinking, what you're reading, and what you've just accomplished. They can also be a way to point your followers to interesting information, get immediate feedback on an idea, or even poll your followers on a specific topic you're trying to learn more about.

Facebook (Facebook.com) is a hugely popular social media site used mainly to connect and stay in touch with friends and colleagues. Although much less formal than LinkedIn, Facebook can still be a powerful online networking tool and a great way to generate leads for your freelance business.

How Wealthy Freelancers Use Social Media

Talk to any freelancer who consistently lands great clients via social media, and five key success principles emerge.

Commit to Active Participation

Social media is not something you sign up for and forget about. If you want to generate activity, you have to become an active participant. You have to join the conversation and contribute ideas and insights—and you have to do it frequently.

Michele Smith (www.MCommunicationsinc.com), a freelance marketing and corporate communications pro who uses Facebook to generate as much as 30 percent of her new business, suggests daily activity on whatever site you use. "Keep your page fresh by letting everyone know what you're working on, what you've completed, or what you're planning," she says. "And post links to finished projects on your page (as long as it's OK with your clients, of course). For prospects, this will not only keep your name top of mind, it will also showcase your work and expertise."

Offer Value First

Another key success principle—and one many freelancers new to social media fail to practice—is offering value first. Social media is no different from a local networking event. You won't get far if all you do is overtly pitch your services to everyone you meet. Instead, provide your social network with tips, ideas, and insights that will help people do their jobs better. And do it much more often than you promote your business.

"You must absolutely offer something of value every time you tweet," says Ruth Perryman (TheQBspecialists.com), a Roseville, California–based freelance QuickBooks consultant. "You can't just tweet promotional information—and even when you do, it needs to be written in a way that helps people." She credits her fast success with social media to this approach. Within just a few weeks of using Twitter in this manner, her website traffic tripled, and she was contacted via Twitter by a franchisor who has since outsourced her entire accounting department to Ruth and her team of freelancers—and is now her largest client.

Contribute Ideas Freely

When contributing ideas to forums, blogs, and other types of social media, share your ideas and advice freely. You don't have to reveal every strategy or methodology you use, but don't hesitate to provide useful advice to the members of your community. Sharing your expert knowledge is today's way of building credibility, trust, and a steady stream of work.

Competitors may be able to copy some of your ideas, but no one can copy you as a multifaceted freelance professional.

Take a Steady, Long-Term Approach

You don't earn someone's trust overnight. Relationships take time to develop and cement—especially online relationships. That's why freelancers who use social media successfully don't treat it as a quick fix. They recognize that results will take time and a steady, concerted effort.

Since becoming an active participant in a number of online forums in 1995, freelance copywriter, marketer, and author Shel Horowitz (www.shelhorowitz.com) has landed close to 200 clients as a direct result of his participation in these forums. In fact, he cites online discussion forums as his single-largest source of new business. His secret: "It's not going to happen overnight. You need about six months of active participation in a forum before you start to see results. And by 'active' I mean participating about three times a week by contributing good answers to participants' questions and providing valuable feedback to the forum members."

Develop a Community

Social media is about much more than conversations. It can also help foster online communities that are centered on a common interest or goal. By starting a group on a specific topic that's of interest to both you and your prospects, you can help members of that community share news and ideas, stimulate relevant discussions around these topics, and get to know each other, all in one spot.

For instance, after losing her job in 2008, Deborah Corn (Ablaze.biz), a freelance project and production manager, created a LinkedIn group to bring together hundreds of professionals in the advertising production business—including agency recruiters, printers, service providers, and other print production professionals. Deborah's group grew exponentially and has close to 5,000 members as of this writing. Through the group, she's now connected to 11.9 million people, 3,642 of which are direct connections.

"This approach has given me tremendous visibility," says Deborah. "When users search the term 'project management and production' within the LinkedIn website, my name almost always comes up. That alone has led to several paid gigs, including a large client for which I've been freelancing for six months now."

Using Direct Mail

Some freelancers are so good at tapping their personal and professional networks, going deeper with existing clients, working local events, and using social media that they can get and stay booked solid for years without having to do much more prospecting. But most of us have to supplement that effort with a prospecting tactic that can predictably generate a steady stream of leads throughout the year. And the best way to do that is with direct mail.

Direct mail enables you to reach hundreds of prospects quickly and cost-effectively. It's also very predictable in that, over time, you'll know roughly how many letters you'll have to mail to generate just one lead. This predictability makes direct mail a very adjustable tactic. As your capacity to take on new clients and your income goals change, you can easily adjust the number and frequency of mailings to reflect your needs. For these reasons, direct mail should become the one prospecting activity you continually run in the background while you carry out other promotional efforts.

Think of direct mail as a seasoned salesperson with a polished script. When your letter carries all the components of a well-crafted message, it's the equivalent of having a top-notch salesperson "pitching" a concept or idea to prospects on your behalf. But unlike in a traditional in-person meeting, your direct-mail recipients can read your message without the typical pressure they might feel when getting a cold call or meeting with a salesperson. Their guards are down. They're more receptive. And if your message is relevant and persuasive, they'll read further and perhaps even respond.

Direct mail is also dependable. This loyal army of "paper salespeople" never complains. It never asks for more vacation time, a better health insurance plan, or higher commission rates. Instead, your loyal army diligently works its way into your prospects' offices and consistently delivers your message. Of course, its success rate may not be as high as that of networking or client referrals, but when you consider how easy it is to mail a few letters every week—and how repeatable this process is—direct mail is one prospecting vehicle you cannot ignore.

What's Working in Direct Mail

Rather than overtly promoting their services or blasting out thousands of postcards or letters (as I did early in my career), wealthy freelancers use a more strategic two-step approach with their direct-mail campaigns.

The first step is to offer prospects relevant and valuable information in the form of a special report or other type of buzz piece (we discuss buzz pieces fully in Secret 3). The letter's main objective is to persuade the prospect to request this buzz piece, which the prospect can do by going to a special page on your website.

The second step involves following up with all prospects (now leads) who downloaded your buzz piece to try to convert as many of them as possible into opportunities and clients.

When done well, this approach helps you capture many more leads while helping you reduce the effort required to turn those leads into opportunities and clients. Here are the elements you'll need to make this strategy work:

- A targeted mailing list
- A persuasive letter
- A solid buzz piece
- A means of handling buzz piece requests
- A means of delivering your buzz piece

Let's take a look at each in a little more detail.

The Mailing List

You can purchase or rent lists from various sources, but no list will be as good as the one you compile manually. Secret 5 offers a number of excellent sources for assembling a mailing list.

Put together your own targeted list using a variety of sources. And be sure to "code" each prospect based on where you got his or her name. That way you can track which sources seem to be yielding the best response.

The Letter

Your prospecting letter should be short (one or two pages max), to the point, and it must be a letter (sorry, no postcards!). Although there are many ways to write a prospecting letter, you'll want to use the following structure, developed by veteran copywriters Bob Bly and Gary Blake:

- Attention
- Problem
- Solution
- Proof
- Action

First, you must grab the reader's *attention* with a powerful headline. You then start out your letter discussing or implying a *problem* that's relevant to your reader and addressed by your buzz piece. From there, you position your buzz piece (the *solution*) as an informative and authoritative resource on the topic. You then go on to briefly tell the reader why you are qualified to provide advice on the topic (*proof*). And you conclude the letter by providing the address of a specific website where the reader can take *action* (download your buzz piece).

I want to show you one of the first letters I used to find prospects for my freelance business. On average, this letter generated a very respectable 5 to 7 percent response rate every time I mailed it. That means for every 100 letters I mailed, 5 to 7 prospects downloaded my special report. That's considerably higher than the 1 percent response many direct marketers shoot for.

Again, the objective of your letter is to persuade prospects to request your buzz piece, which in this example is a special report. That's it! Of course, you can—and should—include a couple sentences about who you are. But the idea here is to generate as many downloads of your buzz piece as possible, not ask for work at this time. (Occasionally, one of your letter recipients will call you to discuss a specific project as a result of reading your letter. If that happens, great! But those calls will be the exceptions to the norm.)

Are You a Software Marketer Looking For a Steadier Stream of Qualified Leads?

May 1, 2004

John Doe
Software Co., Inc.
123 Main St.
Atlanta, GA 30004

Dear John:

What if you could generate more and more quality leads – *consistently* – while getting a higher return on your precious marketing dollars?

In a recent project, I helped a software company increase sales of one of their solutions by 433% in under 30 months, yielding an ROI of over 2,700%.

The secret? High-impact, results-oriented copy...combined with a proven lead generation methodology—a combination that could produce similar results for your company.

I'd like to share with you some proven techniques that could help fine-tune your own lead generation efforts. You'll find them in my new **FREE report**, *10 Proven Steps to Creating a High-Impact "Software Lead Generation Machine."*

To request a copy, simply go to: **www.edgandia.com/report**

Here's a sampling of what you'll learn in this valuable report:

- 9 key questions about your selling process that will help you create more effective lead generation campaigns. The answers will directly determine the number (and quality) of the leads you'll get.

- Why so many software companies use the wrong message when targeting prospects...and how you can avoid this common pitfall.

- 12 proven "offers" you can use in your campaigns to double response rates...while increasing lead quality at the same time.

- Why (and how) using a "creative brief" can help you create higher-impact materials, more quickly...and with *fewer headaches*.

- A simple strategy that could easily increase response rates by 100% - 500%. You may be using it already...but probably <u>not</u> to its fullest extent...*or in the right manner*.

▫ And over a dozen more powerful techniques to boost your response rates, conversion rates, and lead quality...all the necessary ingredients to start creating a **steadier stream of qualified leads.**

So...who am I to be giving advice about lead generation?

I'm a freelance B2B copywriter specializing in the software industry, but I'm also a successful 10-year sales veteran. I've spent half of my sales career in the trenches selling software and IT solutions...so I understand the strategic selling process and what it involves.

I also know the importance of writing copy that aids this process. Targeted, benefit-oriented copy that gets more suspects to engage with you. And copy that gets prospects to move more quickly through your sales funnel.

In fact, I credit my ability for writing powerful, effective copy—the ability to "sell on paper"—for helping me reach and beat sales quotas throughout my career. I've highlighted many of these winning techniques in this report...and I'd like to share them with you. So why not go to **www.edgandia.com/report** and request your free copy now?

And should you need help crafting lead generation materials...or help polishing what you have now...simply contact me at **770-419-3342** or ed@edgandia.com with the details. The consultation is free.

Sincerely,

Ed Gandia
Freelance Copywriter

PS – Could your sales force use a **steadier stream of qualified leads** ? Could your lead generation materials use a boost? For powerful strategies and techniques that can start helping you drive more (and better quality) leads, simply go to:

www.edgandia.com/report

And request your free copy of my new report, 10 Proven Steps to Creating Your Own *High-Impact "Software Lead Generation Machine."*

The Buzz Piece

Again, we cover buzz pieces at length in Secret 3. But for now, just keep in mind that regardless of your profession, the success of your direct-mail efforts depends greatly on the topic, quality, *and* title of your buzz piece. A high-quality piece will speak volumes about the kind of freelancer you are and your knowledge of both the profession you work in and the industries you target.

Handling Buzz Piece Requests

To ensure a successful campaign, you must make it easy for your leads to request and download your buzz piece. If you make the process too complicated for them ("Go to my website, click on 'reports,' then click on 'free reports,' then scroll down …") or if you ask too much of them ("Call me directly to request your report"), you will lose the majority of interested prospects. To avoid that, stick to either the *URL and dedicated landing page* approach or the *fax reply sheet* method (or use both).

The URL and dedicated landing page approach involves creating an extra page on your website dedicated to downloading your buzz piece. This page won't be visible to regular visitors, and your home page won't even have a link pointing to it. Only your letter's recipients will know it exists. After reading your letter, interested prospects can get there by typing in the web address you provide them in the letter. On this page (often called a *landing page*) they should see some brief copy about your buzz piece. Not too much— just enough to assure them that they're in the right place.

Next, under the copy about your buzz piece, insert a short registration form that prompts the lead for his or her name, company name, e-mail address, and phone number. The idea is simple: in exchange for some basic contact information, you provide the visitor with a copy of your buzz piece. However, keep that form short. Ask only for the information I suggested earlier. If it feels like a mortgage application, your prospects won't bother to fill it out. Here's what mine looks like:

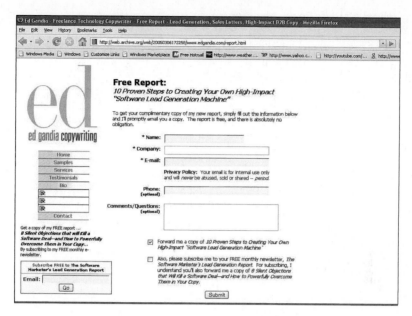

The fax reply sheet method is very similar to the URL-and-landing-page method. The main difference is that rather than sending your prospects to a landing page on your website, you include a fax reply sheet with your letter, which you ask prospects to fill out and fax back to you. Pete Savage has had great success using both methods in his letter campaigns. He's found that a large percentage of respondents will reply via fax rather than go to your landing page. And in some cases, having this second option even increases responses. Here, again, is what mine looks like:

Two Easy Ways to Get Your Free White Paper Guide :

1)   Visit www.EdGandia.com/secrets
2)   Or enter your email below and fax this page to
     678.555.1567.

Enter your email below and FAX to 678.555.1567

21 Ways to Generate
Better Leads
With White Papers

By Ed Gandia

☐   **Yes, please email me your free white paper guide!**

Name: <First Name><Surname>

*Email: _____

We respect your privacy. Your email will NEVER be sold or shared.

☐   **Ed , please call me to discuss a potential copywriting project:**

My phone: _____

Best time to call me is: _____

This white paper guide is full of practical ideas and insights you can put to use immediately, including:

✓ How to best leverage your white paper in the sales cycle — and when to use it for optimal impact.

✓ What you should never include in your paper's title (if you want prospects to read it!).

✓ What's the optimal length of a white paper? Depends on the audience. I'll show you what works best for each one .

✓ The two types of readers you'll need to write for, and how to do it well.

✓ Three simple tips that will help increase your white paper downloads.

Again, to receive your copy, visit www.EdGandia.com/secrets or fill out and fax this sheet to 678.555.1567.

Delivering Your Buzz Piece

Once a lead submits his or her contact information, you can handle delivery of the buzz piece in one of two ways. One approach is to have an auto-responder automatically send an e-mail to the prospect with a web link to that document. An autoresponder is a service that collects a lead's contact information and automatically sends an e-mail with the requested information to that individual. I use AWeber (www.aweber.com), but there are many others out there, including Interspire and GetResponse.

If you don't want to go through the trouble and expense of setting up an autoresponder, you can have your website automatically e-mail you every time someone requests your buzz piece. At that point, you can either manually e-mail the buzz piece or send a direct web link to that file.

The latter is the method I chose to use at first, and it's the one I still prefer. Yes, it involves more work because you'll have to manually e-mail the buzz piece to every respondent. But this approach also enables you to personalize your e-mail message, which can be a nice touch. Of course, if you're not always in front of a computer, or if you have a full-time job that prevents you from checking your personal e-mail a few times a day, then the autoresponder is the way to go.

Wealthy Takeaways

- High-impact prospecting is about generating quality leads that have a high chance of turning into clients.

- Wealthy freelancers concentrate their time, effort, and budgets on prospecting tactics and approaches that produce the best results for the time and money invested.

- Virtually every wealthy freelancer employs one or more of the following five tactics: tapping their network, getting more out of existing clients, investing in smart local networking, leveraging social media, and employing direct mail.

- Approaching people you already know—personally or professionally—about your freelance business is always the best place to start prospecting.

- Besides being excellent sources of referrals, existing clients can also be great sources of additional work.

- The secret to successful local networking is to focus on only one or two organizations; become active in each one; and treat it as a long-term initiative, not a quick fix.

- Thousands of freelancers are using social media to generate leads, opportunities, and clients by participating actively, offering value first, contributing ideas freely, taking a long-term approach, and developing targeted communities.

- Direct mail should become the one prospecting activity you continually run in the background while you carry out other promotional efforts.

- Rather than blasting out thousands of postcards or letters to overtly promote your services, use direct mail to promote a high-quality buzz piece that positions you as an expert in your field.

Secret 5: Cultivate Repeat and Referral Business

Pete Savage

"I have a handful of clients who account for the majority of my income."

"I get most of my business through referrals."

When I was starting out as a freelancer, I used to hate it when I heard other freelancers say these things! There I was, slugging away, trying to make a living on small projects from lousy clients, while some other freelancers seemed to have it made. Could it be they were really just sitting there, leisurely lapping up all the new business that came their way?

Eventually I learned, of course, that it does take *some* effort to get repeat and referral business, but it certainly is a much easier way to grow and sustain your business versus constantly fishing for new clients.

Think of all the marketing effort you have to exert to get someone's attention for the first time. Take a sales letter, for example. Writing, graphic design work, paper, ink, printing, envelopes, and postage all require a certain amount of your time, energy, and money. Compare this with the effort it takes to pick up a ringing phone and listen as your client says, "We've got another job for you." I know which scenario I prefer!

In this chapter, we go over the things you must do to get your clients excited about sending more business your way and passing your name around. The techniques revealed in this chapter really are the easiest way to grow your freelance business and, if you focus your energy on doing these things right, you, too, can reach that point where the vast majority of your business *comes to you!*

It Pays to Advertise

A few years ago, I witnessed one of the most effective self-promotion campaigns I have ever seen. It happened one night at the Air Canada Centre in Toronto, partway through a U2 concert.

My wife and I were sitting in decent lower bowl seats, a little off to the side. Three members of U2 were performing on stage. Bono, the band's front man, was singing and parading around on a long, semi-circular platform that extended out into the massive audience about 50 rows deep. This exaggerated stage enabled him to get closer to thousands more fans throughout the show.

At one point, I noticed a fan standing 10 or so feet back from the platform who was waving a large homemade sign. Each time Bono walked by, the fan thrust the sign up in the air and waved it madly. Bono eventually saw it, too, and squinted to read it. What he read moved him to take immediate action!

I couldn't see the sign, but I could see Bono's reaction. He walked toward the sign's owner and made a pointing gesture, singling him out amidst a crowd of thousands. Then with a wave of his hand, Bono motioned that this fan be brought up onto the platform! Nearby fans, happy to oblige the wish of their crooning idol, helped jockey the fan through the tightly packed crowd and hoist him up onto the platform in unison. There stood the fan, face to face with the rock star he'd been desperately trying to flag down. He was still clutching the sign. Bono took it.

He looked it over again, as if to read it carefully and think of something to say. Then he looked out into the crowd, raised his microphone to his mouth and said, "Well … I guess it pays to advertise." With that, he held the sign up high, for everyone to see. And that's when I read the five words that were written in big, black capital letters on the homemade poster. Seeing the words on the sign, it was plain to see why Bono had yanked this man, and not some other person, out from the crowd of thousands. The sign read:

ME + GUITAR = PEOPLE GET READY

I looked again at the fan and noticed he now had a guitar slung over his shoulder! (A stagehand must have brought it out to him.) The band, following Bono's lead, suddenly broke into a rendition of the Curtis Mayfield hit "People Get Ready." The mesmerized fan, with nothing but the obvious left to do, began strumming the guitar while Bono stood beside him and sang.

That fan was rewarded because he used a creative method to advertise his abilities. Without this sign proclaiming his talents, how else would Bono know that this fan in particular was willing and able to hop up on stage and perform the song?

The same goes for you when trying to get closer to your clients. Unless you *tell* them what you're capable of, they may never know the full breadth of what you have to offer. This is why, if you want clients to reward you with more business, you, too, (no pun intended) must "wave a sign" that advertises what you're capable of. Following are a few easy but effective ways to do just that.

Itemize Your Services on Your Website

Maybe you're a freelance graphic artist and your client hired you to design a logo and stationery. But does she know you also design websites? She would, if she saw "Website Design" as one of the services specifically listed on your website.

On my website, I don't just say I offer "copywriting" and leave it at that. Instead, I have a dedicated "Services" page that lists more than a dozen specific copywriting services I provide. Here's the list:

Sales Letters

Direct-Mail Packages

E-Mail Marketing Campaigns

Newsletters and E-Newsletters

Landing Pages

Websites

Webinars/Teleseminars

Online Video Ad Scripting

Case Studies

Testimonial Ten-Pack™

White Papers

E-Books and Business Booklets

Thought Leadership Articles

E-Mail Templates (for sales force)

Letter Templates (for sales force)

Sales Presentations

Brochures and Sales Sheets

Proposals (on a limited basis)

Thanks to this list, a marketing director who wants to hire me to write a sales letter now but also has to crank out a white paper, two sales presentations, a webinar, and a case study for his sales team next month will realize he's hit the talent jackpot!

Send Out Thousands of E-Mail Advertisements for Free!

What if you could place an advertisement in the one spot where every client or prospect was virtually guaranteed to see it? Well, you can, and it won't cost you a dime to advertise there.

I'm talking about the space at the bottom of your own e-mail messages, right below your name. That's right, your e-mail signature is a great place to list a handful of services you wish to promote. You don't have to come up with anything complicated or fancy. Here's a simple example of a good e-mail signature that gets the message across:

> **Courtney Jameson** — *Graphic Designer*
> *Direct Mail — E-Mail — Landing Pages — Case Studies*
> *e: courtney@herwebsiteurl.com   p: 123-456-7890*

Create a Fee Schedule

A fee schedule is easy to create. Start by making a two-column document on your computer. In the left column, list your services. In the right column, list your fees (or fee range) for each service. That's it! (See Secret 7 for an example and get more coverage of fee schedules.)

You can now be sure every new client of yours gets a fee schedule. What's more, you can update this every six months and send a new copy to all your clients. This is an effective tool to have in your marketing arsenal because it's so disarming. It's a great advertisement for all your services, but it doesn't look anything like an ad. That means clients are more likely to read it and hang on to it.

After receiving my fee schedule, one client of mine, an experienced marketing manager for a huge blue-chip company, told me she'd never seen one before and that it would be a great help to her when budgeting projects. I got a lot of business from that client over the next several years. Another client once told me, "The fact that you have a fee schedule tells me you know what you're doing. I like that you can give me a specific price or range on a project, rather than say, 'Well, it depends.' When freelancers tell me, 'It depends,' I take it to mean they've never done that project before, or they have no idea whether or not their services are fairly priced." Since receiving the fee schedule, this client has essentially gone shopping and "ordered" a slew of new projects from me. Having a fee schedule also impresses potential new clients and motivates them to hire you, as Steve explains in Secret 7.

Say you're a graphic designer and you've never designed a banner ad but you'd like to. What's stopping you from putting "Banner Ad" on your fee schedule? Nothing! Your fee schedule should include all the services you're capable of doing even if they're new to you. When clients see a service listed in your fee schedule, they will of course assume you can deliver it. Perception is reality! So if you know you're *capable* of delivering a service that's new to you, go ahead and include it on your fee schedule.

Using techniques to advertise your services lets clients know about the breadth of services you offer, setting the stage for various more projects to come your way.

Get the Basics Right

For clients to *want* to give you additional work, or pass your name on to a friend, you must maintain a handful of basic performance standards on every project:

1. Be a joy to work with.

2. Be professional.

3. Deliver outstanding work.

4. Be flexible.

5. Thank clients frequently.

These are indeed *basic* standards, but they're worthy of discussion here because, surprisingly, not all freelancers adhere to them on every job. Ignore these basics, however, and you blow your chances of getting repeat or referral business from your existing clients.

With that in mind, let's go over the five basic performance-standard credos that should be central to your freelance practice.

Be a Joy to Work With

There's no future for the rude, short-tempered, or arrogant freelancer. Don't be unpleasant to work with by heaving an audible sigh when the client asks for minor revisions or changes to your creative work.

Make it your mission to be the person who delivers excellent work on every project, while making the entire process a treat for the client.

Be Professional

If you call yourself a professional, you must act professionally. This means much more than simply meeting deadlines, keeping promises, and the like. This means you take ownership of the work you engage in.

You work *with* a client to get a project finished. You eschew the "I've done my part; now the ball's in the client's court" attitude so many freelancers adopt in favor of a more positive, collaborative outlook. You accept feedback with confidence and humility, and you strive to make clients happy.

Deliver Outstanding Work

On every project, put forth your best effort and deliver your best work. Avoid rushing to complete jobs, and try not to cram your schedule so tight with deadlines that you're always working under time pressure to just get projects out the door. The quality of your work will suffer, and so will your chances of securing repeat business.

Speaking of quality, be sure the work you submit to clients has passed through some sort of quality-control process. Whatever you produce, be sure your work has been proofread, checked for errors, vetted against the specifications outlined by your client, etc. Consistently delivering outstanding, high-quality work is the best way to ensure you get more!

Be Flexible

Not all projects will go smoothly. You might encounter delays because someone in your client's company is unreachable for a day or two. A certain phase might get put on hold. Or the scope might change considerably midway through the project. These things happen, so you must expect them and roll with them.

The difference between average and top-earning freelancers is that the top earners always try to create win-win outcomes for themselves and their clients, rather than complain and get deflated when a project doesn't go according to plan.

Thank Clients Frequently

Your clients are human beings. They appreciate sincere gestures and acts of kindness just like everyone else. Let your clients know you appreciate their business. A handwritten thank you card sent through the mail is a high-impact and low-cost way to do just that. You don't have to send a card out for every project, but certainly send at least one at the beginning of your first engagement. As your relationship grows, you can even go a few steps further by expressing your appreciation with a small, suitable gift such as a gift card for a favorite coffee shop, a bottle of wine, chocolates, flowers, or a gift basket.

I'm sure you agree, living up to these basic standards is not hard. And the truth is, when you adhere to these principles alone, additional work and referrals from current clients will naturally flow your way.

Describe What You Do

Develop a succinct statement that clearly describes what you do so others can easily remember it. Gordon Graham (ThatWhitePaperGuy. com) is a freelance writer who writes white papers. As you can see by his website URL, he bills himself as "That White Paper Guy." There's no mistaking what kind of service Gordon offers!

However, there's a lot more you can do to speed the flow of repeat and referral business in your direction. It's all about taking action!

Action Tips for Earning Repeat Business

These action tips will help you get more business, and referrals, from current clients. They're not hard to execute, but they do require some extra effort on your part.

The good news for you, however, is that very few freelancers spend the extra time and energy these actions require. Exert this extra effort, and you're guaranteed to reap the rewards!

Learn About Your Client's *Business*

Don't just limit your research to the bare minimum required to complete a single project. Learn as much as you can about your client's business as a whole. You can learn a lot about a company, its industry, and the market it serves using the Internet. You can also learn by asking your client contact specific questions. Ask about the mandate of her department. Ask about the organization's strategic goals. Probe to uncover its challenges and where it sees opportunities for growth.

When you develop this knowledge, you make it easier for clients to send work your way because you know the company, the industry, and the lingo. It becomes easier and faster to work with you rather than another freelancer because you're the one who's already up to speed.

This really is a cornerstone technique. The success you have with the rest of the action tips in this section will increase when you fully understand your client's business.

Ask for More Work

What's the quickest way to get more business? Just ask! Early on in a project, after I've taken my client through my standard list of preliminary questions, I like to open up the door for future work with this simple sentence: "So what comes next in your marketing plan once this project is done?"

When asked in a conversational, casual tone, this is a very nonthreatening question. It's a great way to get a glimpse of any other projects that might be on the horizon for you to bid on. Some clients won't have a very detailed answer for you, and others simply won't have any firm plans worth talking about. But sometimes you'll hear the type of answer you're hoping for: "Oh, we're planning a series of white papers on this subject as well. We'll get you to quote on those, too."

What about referrals? Should you come right out and ask clients for referrals? Of course! I show you how later in this chapter. In the meantime, the next tip shows you how to get introduced (which is an implied referral) to other people *within* your clients' company.

Ask to Be Introduced to Others Within the Organization

Once you grow more familiar with your client's business and you've built up a decent track record with your main contact, it's okay to ask "Are there any other people in your company who might need help with *[insert your service here]*?" If your contact mentions someone else, ask to be introduced! So if your contact says, "Well, Sandra Thompson is our public relations person, and she might use those services," all you need to say is, "Oh, would you mind introducing me to Sandra?"

You'll probably get an introduction but not necessarily in person. People often introduce others over e-mail now, which is actually great news for you in this scenario. If you're introduced to Sandra via e-mail, you can reply with a short e-mail "Hello" and a summary of the work you've already completed for her company to demonstrate your deep understanding.

Offer a "Lunch and Learn"

What's your area of expertise? Search engine optimization? Social media? Writing white papers? Put together an informative presentation on the subject; pack it full of relevant, high-value content; and offer to deliver it to your client's team in the form of a "lunch and learn" on their premises. This technique yields benefits all around. For your client, the staff will get some free training (and free lunch!). The benefits to you are twofold:

1. You elevate your perceived status in the eyes of your main contact.

2. You get to meet other people within the company, who don't yet know you but may have need for your services.

I recently put on a lunch and learn on the topic of direct mail for a client of mine, and 15 marketing people showed up! Within a week, I had one project from that presentation, which paid for the lunch tab many times over. And now I have more than a dozen new, warm prospects to call on.

Get to Know Your Contacts Personally

A lot of advice for freelancers shuns the notion of personal contact with clients. "It takes up too much time," is the common rationale. But it's hard to make personal connections with people when your communication is limited to phone calls and e-mails. (It's not impossible, just harder.) If your clients are located close by, take advantage of this by building your relationship with personal contact. Don't worry, I'm not suggesting you spring for orchestra-level seats to *Phantom of the Opera*, but maybe treat some select clients to lunch once in a while or meet up with them for a quick coffee.

I like to bring a tray of Starbucks coffees to my local clients whenever I visit their offices. This gesture always gets a round of smiles and genuine thank yous. More importantly, it creates a relaxed tone that invariably opens up a few minutes of casual, personal banter before we get down to business.

If you think these personal niceties between clients and freelancers is all an act, think again. The fact is, you may actually genuinely enjoy interacting with some clients on a personal level. And—surprise!—they may genuinely enjoy your company just as much. A business owner client of mine once phoned to invite me to his company's Christmas party at a local restaurant. Outside of family members, I was the only nonemployee there. This was very flattering, and it did wonders for our business relationship; I continued to get a lot of work from his company.

Don't be afraid to get to know clients on a personal level. Your lunch together just might be the highlight of a client's otherwise unpleasant day! And being a bright spot in the heart and mind of someone who has the authority to send projects your way is a great thing.

Just remember that getting to know your clients on a personal level and treating them well is an add-on, *not a substitute*, for delivering top-notch work!

Suggest New and Additional Projects

Don't just be an order-taker. Suggest projects you feel will help your clients achieve their goals.

If a client of yours markets a complicated technology, suggest a frequently asked questions page for their website. If your main client contact is the director of marketing, and there's a gap between sales and marketing departments (which there almost always is in every company), suggest a survey of the sales force where you compile and report on the results. If you're being hired to write a white paper, suggest a press release to go with it. Being asked to design a direct-mail campaign? Suggest that you also design a series of promotional e-mails and a landing page as well.

Give Before You Get

How do you feel when you're on the receiving end of a kind gesture? You feel all warm and fuzzy, right? And oftentimes you feel compelled to do a good turn right back. This is called the principle of reciprocity, and marketers have been leveraging the power of this principle for decades: free samples in grocery stores, a free mug when you apply for a credit card, and free T-shirts at trade shows are all high-return marketing tactics that leverage this principle.

Granted, these "trinkets and trash" handed out by savvy corporate marketers are very transparent, but they work. And you can be a lot more genuine in your efforts to do something helpful for a client. Here's a great story about giving before you get, told by Ed Gandia …

> I was talking casually with a client about some of the big accounts he and his company were trying to land. As I listened to him, I realized that I personally knew someone who was an 18-year executive in one of those target companies.

So I called up my friend and set up a conference call. In that call, my friend was able to provide my client with invaluable insight into the target company (including the names of some key decision makers). Needless to say, my client was very appreciative of this gesture. They recognized that I had gone above and beyond for them.

Now who do you think this client is going to call the next time they need more consulting or copywriting work? They'll be calling Ed first!

Be Selective

Don't worry, you're not going to apply each one of these action items with every single client you come across. Not every client of yours is a good prospect for repeat business over the long term. There may be several reasons why. Some clients may be unappealing to you in some way, because they're either rude, disagreeable, or unreasonable in their expectations. Others may take too long to pay your invoices. Others may be great to work with, and pay up on time, but have no real need for more of your services beyond one or two key projects.

With this in mind, be selective as you cull your client list for the real gems with whom you wish to deepen your relationship. How do you identify which clients should be the focus of your efforts? Here are a few tips:

- Remember the list of standards we talked about in Secret 1? Take a look at the standards you set for your business. Give every client you work with a score out of 10 based on adherence to your standards. Any client who scores an 8 or higher should be approached for more business.

- Ask yourself these basic questions about the client: Do you enjoy performing the work? Do you understand the industry and the marketplace this client serves? Are you a good "fit" with his business? If you answer yes, asking for additional work is a good idea.

- Ask every client about his experience and future plans regarding freelancers. You can ask him even before the project is getting underway by saying, "Is this project the result of a one-time need, or will you have ongoing need for freelancers to help you meet your goals?"

Referrals—Who, When, and How Should You Ask?

"You don't get if you don't ask!" That's something I learned from a former sales manager of mine back when I was in the corporate world. It's a good mantra to keep in mind for freelancers, too. If you want to be a wealthy freelancer, you need to get into the habit of regularly asking for referrals.

Let's identify who can send you referrals and exactly when and how you should ask for them.

Who Should You Ask?

Not all clients will be a great source of repeat business, but *virtually any client* may have the potential to hook you up with friends or colleagues of his who need your services.

The key is to ask. It's up to you to ask because most clients—even good ones—won't automatically assume you're looking for referrals, especially if they view you as having a vibrant freelance business. Ironically, the more successful your business *appears*, the greater the odds are that your client will assume you're *not* interested in receiving referrals! They'll assume you don't need them!

How do I know this is true? Because I've been surprised several times by clients asking me, almost apologetically, for *permission* to send a referral my way! They'll say something like, "I have a friend who needs some copywriting help with his company … but you're probably not even taking on new clients right now, are you?" Or "I don't know if you're even looking for new clients right now, but I know some people who could use your services. Do you mind if I give them your name?" (Keep reading for tips on exactly how to respond to this.) So you should absolutely come right out and ask *each one* of your clients to refer you to his or her friends, colleagues, and contacts.

It's human nature to want to help. And lots of people love to play match-maker, so do let go of any hang-ups you may have about asking for referrals. It's not cheesy, salesly, or desperate. It's a very common, very acceptable practice in the business world, and it's very easy to get referrals when you know exactly when and how to ask for them.

Make Friends with Nonclient Referral Sources

When it comes to referrals, new business doesn't always have to come from your clients. You can pick up business from a referral source, which is simply another professional, freelancer or not, who can send business your way. Steve Slaunwhite tells a story that illustrates just how lucrative this type of informal partnership can be:

> Early in my copywriting career I invited a local freelance designer out for a coffee. We met, drank overpriced café lattes, and showed each other our portfolios. I told him I was impressed with his work and was confident I could recommend his services to my clients and prospects.
>
> He said he could do the same for me, too.
>
> That was over eight years ago. Since that time, that freelance designer—who eventually went on to found a successful B2B design firm—has referred more than two hundred thousand dollars in business my way!

That's quite a nice return on a $4 cup of coffee! Steve even has a great script for reaching out to someone—even someone you've never met—who you think might be a great referral source:

> Hi Rick. This is Doug Anderson. I'm a freelance copywriter, and I noticed on your website that we both target the same market: business-to-business companies. i often get asked by clients to recommend a design firm. And I'm sure you get asked to refer copywriters from time to time, too. Should we be talking? I'd be happy to buy you a coffee next time I'm in the area ....

When Should You Ask?

Most of the techniques for asking for repeat and referral business require that you build up a bit of a reputation with the client before you make your move. You wouldn't fly to Vegas and get married on a first date, right? Likewise, you should establish a baseline relationship with your client before offering to get more serious.

When it comes to asking for a referral, timing is *everything*. My friend Allison Graham, author of *Business Cards to Business Relationships* (elevatepress, 2008), calls the act of sending someone a referral "the single greatest business compliment ever." She has this to say about the importance of timing:

> You can't stuff a marshmallow into a piggybank. No matter how hard you try, it just won't squish through the slot. Asking a contact for a referral before you have established trust or developed a business relationship will generate the same frustration for *both* of you.

So when exactly is the right time to ask for a referral? The answer is, as soon as you've *earned* the right to do so! And when exactly is that? Well, it's actually quite easy for us freelancers to know when we've earned this right because the work we deliver tends to be project based, with definite start and stop dates.

You've earned the right to ask for referrals when you've delivered the project and your client is happy with the result. *That* is precisely when you ask—exactly one moment after your client tells you how happy you've made him or her. Do *not* wait a month, a week, or even a day later to go back to the client and ask.

Consider this: when is the better time to kiss someone? At the end of a romantic candlelit dinner, when both you and your date are enjoying a second glass of wine, holding hands, and looking dreamily into each other's eyes? Or eight days later, at 2:30 on Sunday afternoon when you're driving by the object of your affection's house and you see him or her outside, cutting the front lawn? (*SCREEECH! "Hey! Fancy bumping into you again! Hot date, wasn't it? Wanna smooch?"*)

How Should You Ask?

Asking for referrals is no big deal. Provided the timing is right, there's no reason to worry that you'll look pushy, presumptuous, or out of place. To boost your chances of success, however, it's important to know just *how* to ask your client for referrals.

For example, if you just blurt out, "Do you know anyone who needs a photographer right now?" like an overbearing game show host, what answer are you likely to hear back?

"Ummm ... ahhh ... hmmm ... no."

End of conversation. Asking the question in that manner puts your client on the spot. It makes her brain lock up.

Instead, say something like this, which uses very casual language to make a very specific request:

> Referrals are the primary source of how I grow my business. And since you're happy with the way this project has turned out, I wonder if I can ask you for the names of three people who might have a need for my services—now or sometime in the future. Would that be okay?

Happy clients will say yes. And then you ask for the three names. You may only get two—or one—but consider this: if you ask 15 people for three names this year, and you get an average of two names each time, that's *30* potentially warm prospects placed right in your lap!

$ Success Story

Develop and Follow a Simple Referral System

Asking for referrals in a systematic way can add predictability to what may be an otherwise erratic method for growing your list of prospects and clients. Sharon Hess, a freelance office financial manager and professional organizer (www.MommyManagementInc. com) who launched her solo business in 2001, can attest to that.

Sharon's prospecting plan was straightforward: upon completing a project for a client, ask for at least one referral from that client. To encourage clients to make referrals, she offered an incentive. "For every referral and/or referral letter I received, I gave the client one free hour of organizing on their next project," she explains. "I found that clients were happy to refer me. Also, the potential clients they referred me to were usually very receptive to my services. And of course, once they hired me, I would also ask *them* for referrals."

Within a few months of launching her business, Sharon was booked solid, and her referrals eventually led her to bookkeeping and bill-paying projects with a few small businesses and nonprofits. Although these offerings were not among Sharon's initial list of services, she says the financial management projects are recurring, which helps add more stability to her income.

"I wouldn't have enjoyed the rapid success I achieved had it not been for my referral strategy," says Sharon. "When you do good work and you make your clients' lives easier, it's easy to get great referrals that lead to even greater opportunities. All you have to do is ask!"

Be Referral-Ready!

Recall what I said earlier in this chapter: sometimes clients will actually ask you for your permission to introduce you to someone or pass your name along! When this happens to you, say this:

> Oh, I'm glad you asked! Actually, referrals from clients I respect and enjoy working with is my preferred way to grow my business, so I'd be very happy to talk to your friend (or colleague). And thanks for offering to make the introduction.

If you enthusiastically show a client that you appreciate this referral gesture, he or she is likely to repeat it again.

One final tip: always keep track of who referred you to whom. Send a thank you card to any client who makes a referral, and treat these clients especially well. Over coffee or lunch outings, mention how much you appreciate the referrals and introductions and how those connections have benefited both parties. Seeing the results of their matchmaking efforts will make your clients feel good, and they'll want to keep connecting you with people you can help.

Wealthy Takeaways

- Getting repeat business and referrals from existing clients is easier, faster, and less costly than landing new business from brand-new clients.

- Develop a succinct statement that clearly describes what you do, so others can easily remember it.

- Specifically advertise your services so clients are aware of your breadth of services. Use your website and e-mails, and create a fee schedule to advertise without appearing too salesly.

- Make it a policy to adhere to basic performance standards. These are the gateway to earning more business from a client.

- Commit to learning about and really understanding your client's business. It will further entrench your relationship and provide a springboard from which you can execute other recommended tactics that will earn you repeat business.

- Give before you get. Make it a point to help others (other clients, fellow freelancers) without the condition that you have to be helped in return—it will happen anyway!

- Be selective. Not every client will be a good prospect for more business over the long term. Take the time to assess each client and focus your efforts for generating repeat business on these clients only.

- *Ask* for referrals! The best time to ask for referrals is when you have delivered on a project and the client is happy. Seize the moment!

- Cultivate nonclient referral sources by reaching out to people in your market who can send work your way—and who you can send work to as well.

Secret 6: Nurture Prospects Perpetually

Ed Gandia

I worked as a sales professional for 12 years before becoming a full-time freelancer. I loved sales! But one thing I always seemed to lack was a steady stream of good leads—meaning prospects who indicated interest in my product.

When you're a salesperson, leads are your lifeblood. A constant flow of good leads keeps you from having to spend a lot of time making cold calls (yuck!). And if your job hinges on meeting your sales quota every quarter, you need new leads all the time. Unfortunately, in every company I worked, the marketing department didn't seem to have the same urgency I did. The leads they would give me were … well, worthless! So it wasn't long before I realized that if I wanted to put food on the table, I had to find my own leads. So I began to write and send sales letters to prospects, at my own expense. And within a few short weeks, I had more sales leads than I could handle—and my sales shot through the roof!

As I studied my direct-mail results, I found an interesting pattern. I noticed that only about 10 percent of the leads I was generating were actually ready or willing to talk with me about my product. That was no surprise. But what shocked me was how many of the other 90 percent (the ones who weren't ready when they first contacted me) bought from me 3, 6, or 12 months later—as long as I stayed in touch! In fact, at one point, one third of all my new business was coming from this group of "not ready yet" leads!

By staying on their radar screen in a nonthreatening way, I was the first person they thought of when the timing was right. As a result, the cost of my mailing efforts began to drop (I no longer needed to generate as many leads to make one sale). And I quickly rose to the top sales position in my division. Since then, I've implemented this same "staying in touch" strategy in my freelance business.

In fact, I've found that much of the difference between just "getting by" and earning an executive-level income as a freelance professional lies in what you do with prospects who are not ready to hire you today.

The Value of the "Not Today" Crowd

According to Brian Carroll, CEO of InTouch, Inc., and author of the popular book *Lead Generation for the Complex Sale: Boost the Quality and Quantity of Leads to Increase Your ROI* (McGraw Hill, 2006), at any given point, only about 5 to 15 percent of prospects for your services are either actively looking for or considering what you offer. But Carroll notes that as many as half of the remaining 85 to 95 percent of leads will typically buy the services you provide—either from you or from one of your competitors—over the following 18 to 24 months.

That's huge!

What's more, a research study conducted for Cahners Business Information (now Reed Business Information) on 40,000 leads generated through various marketing efforts found that six months after inquiring, 23 percent of those leads had bought the product or service they had inquired about, either from the original vendor or from a competitor. And 67 percent said they were still in the market, planning to buy. In other words, six months after their initial inquiry, a whopping 90 percent of buyers had either bought the product or service or were still looking for a vendor!

Although these figures are based on the marketing activities of companies that sell expensive and complex products and services, I've found that they're not far off for most freelance businesses. The three of us have landed a tremendous amount of work just by staying in touch with longer-term prospects. And in Steve Slaunwhite's case, his biggest and best copywriting client today was the result of a lead he stayed in touch with for more than two and a half years before they hired him.

Putting the Numbers in Perspective

To put these statistics in perspective, let's say you recently sent out a lead-generating letter to 150 highly targeted potential prospects. You offered them a special report on a topic that's of interest to them and somehow tied to the work you do. Two weeks later, seven of those potential prospects have downloaded your report, representing a 4.7 percent response rate. (Hey, not bad!)

After a few follow-up phone calls, you connect with one of these seven leads and learn that she may soon have a project for which you are a good fit. Although it's too early to tell if this lead will actually turn into a client, further questioning reveals that she is definitely a good lead for you. Let's call this one a "longer-term lead."

A few more attempts to connect with the other six respondents lead to brief conversations with two of them. But unfortunately, neither has a need for your services at the moment. The other four individuals never return your calls or e-mails, so there's no way of knowing where they stand.

So the final tally looks like this:

- One good lead
- Two longer-term leads
- Four unresponsive leads

Now what do you think most freelancers would do at this point? You guessed it. They'll spend most (if not all) of their efforts trying to turn their one good lead into a client. Sure, they'll follow up once or twice with the other two longer-term leads, but after two or three more attempts, most freelancers will simply give up on them. And the four unresponsive leads? Forget it. Those are history!

What's Missing? Timing and Trust

This common scenario begs two questions:

- Why would someone respond to your mailing yet never bother to call or e-mail you back?

- Why would someone show interest but never bother to follow through?

There are a couple reasons for this. When you market your services to a select list of prospects, you have a great deal of control over the industries you target, the specific organizations you go after, and the specific individuals within those organizations you reach out to. What you have no control over, however, are the *current needs* of those organizations. If there's currently not a project in the pipeline or even a budget for one, you're not going to land a project that day.

Trust is another key factor in converting a lead to a client. Say you just met the ideal prospect at a local networking event. He seems sincere in his desire to want to learn more about your services. He even mentions a couple projects for which you could be a good fit. So you exchange business cards and follow up a few times over the next month—yet receive no return calls or e-mails.

What happened here? Where did you go wrong? Did he change his mind? Did he find someone else? Probably not. More than likely, he simply doesn't yet feel 100 percent comfortable with you, at least not comfortable enough to award you a project. It's a trust issue.

Unfortunately, you can't just build trust overnight. It takes time. It also takes patience and a sincere desire to establish a meaningful connection with your prospects. To do that effectively, you need a smart, methodical, and sincere lead-nurturing effort—a *wealthy* lead-nurturing strategy that's focused on starting and sustaining a meaningful conversation with your "not today" leads.

Start a Meaningful Dialogue with All Prospects

According to InTouch's Carroll, effective lead nurturing is all about starting a meaningful dialogue with this "not today" group (your longer-term leads), regardless of their timing in hiring you. The objective is to work diligently to stay in touch with these people over the long haul. Not with calls to see if they have a project for you. Not with poorly conceived and scripted e-mails and voicemail messages. Not with "hire me for your next project" postcards. But with carefully timed, value-added information.

And when you think about it, this approach makes perfect sense. When prospects respond to one of your marketing efforts—whether it was a direct-mail campaign, an e-mail blast, an inquiry from a Google search, or a referral from someone in your network—they have expressed interest. They have responded to your "call to action." Many of them are qualified to do business with you. And you may even have had some honest dialogue with a few of these individuals.

In other words, you've already done a big chunk of the heavy lifting: you've persuaded them to respond to *something!* The challenge now is to stay in touch without being annoying or offensive. That way, the next time they need a freelancer in your profession, you're the first person they think of.

Must-Haves: Personalization and Sincerity

Before we get too far into the lead-nurturing mechanics, I want to point out two essential ingredients for succeeding with lead nurturing: personalization and sincerity. Wealthy freelancers understand that personalizing each interaction is key. And being sincere in your desire to stay in touch with longer-term leads is absolutely critical to a successful nurturing strategy.

Personalization is about much more than a handwritten envelope or note. It's about matching everything you send to what you know about each individual on your nurturing list. In other words, what you send must be highly relevant and useful to each recipient, even if it means you have to send something different to everyone on your list. This is not a time to strive for efficiency, automation, and mass mailing. Rather, it's an opportunity to show that you care enough to take the time to stay in touch in a meaningful way.

This brings up another important point: your efforts to stay in touch must come across as genuine and sincere. Whatever you send to the people on your list—as well as *how* you communicate with them—must clearly show that you're committed to developing a productive and valuable dialogue, even if these leads aren't ready to hire you anytime in the immediate future. This is not something you can fake. So if your motives are anything but genuine and sincere, you may want to rethink lead nurturing as a strategy.

Key Components of a Wealthy Lead-Nurturing Program

I can hear you already: "This lead-nurturing stuff sounds like a lot of work, Ed!"

Well, it's really not that bad. Especially when you consider the time, effort, and money you'll save as you concentrate more on the leads who have already shown interest, rather than reaching out to a new list of prospects every time. Plus, it's actually a very simple process if you follow the steps I'm about to outline.

Basically, a wealthy lead-nurturing program involves the following:

- Developing or compiling an information library
- Using multiple forms of media
- Leveraging the power of frequency
- Implementing a simple management system

Let's dig a little deeper into each of these.

Develop a Library of Value-Added Information

The first thing you must do before you start actively nurturing long-term opportunities is to develop and assemble a library of value-added content. I've found that assembling a good library is a great motivator to get you moving forward with your lead-nurturing strategy. It also makes it easier to nurture your prospects more consistently because you won't be scrambling to find good, relevant information to send out when you need it.

Your content library doesn't have to be massive. A dozen or so items will be enough to get you started. Also, not every item needs to be in printed form. You can have a physical file for printed materials and a file on your computer with digital documents and links to a variety of articles on the web.

How do you find good, relevant information for your library? What types of items should you try to develop or assemble? Here are some categories to consider:

Articles you've written. If you write a newsletter and have a few articles lying around from previous issues, move the best ones to your library.

Relevant, insightful, and well-written self-authored articles make excellent nurturing material. They give you credibility, position you as an expert on the topic, and provide your leads with ideas and insights that could help them do their jobs better.

Reports or white papers. Have you written a report or white paper on a topic that would be of interest to your target audience? If so, this can be a powerful nurturing piece. Here again, reports and white papers give you credibility while offering value to readers.

Don't have a meaty report you can share? Not a problem! Try assembling one with previously published articles that touch on a common theme. For instance, you may be able to create a report titled "Five Free Design Tools for Nondesigners" based on five separate articles you've written in the past, each describing a useful and easy-to-use tool for beginners.

Success stories. Also known as "case studies" in marketing-speak, success stories are short articles that describe how you've helped a client solve a specific challenge and how the client specifically benefited from your service.

If you have one or two case studies already written, they can make fantastic nurturing material. If you don't have any but have a few client successes that would make for a great story, this may be a good time to approach those clients. Ask for their permission to draft a simple summary of how you've helped them. And be sure to include a few quotes from the client, especially in the results area of the story. Keep it brief, avoid hype, and have the client give you final approval on the document before you use it. Finally, have it proofread by a professional. You want these pieces to be error-free and polished. So if writing isn't your thing, consider hiring—or trading services with—a good freelance writer.

Third-party content. Your nurturing content library doesn't have to be completely self-authored. In fact, it's better to have a good mix of self-authored content and third-party information. Assemble a good list of interesting and relevant third-party content in the way of articles, blog posts, reports, white papers, success stories, reference material, survey results, and statistics.

Books. If you work in a field in which each new client is worth thousands of dollars over the course of a year, you may want to consider adding books to your nurturing library. I know, I know—books can get expensive. But here's the thing: it's not every day that you get a free book in the mail, especially one that's relevant and useful to what you do for a living. Plus, few people will ever throw away a book. Sure, they may give it away, but for the most part, they'll either put it on a bookshelf or take it home to read. Pick books that are timely, relevant to the prospect, tied somehow to what you do, and written by credible sources.

Press releases. Have you recently written a press release on a big client win, a noteworthy success with an existing client, or a new service offering? Add it to your library! But don't limit press releases to news about you and your business. Seek out interesting stories about new trends, statistics, events, and products that would be of interest to the people on your list.

Also, keep an eye out for news related to the companies you're nurturing. Major accomplishments, new product launches, changes in leadership, and other compelling events can be a great excuse to contact your lead in that company with a quick note of congratulations or acknowledgment. It shows that you're paying attention and care enough about that person to take the time.

🄵 Wealthy Tip

One easy way to keep abreast of what's going on with the companies on your nurturing list is to sign up for Google Alerts (Google.com/alerts). With this free service, you can type in a company's name and have Google send you e-mail alerts anytime that name appears in a press release, blog post, or any other type of news announcement.

New services or solutions. You don't need to write a press release to tell your longer-term leads about new ways you can help them. You can also do this in other creative ways. For instance, if you've recently partnered with another freelancer to deliver a more complete service, draft a one-page document that describes the service, lists all the deliverables, explains what's involved, describes your process or system, discusses the results clients can expect, and lists the advantages of using you instead of another provider. When that document is polished, add it to your nurturing library!

Event invitations. If you come across a live or online event that would be of high interest to one or more individuals on your nurturing list, let them know about it. If you choose carefully and don't overdo these announcements, your leads will appreciate your thinking of them.

Videos and podcasts. Whether it's a video you've put together with some practical and relevant tips, or a podcast you came across that would be relevant and valuable to your audience, rich media can be a great way to stay in touch while adding value. Rich media expands and enhances content, engaging viewers or listeners in ways that text simply can't do.

Helpful tools. If you come across helpful and practical tools, utilities, software, or websites that would help your leads do their jobs more easily, add them to your library. People are constantly looking for tools that will save them time, money, and hassle—especially if they're free. Become the person who brings those valuable ideas to their attention. They won't forget you!

Use Multiple Media

Another key ingredient of a wealthy lead-nurturing program is the use of multiple forms of media to touch those longer-term opportunities over time. "There's really no way of knowing which medium is going to work best for any individual or company in any given campaign," says Dan McDade, president of PointClear (www.pointclear.com), an Atlanta-based prospect development company. "That makes it prudent to spread your bets across multiple media, with multiple touches."

Using multiple media not only diversifies your efforts but also adds variety to your messages, which can help cut through the noise of junk mail and flooded e-mail and voicemail inboxes. There are three basic media you'll want to use in a rotating fashion:

- Postal mail
- E-mail
- Phone

Postal mail. When done correctly, postal mail gets attention. In fact, it's one of my favorite media for a number of reasons. For one, the physical nature of mail tends to give letters more attention than e-mail and voicemail.

Also, with so much marketing communication moving online, personalized letters can now stand out a bit more than they used to, which helps get them past your prospect's administrative assistant and other "gatekeepers."

When it comes to postal mail, simplicity is key. Stuff your printed nurturing piece into either a standard #10 envelope or yellow oversize envelope (a 9×12-inch envelope works). Include either a sticky note or a cardstock note with a personalized *handwritten* message, such as this:

> Hi John,
>
> Came across this article recently. Thought you'd find it interesting.
>
> Ed

Throw in your business card, handwrite the envelope, and you're good to go! Few people ever get mail like this anymore, so your piece *will* stand out.

E-mail. There are great benefits to using e-mail for lead nurturing. It's efficient. Recipients get e-mails right away. And there's usually no gatekeeper, so the chances of getting through to prospects can be higher than with postal mail.

Unfortunately, most prospects today are inundated with e-mail. Plus, many people consider their e-mail inboxes sacred zones. Any e-mail that's perceived to be an unsolicited promotion may be seen as spam and often is deleted before it's even read. To avoid this, keep your e-mails short, personalized, and sincere. Remind recipients right away where they know you from, and get to the point immediately by providing the URL to the website, article, or report you're suggesting she read. Tell her what it is, and quickly explain why you think she would find it valuable. Then wish her well and move on.

Phone. Finally, throw a few phone calls into your nurturing mix. The telephone is a very personal and interactive medium that enables you to have a richer dialogue. One downside to using the phone these days is that many prospects have their calls set to roll into voicemail. However, rather than seeing voicemail as a negative, you can turn it into an ally with the right strategy and approach. The secret is to craft a very natural, conversational, and brief message prior to making lead-nurturing calls.

Let me warn you, though: even if you're good on the phone, don't wing this. Write out what you're going to say, and practice saying it at least six or seven times or until it sounds natural and relaxed. Here's an example of a good nurturing voicemail message:

> Hi Jill. Ed Gandia here. I'm the business-to-business copywriter you contacted back in March. I'm calling because I just got an e-mail about a free breakfast event that Acme Corp. is holding in your area on May 15. The seminar is on using Twitter and other social media marketing tools to drive leads in complex selling situations. Thought you might be interested in checking it out. The information and registration form are at www.Acme.com/SocialMediaSeminar. Anyway, hope you're doing well. If you need me for anything, I'm at 770-555-1876. Take care.

Simple, relaxed, to the point, sincere, and nonpromotional. That's the approach few service providers take. And it's the approach that will get you noticed—and eventually hired!

The Importance of Frequency

As we've discussed, effective lead nurturing consists of repeated efforts over a period of time. A series of value-added touches over the course of 12 to 24 months helps build trust and credibility while increasing the chances you'll be the first to pop up on a prospect's radar when the right opportunity comes along.

But what separates wealthy freelancers from their competitors is how judicious they are when it comes to the frequency of touches. Wealthy freelancers know how to maintain a fine balance between staying in touch and being perceived as a pest.

What's the best level of frequency? Frankly, there's no magic formula. Popularized years ago by marketing expert Dr. Jeffrey Lant, the "Rule of Seven" states that it takes an average of seven touches over an 18-month period to get a longer-term lead to convert to a client—or at least to a good lead. That's the equivalent of one touch every 10 weeks or so.

Mac McIntosh, president of Mac McIntosh, Inc. (www.sales-lead-experts. com), a consulting firm specializing in business-to-business lead generation, suggests that freelancers touch base with their longer-term leads once every four weeks. "However, usefulness and relevance are key," he says. "Everything you send must be perceived as valuable by your prospect." PointClear's McDade suggests that the frequency and mix of media are dependent on each prospect's situation. "For some, specifically in cases where there are long-term contracts in place with other freelancers, less frequent contact with lower-cost media is appropriate," he says. "But if a prospect is qualified, and hiring you could depend on unforeseen events or 'triggers' (such as senior management change, a merger, or rebranding effort), then more frequent and more expensive media should be used."

Having tried different approaches and levels of frequency over the last few years, I've found that touching base with each lead in my nurturing list every other month is a good balance. I also recommend rotating from postal mail to e-mail to phone. Naturally, you'll have to experiment with a level of frequency that works best for you and your target market. Above all, use common sense. If a few of your long-term leads give you several indications that they may be ready to reengage with you sooner, you may want to increase the frequency of your contact to once a month.

Managing the Lead-Nurturing Process

All this sounds good on paper. But is it practical for a one-person business with 10 spinning plates in the air at any given time? Yes, it is! To make it all work, you'll need the following:

- A good content library
- An easy-to-use contact management system or a spreadsheet program
- A simple nurturing schedule

We've already covered the content library, but let's take a look at the other two items on the list.

Contact Management System

A contact management system can help you manage your lead-nurturing efforts more efficiently by enabling you to tag specific leads with a nurturing status, making it easier to create a contact list whenever you need to send out your nurturing materials.

Microsoft Outlook is a great starting point for PC users. ACT! is another good option that's affordable and relatively simple to use. But for those of you who are just starting out—or who just want to keep it as simple as possible—a spreadsheet program will work just fine. Not only is it a cheaper alternative, it's easier than learning a new contact management system.

Nurturing Schedule

You'll also need a simple schedule that makes it easy to track what you need to send and when. Let's look at a sample schedule.

Sample Nurturing Schedule

Date	Action/Deliverable
Oct	Mail article of interest
Dec	"Touch base" with a phone call/voicemail
Feb	E-mail URL of results from an industry survey
Apr	Mail client success story with a personal note
Jun	"Touch base" with a phone call/voicemail
Aug	Mail report or white paper with a Post-it note attached
Oct	E-mail URL of helpful checklist or self-assessment quiz
Dec	Call to invite them to download a podcast
Feb	Mail article of interest with a personal note
Apr	E-mail URL of a relevant online video
Jun	"Touch base" with a phone call/voicemail
Aug	Mail article of interest with a Post-it note attached
Oct	E-mail URL of results summary from some sort of survey

When it comes to your schedule, the sequence of items you settle on is not nearly as important as being diligent about touching base with your nurturing leads every other month. I recommend taking some time to go through your content library and draft a basic schedule that takes advantage of the different types of content and media available to you. Use a spreadsheet to track your schedule, and save that file to the folder that houses all your nurturing files. Then every other month, set aside a couple hours to run through the process. Start by referencing your spreadsheet of longer-term leads (or running a report in your contact management system for all leads tagged as nurturing). From there, send each individual on that list the designated piece from your schedule, regardless of when you added them to your nurturing list. (You may have a few brand-new additions mixed in with older leads.)

Again, you don't want to send everyone the same content. If this month's lead-nurturing item is a relevant article, look at each individual separately and choose an article from your content library that would best suit that person. Base your decision on what you know about the individual and his industry, interests, and job function. Finally, make a note in your system or spreadsheet on what you sent each prospect. That way you won't send them the same thing again by accident. (I've done that before. It's embarrassing!)

Does My Newsletter Count?

What if you have an e-mail newsletter? Is that considered a touch-point in terms of nurturing longer-term leads? Absolutely! How you weave your newsletter into your schedule is up to you. Just don't depend on your newsletter alone to do all the work. Add other media and content types as described in this chapter.

One idea would be to publish your newsletter every other month. That way you can send something more personalized in the months when your newsletter doesn't go out. You can also keep publishing monthly (if this is what you're already doing), but space out your other nurturing touch-points so prospects don't get two pieces of communication from you in the same week.

When to Move On

There will come a point when you'll have to decide whether it's worth staying in touch with some of the longer-term leads on your list. In some cases, that decision will be made for you. For instance, an individual may leave the company, or a full-time position may be created that keeps the company from needing freelancers to fill any gaps. But in most cases, it will be a decision you'll have to make on a case-by-case basis.

As previously stated, many experts recommend nurturing long-term leads for 12 to 24 months. However, I suggest you evaluate your nurturing list once a year and decide who's worth staying in touch with beyond that point. In many cases, prospects who seemed to be promising long-term leads at first may no longer be receptive to your services.

Wealthy Takeaways

- Much of the difference between just getting by and earning an executive-level income as a freelance professional lies in what you do with prospects who are *not* ready to hire you today.

- At any given point, only about 5 to 15 percent of viable prospects for your services are either actively looking for or considering what you offer. Yet as many as half of those who aren't looking for a freelancer today will typically buy the services you provide—either from you or from one of your competitors—over the following 18 to 24 months.

- Effective lead nurturing is all about starting a meaningful dialogue with your "not today" group (your longer-term leads), regardless of their timing in hiring you.

- By staying on your long-term prospects' radar screens in a nonthreatening way, you'll often be the first person they think of when the timing is right.

- When done right, lead nurturing dramatically reduces your marketing costs in the long run by increasing the overall quality of your leads.

- A wealthy lead-nurturing program involves developing or compiling an information library, using multiple forms of media, leveraging the power of frequency, and implementing a simple management system.

- Evaluate your nurturing list once a year and decide who's worth staying in touch with. In many cases, prospects who seemed to be promising long-term leads at first may no longer be receptive to your services.

Secret 7: Price Your Services for Success

Steve Slaunwhite

A prospective client calls you to ask, "How much do you charge to *[fill in the blank]*?" How you address this inquiry will have an enormous impact on whether or not you get the project, how much money you make, your future dealings with that client, and even the quality of your freelance life.

Am I exaggerating? I think not. Let me give you a few quick examples to illustrate just how important pricing is to the success of your business.

Say you're a freelance writer and you get asked to quote a 10-page website. The problem is, you have no idea how much to charge for such a project, so you guess. Unfortunately, your guesstimate is way too high, the client balks, you don't get the job because the client thinks you're ridiculously expensive, and you never hear back from him again. Ouch!

Here's another typical scenario: imagine you're a web designer and get an opportunity to quote on a company logo design. You desperately want the job, so you quote a low price in the hopes the client will jump at the chance to work with you so cheaply. That might happen. But if it does, what have you really accomplished? All you've done is get a big project where you'll be working for hours while getting paid peanuts. Worse, you'll probably be stuck at that low-ball price level for any future projects the client may have for you—perhaps forever. Ugh!

What's more likely to happen is that the client will *not* hire you. Why? Because your low rate flags you as an amateur (even if you aren't). If the client wants quality work done for his important logo design, he will assume correctly that this requires the services of a top-drawer professional. And to him, your bargain-basement price places you firmly in the opposite category. Not a good thing!

Even if you price your services at a reasonable, professional level, you can still fumble the ball and lose the game. Vickie, a freelance WordPress consultant I was chatting with recently, sent a proposal to a prospective client and was certain she'd get the job. She waited patiently for a couple weeks but didn't hear anything. Finally, she picked up the phone and called. To her disappointment, she discovered that the client had hired someone else. Why? Because the client had a concern about her payment terms. As Vickie puts it, "I could have easily cleared that up if only I'd known." And she would have known … *if* she had followed up sooner. Unfortunately, that other freelancer now has his foot firmly in the door, and the chances of Vickie getting another opportunity with that client are slim to none.

I could give you more examples of how pricing and quoting affect your level of success, but you get the idea. How you price your freelance services can mean the difference between a business where you're consistently working on great projects that pay well, to one where your schedule is filled with low-paying work—or, worse, no work at all.

Wealthy freelancers quote top rates and *still* win the work. They accomplish this by using the pricing strategies I explain in this chapter. Some of these ideas may seem a little strange to you at first—and may even run counter to what you've learned elsewhere about pricing and quoting. But I encourage you to keep an open mind and give these strategies a try. If you do, your quotation "win rate" and project income can increase substantially.

So let's get started with the first, and perhaps most controversial, pricing strategy ….

How Much Are You and Your Time Worth?

When a prospective client asks you for a quotation, you basically have two options: you can quote an hourly rate, or you can quote a fixed project price.

Charging an Hourly Rate—Easy, Right?

On the surface, charging a client an hourly rate for your freelance services seems like the simplest approach. (But as you'll discover in just a moment, it's anything but.) You simply say in your quotation, "My fee is $X per hour." Many freelancers price their services this way, and I can understand why. It's nice to know you're earning a set amount of money for every hour you put into a client's website, speech, illustration, or other freelance project. It's comforting—like a warm, fuzzy blanket.

But it's all just an illusion. Charging clients by the hour is fraught with problems and severely limits your income potential. Let's go over some of the reasons why hourly rate pricing is not the wealthy freelancer way.

Clients don't like it. To them, it's too much like writing you a blank check. In his book, *It Sure Beats Working: 29 Quirky Stories and Practical Business Lessons for the First-Time, Mid-Life, Solo Professional* (BookSurge, 2007), successful freelancer Michael Katz reports, "When I was billing my clients an hourly rate, I could actually hear them speaking faster when on the phone ...."

You have to provide a project price anyway. Think about it. If you're hiring a contractor to renovate your kitchen and he explains his fee is "$65 per hour," what is your next question going to be? You're going to ask him how long the job will take. Otherwise, you'll feel the urge to stand over him with a stopwatch while he works in the hopes he'll hurry up! So you're going to have to estimate your hours, which is a *de facto* project price.

You get paid less the faster and better you get. If your specialty is writing executive speeches, aren't you going to be able to crank out your fiftieth in half the time it took you to write your first? Isn't that fiftieth speech going to be better; perhaps even your best yet? And shouldn't you be paid more for that level of expertise? Of course you should. But if you bill by the hour, you won't.

You have to track your time. Some clients demand to see a detailed report of the hours you've spent on a project. But how do you account for ideas you get while mowing the lawn? Or work you do in your head as you drive to your kid's soccer game? Trust me, keeping timesheets for clients is a big hassle.

Your income is limited. When you bill by the hour, your income is determined by the number of hours you work times your hourly rate. If your rate is $45 per hour and you spend 25 hours per week on client projects (remember, you'll need to spend time on such nonbillable tasks as bookkeeping and marketing), your income will be about $45,000 per year. Not bad … but it will never get much better.

You become a commodity. When you bill by the hour, clients tend to judge you by your hourly rate, not by the value you bring to the project. This opens the door to other freelancers with similar qualifications who could potentially replace you, simply by offering a lower hourly rate!

As you can see, charging an hourly rate only seems simple. It actually creates a lot of problems that get in the way of becoming a wealthy freelancer.

Be a Project Pricer

Now let's take a look at the alternative: project pricing. This involves providing a client with one fixed price—or at least a solid ballpark estimate—for the project work.

For example, if you were a graphic designer pricing a four-panel brochure, your quotation would say something like this:

> My fee to design a four-panel sales brochure to promote the new ACME Gizmo is $2,500. That fee includes two rounds of design revisions and the final artwork files submitted to you in the proper format for printing.

If you get the job, the client will have no idea how many hours you spend on the project (and in fact, won't care). You can get the job done in 5 hours or 20. That's one of the benefits of being a project pricer. You don't have to prepare timesheets for your client.

Another advantage is this interesting phenomenon: a client may balk at paying you $100 an hour for 10 hours of work, but will have no objection to a project price of $1,000 for the same project. Why? It's all in the way a client looks at it. If your hourly rate is more than her hourly salary, she may think you're asking too much. A fixed-project price, however, takes that salary comparison out of the equation, making the client stop and consider if the *project* is worth the price instead of whether or not *you* are worth your hourly fee.

And you can make a lot more money as a project pricer because you benefit financially by being faster and better. For example, I'm very good at writing effective sales letters. I've written hundreds over the years and know the best strategies and formats. I can craft a winner in about four hours and charge upward of $1,600. Clients have no problem paying that project price because a successful sales letter is so valuable to them. However, I'm sure I'd meet with serious resistance if I said my fee was $400 per hour!

Exception to the Rule

How do you quote a project price if you don't know exactly what the project requirements are? You can't. Say, for example, a client wants you to write a website but doesn't yet know how many pages of copy are required. In this situation, it makes sense to bill hourly until the project scope is better understood, at which point you can switch to a project price for the balance of the job.

Being a project pricer lifts your income ceiling. Indeed, it shatters it completely. As you gain more experience, and get better and faster, your income increases accordingly—as it should. Project pricing rewards you for getting good. Billing by the hour does exactly the opposite.

But perhaps the most compelling reason of all to be a project pricer is that clients prefer it. It eliminates price uncertainty. Often, when a client calls me and asks how I price my services, I can almost hear a sigh of relief when I explain that he will be quoted a fixed project price. An hourly rate worries a client. A project price makes it easier for him to say yes and give you the go-ahead. And that, of course, is what you want!

Worried About Not Being Paid for Overtime?

"Wait a minute!" I hear someone saying. "What if I quote a project price, say $1,500, and the client takes advantage of the situation? He demands endless revisions, keeps changing his mind about what he wants, schedules endless meetings, or otherwise causes me to work on the project much longer than I expected to?"

That can happen. But if you're careful about how you quote the job, it won't happen very often.

Before you propose a project price, you must ask the questions required to determine how much work is involved. You also have to clearly spell out your policy regarding attending meetings, handling revisions, dealing with project changes, and so forth.

Compared to an hourly rate, being a project pricer takes a little more upfront work, but the extra effort is worth it. You'll win more projects at better prices and earn more income as your knowledge and skills grow. I've worked with some freelancers who have doubled their income simply by switching to a project price model. No wonder just about every wealthy freelancer I know prices their services this way. My suggestion? Join the club!

Create a Fee Schedule

Your dentist informs you that you have a cavity that needs to be filled. You ask, "How much is that going to cost?" She replies, "Hmm, let's see, not sure, ... well, I'll get back to you with a quote." That hardly instills confidence in the person who's about to drill a hole in your tooth! The good news is, a dentist is likely *not* going to reply in that way. Why? Because she probably has a fee schedule detailing her prices for a broad range of procedures. She's not going to *um* and *ah*. Instead, she's going to state with matter-of-fact confidence, "The fee is $192."

That's just one of the many benefits of developing a fee schedule. It inspires confidence and, as a result, prospective clients are more likely to say yes to your price.

Fee Schedules Up Close

A fee schedule is simply a document that lists your services and corresponding fees. Here's an excerpt from the fee schedule of a freelance web writer:

Website—Front Page	$750 to $1,250
Website—Bio Page	$250 to 500 per bio
Website—Services Page	$500 to $750 per description
E-Mail—Newsletter	$750 to $1,500 per issue
E-Mail—Announcement	$500 to $1,000
Blog Ghostwriting	$500 per post

Notice that this freelancer quotes a fee *range* rather than a fixed price. This gives her the wiggle room she needs to consider individual client and project requirements. After all, not every website front page is the same.

A fee schedule makes the entire process of determining a price and quoting a job a lot less stressful and time-consuming. I know some freelancers who agonize for hours preparing a quotation. I get frantic calls all the time from colleagues in my field (copywriting) asking, "Steve, I have to quote a media kit and I don't have a clue what price to charge! Help!" When you have a fee schedule, that's not a problem.

A fee schedule also helps deter low-paying clients. Unfortunately, there are plenty of them out there, waiting to toss you crumbs in exchange for your talents and knowledge. Unless you need to grab some of that work to pay the bills—we've all been there—you'll want to discourage these types of clients before they waste too much of your time. Showing them your fee schedule is a great way to do that. No wonder expensive restaurants post their menus outside their front doors!

But the most important benefit of having a fee schedule is that it enables you to quote a ballpark price right away. And as you'll find out in the next section, this is key to winning more work.

Determining Your Prices

Perhaps the most challenging aspect of creating a fee schedule is working out what your fees are in the first place. This requires some research on your part. You have to find out what the going professional rates are for the services you offer.

Notice I said *professional* rates? Lots of designers charge $150 for a stationery design, but they're firmly where you don't want to be—in the bargain-basement category. Professional branding designers charge considerably more, and you have to know what those rates are so you can set your fees accordingly.

Depending on your experience in your particular freelance field, you may intuitively know what to charge for particular types of projects. But what if you don't? Here are some tips for finding out:

Create your own price club. Over the years, I've built relationships with several colleagues I'm comfortable calling to ask for pricing information and advice. We call it our "price club." I just pick up the phone and say, "Hey, Dianna. How much do you charge to write a press release?" You can set up the same arrangement with colleagues you know.

Freelance websites. Some freelance professionals post their fee schedules on their websites. Isn't that convenient! Find some of these sites, and you'll gain useful insights into pricing in your freelance field. Be careful, though: just because a freelancer posts his fee schedule online doesn't necessarily mean those rates are reflective of what professionals should be charging. Christy Wagner, editor of this book, suggests that you review at least three such websites and then average the prices. I agree!

Professional associations. Many professional associations for writers, photographers, graphic designers, and so forth publish pricing guidelines. The American Society of Journalists and Authors, an association I belong to, provides its members with a schedule of going rates for a long list of writing projects.

Your prospects and clients. This is often your best source of pricing information. Here's a tip: quote prospective clients a little higher than you normally do when your schedule is full and you don't really need the work. It's a great way to find the "price ceiling."

You won't create the perfect fee schedule overnight. It's always going to be a work in progress. Expect to make adjustments as you gain experience with pricing and learn more about how much you can get for the types of projects you handle. If in doubt about what to charge for something, be daring and set your price a little higher than you think clients would be willing to pay. You might be pleasantly surprised when you quote that price and get the job!

Your Time and Talents May Be Worth More Than You Think

For many years, freelancer Debbie Charette charged clients $750 to write a case study (a product success story). Because she could write these fairly quickly, the job was profitable for her. However, when she got busy, she took a chance and quoted a few new prospects a higher rate: $1,250. Her new price was met with no resistance. Obviously, clients valued having these important marketing pieces done professionally and were more than willing to pay a higher fee. By taking a chance and raising her rates, she increased her project income by more than 65 percent!

"But Every Project Is Different!"

With few exceptions, no two freelance projects are exactly the same. So how can you develop a fee schedule that's in any way accurate?

Keep in mind that the purpose of a fee schedule is to give clients an idea of your professional rates and to allow you to quote a ballpark fee. Your fee schedule is not meant to be a definitive price list clients can use to place an order for your services. It's meant, instead, to be a guide.

That's why I recommend you list a fee *range* for each of the types of projects you handle, rather than a single fee, as shown in the earlier fee schedule example. That gives you the opportunity to customize the project price accordingly as you learn more about its scope and requirements.

Another technique to deal with this issue is to feature a "typical project" on your fee schedule. Say you're quoting the design of a website. In your fee schedule, you could say something like this:

> Website design that includes one home-page template and one inside-page template. Sourcing of up to five royalty-free images. Uploading and testing. $2,500 to $3,500.

This approach enables you to provide a ballpark price for a typical website and then come up with an actual price later on when you get more details on the project. A client is hardly going to be surprised to learn that it's going to cost extra for you to install a shopping cart program and a blog.

Ballpark It Before You Quote

The phone rings. It's a prospective client, and she wants to discuss a possible project with you. You're excited. Then as the conversation progresses, the inevitable topic of price comes up. She wants to know approximately how much you're going to charge for the work. How do you reply?

At this point, most freelancers would say, "Let me get some project details, and I'll get back to you with a quotation." That might sound like a reasonable way to proceed, but it actually lowers your chances of winning the work. What you should do instead is give the client a ballpark price right away. Then submit a formal quotation or proposal later on to nail down the exact price.

Why ballpark your project price during that first conversation? First of all, it allows you to deal with price issues right away. Say you don't talk about price on the initial call but instead work out a formal quotation and send it a day or two later. If the client has an issue with the price, she may choose not to talk to you about it—preferring, instead, to go with the next freelancer on her list. You've lost the opportunity. However, if you ballpark your fee while you have the client on the phone, you have a chance to deal with any price objections that may be standing in the way of your getting the work.

Recently, I was discussing a website writing project with a prospective client. He didn't ask about price, but I volunteered a ballpark figure anyway. I'm glad I did! I discovered that his budget was already set in stone and was about $1,000 *less* than my estimated fee. Fortunately, we were able to work out a compromise and I got the job. But that might not have happened if I presented him with a formal proposal a day or two later featuring a price he couldn't afford.

Ballparking your price also saves you a lot of time and energy. What if a prospective client is cheap and not willing to pay professional rates for professional work? Wouldn't you rather find that out right away instead of wasting an hour or two (or even more) preparing and submitting a formal proposal?

Finally, when you quote a ballpark price, some clients will be satisfied and give you the go-ahead right away. I've had many projects where I quoted a ballpark price and the client said, "Yes, that sounds fine. When can we get started?" After that, the formal quotation I sent a day or two later was just a formality. The project was already mine!

How do you come up with a ballpark figure? That's easy. You simply look at your fee schedule. Unless the project is highly unusual or something you've never handled before, quoting an estimate over the phone or in person is relatively easy.

Ask the "Expected Results" Question

When you ask a renovation contractor for a price to install new tile flooring in your bathroom, what are you really asking for? The cost to glue 78 tiles in place? Or the price to get a beautiful new floor you and your family will enjoy for years?

My guess is the latter. You want that shiny new floor!

Your prospective clients feel the same way. They may ask you for a price to do this or that, but what they really want is *the result* of what you do. When they ask you to design a new brochure, what they really want is an effective tool to help them increase sales. When they ask you to write an e-mail newsletter, what they really want is to keep their customers engaged and buying. When they ask you to craft a press release, what they really want is to create a buzz about their new expansion.

In my experience, the more you position your freelance services around the *results* you can help a client achieve, the more likely you are to get the job—at the price you want.

So what does this have to do with pricing and quoting? When you provide a prospective client with a ballpark price or send in a formal quotation, clearly explain how your services can help the client get the result she wants. You find that out by asking what I call the "expected results" question.

The expected results question is simply any variation of, "What exactly do you need this project to accomplish?" Here are some examples:

"What exactly do you need this press release to accomplish?"

"How many leads are you hoping this direct-mail letter will generate for your sales force?"

"What do you need this e-mail newsletter to accomplish for your company?"

"What are you hoping this new logo design will do for your organization?"

Always, *always* ask the expected results question. The very fact that you ask it oftentimes impresses the client, setting you apart from other freelancers who may also be quoting on the project. It shows that you care about what the client is trying to achieve, rather than just wanting to get the job.

For example, say you're asked to quote on doing a photo shoot for the senior executives of a company. You ask, "What exactly do you need these photos to accomplish?" The reply you're likely to get is, "Excellent question." (I know because that's the response I hear all the time.) The conversation will then continue on the topic of project goals and how your freelance services can help the client achieve them. Hopefully, perhaps even likely, the client will be thinking, "Wow. This photographer really knows his stuff. He gets what we're trying to accomplish. Let's hire him!"

Just asking the expected results question can dramatically increase your chances of getting the job. But you can also use the client's answer to make your formal quotation or proposal a lot more persuasive.

If you're submitting a quotation to craft a press release, for example, you might describe the project in this way:

> Thank you for the opportunity to quote you on my PR consulting services. As I understand it, the project is to write a two-page press release. My fee for this project will be ….

That's fairly typical. But look at how much more compelling the quote becomes when you incorporate the client's answer to the expected results question.

Thank you for the opportunity to quote you on my PR consulting services. As I understand it, the project is to write a two-page press release. The objective of this piece is to gain the interest of trade magazine editors in your industry and motivate them to publish news and stories featuring your new product. My fee to help you accomplish this will be ....

I'm sure you'll agree that the second example is much more convincing. Why? Because, to use my earlier bathroom renovation example, it focuses on the shiny new floor (the result), not just the laying of tiles (the work).

When the Client Says, "Your Price Is Too High!"

"We just don't have the budget for that."

"Your price is a lot higher than we expected to pay."

"The freelancer we used before only charged half that amount."

There's no getting around it. If you're going to quote a professional rate for your freelance services, you're going to meet with some price resistance. It goes with the territory. In fact, if you're getting no resistance when you quote a ballpark price, your fees are probably too low! As legendary freelancer Bob Bly once told me, "You want a prospect to agree to your price, but not too quickly!"

So what do you say when a client says some variation of the phrase, "Your price is too high"? Regardless of the price objection, and why, you may still be able to salvage the job—if you're smart. Here's a script of what I say when a client has a concern about a price I quoted:

I can appreciate your concern. Although that fee range is typical of what professionals charge for this type of project, I'm sure we can work something out. How much were you expecting to budget for this work?

That puts the ball firmly in the client's court, and she'll probably make you an offer. If that offer isn't too far off your original ballpark estimate, you may be able to do business with her after all. For example, if your ballpark is $3,000 and the client explains she can only pay $2,500, chances are pretty good you can work something out—probably for a meet-in-the-middle price of $2,750.

Negotiate, Negotiate, Negotiate

However, don't just drop your price for no other reason than the client's objection to it. Negotiate an exchange of value instead. That involves offering the client an alternative plan that gets her what she wants—your freelance service—and gets you what you deserve—your professional fee. Here are a few ideas for doing just that.

Offer to get the job done faster. If the client wants the job done in three weeks and you can do it in two, offer to do that as a bonus. The client may be willing to pay your price in exchange for getting the project done sooner. It's a stress reliever.

Throw in an extra. Can you offer some value-added extra that doesn't cost you a lot of additional time and money? Perhaps you can submit the press release to the media company, saving your client time? Or create five logo concepts for the client to choose from instead of the quoted three? A client may be willing to pay your full fee for the extra service.

Offer a discount for paying your full fee in advance. I learned this technique in Alan Weiss's excellent book, *Million Dollar Consulting: The Professional's Guide to Growing a Practice* (McGraw-Hill, 2002). I say to the client, "I offer a 10 percent discount when my quoted project fee is paid in advance." That savings may be all the client needs to award you the work. And it sure is nice to get that cash in the bank right away!

Ask for more time to get the project done. For many freelancers, getting a few extra days or weeks to do the job is a real benefit—one that may be worth being paid a little less. So if the client wants a better price, offer a discount if you can get four weeks to do the job instead of two.

Offer a volume discount. Query the client about upcoming projects and offer him a package deal. For example, if you've just provided a ballpark quote for a new sales brochure, ask the client about other sales materials that may be needed, such as a web page and advertisement. Then offer a lower overall price for all three projects.

Did you notice a theme throughout these negotiating tips? None involve lowering your price for no other reason than to just get the job. There's always a compromise between you and the client.

Why Not Just Lower Your Price to Meet a Client's Budget?

"The most we can pay is $950. Take it or leave it," the client says. So you take it. What's wrong with that? Well, you've just signaled to the client that it's easy to get a lower price from you. All that's required is a little push. And trust me, she'll give you that push every time she needs your services. Not a nice way to work!

Resolving Price Issues Politely and Professionally

Here's an example of a typical conversation dealing with a "Your price is too high!" issue:

Freelancer: "Based on what you've told me so far about the project, my ballpark fee would be $2,000 to $2,500. I will, of course, send you a formal quotation with an exact fee later today."

Client: "Oh. Um. Well, actually, that price is higher than we expected to pay. In fact, I'm sure we don't have the budget."

Freelancer: I can appreciate that. Although that fee range is typical of what professionals charge for this type of project, I'm sure we can work something out. How much did you budget for this work?"

Client: Well, Dave, we had planned to pay about $1,500."

Freelancer: Okay, let's discuss how we can tweak this project to meet both of our needs. You want three concepts of the same advertisement so you can select which one you like best. Plus, of course, completed artwork and copy for the ad concept you decide to run with. Do you think you could work with two concepts instead of three? And allow me an extra week to get the entire job done?"

Client: "You could do that for $1,500?"

Freelancer: "Under those circumstances, yes, I can."

Client: "That works for us. Send me your quote and I'll sign it back today."

Negotiation doesn't have to be confrontational. As this example illustrates, it can be friendly and helpful. You're working with the client to get him what he wants, without compromising on your professional rates. I find that clients often have more respect for me when I stand up for my rates—and respect, of course, leads to more work from that client. I doubt that would happen if I dropped my price for no reason.

Follow Up—Fast

Okay. You've discussed the project with the prospective client, quoted a ball-park price, found that the fee range was acceptable, and sent in your quote. Now you're waiting anxiously to hear back. How long should you do that before picking up the phone to follow up? Two days? A week? My answer may surprise you.

You should follow up on a project quotation *the same day.*

Why so soon? You want to take advantage of the momentum. Your prospect is already in motion to hire a freelancer. Otherwise, she wouldn't have contacted you to discuss the project in the first place! So you want to keep that ball rolling … rolling toward the client saying yes and giving you the job!

Making the follow-up call the same day (or, at the very least, early the next morning) substantially increases your chances of winning the work. Conversely, waiting too long to follow up lowers your chances much more than you might think.

So when you do make that follow-up call, what do you say?

Don't Talk About Price

Here comes another surprise: don't talk about your price when following up on a quotation. Instead, talk about getting started on the project and the next steps involved. That's right. Assume you've got it!

When I make a follow-up call, I'll often say something like, "Hi Joan. I e-mailed the proposal to you earlier this afternoon. The next step is for me to study the background materials on the project and create an outline. I can get started on that right away. Okay with you?"

Sound bold? It really isn't. After all, you've quoted the job, and unless the client has some objection, then "getting started" is the logical next step. And remember, you've dealt with any price issues when you ballparked your project fee during the initial conversation with the client. So there shouldn't be any problem in that area—unless you bring up the topic!

Try this technique! You'll be amazed by how many clients respond with, "Yes, that's okay with me. Please get started. I'll sign back the quote today." Then you're off to the races.

When You Can't Get in Touch

Sometimes, despite your best efforts to follow up, the client doesn't get back to you. You call, send e-mails, but hear nothing. What do you do?

Here's a great technique I refer to as my "Hail Mary pass." If I've been attempting to follow up on an outstanding quotation, but the client isn't returning my call or e-mails, I'll send a final e-mail that looks something like this:

> Dave, I've been trying to get hold of you about that press release you wanted. At this point, I still have room in my schedule for this project. Would you please reply to this e-mail and let me know how you'd like to proceed. Thanks!
>
> [ ] Yes, your quotation is fine. Please get started.
>
> [ ] No, we've made other plans. Thank you for quoting.
>
> [ ] Maybe. But we haven't made a final decision yet. Please touch base again [insert date].

This multiple choice e-mail may seem silly, but it works like a charm. I almost always get a reply, usually with something like, "Steve, sorry I didn't get back to you sooner. We've had some delays at our end, but we're ready to proceed now. Please go ahead with the project." And even if I learn I didn't get the job, at least I know where I stand.

Wealthy Takeaways

- Be a project pricer. Provide clients with a fixed price for the project rather than an hourly fee. That way, you'll make more money the faster and better your get.

- Get a clear understanding of the scope of a project in advance before you quote a price. You want to gain a rough understanding of how long the job is going to take you to complete. Be sure to factor the possibility of client-requested revisions.

- Develop a fee schedule. This is a list of typical projects you handle along with your fee range for each.

- Always provide the client with a ballpark quote during the initial project discussion. You want to be able to deal with any price issues in advance, before you submit a formal quotation.

- Never drop your price just because the client complains it's too high. Negotiate an exchange of value.

- Follow up quickly on price quotations and proposals, and when you do, don't ask about the price. Instead, ask about getting started on the project.

Secret 8: Bring Focus to Your Freelance Business

Pete Savage

What if attracting a flow of new clients to your freelance business were as easy as going to a trade show, introducing yourself to some people, and asking them about their business—wouldn't that be great? Well, that's exactly what life is like for Pam Magnuson, a freelance copywriter who focuses on writing marketing materials for nutraceuticals companies. "I usually attend the two major trade shows in my industry, one in Las Vegas and one in Anaheim, where I'll be exposed to about 2,500 to 3,000 companies who may require my services," Pam explains.

Imagine getting face to face with up to 3,000 potential prospects! "At the shows, I just troll up and down the isles and introduce myself to people so I can talk with them about their products. I take notes on what they say, I leave a brochure or my business card, and I keep going. Several people will ask me to contact them after the trade show, which I of course do. I've met a lot of leads and I get a lot of business this way."

How about getting business by simply writing articles that appear in popular trade journals? Pam does this, too. "I've been published in four or five different major industry journals," says Pam, "and every single time I get several leads and at least one new project."

Now, if you're ready to label Pam's success as unattainable because she's a seasoned pro who's been freelancing for 25 years, don't. In fact, Pam hasn't been freelancing for 25 years. Or 10 years. Or even 5. No, as of the time of writing, Pam has been a freelance copywriter for just *3* years!

And yet, clients are flowing to Pam from all directions. "I also get lots of business from word of mouth and from my website, which is ranked highly by the search engines." Sounds like Pam's got it made, right? So why is Pam thriving while so many other freelancers are barely surviving? What makes the difference? Is it her own unwavering belief in herself? Her perseverance? Her talent? Well, it's a combination of all these things, plus something else.

Yes, belief, talent, and hard work can help you achieve temporary bursts of success as a freelancer. But these things alone didn't bring Pam to those trade shows or help her get published in coveted trade journals. Another important ingredient has fueled Pam's success. What is it? Let me explain with a little story …

Picture this: you're sitting at an outdoor café, enjoying your favorite coffee and reading the newspaper. It's warm and sunny outside. You're feeling very peaceful and relaxed when, out of nowhere, you suddenly notice a swirl of smoke curling right up in front of your nose. You glance around to see where it's coming from when, to your utter surprise, you realize the smoke is coming from your newspaper! You can see it swirling up from a tiny little ring of smoldering paper, but before you have a chance to react, that little smoldering circle ignites into a flickering flame! Your newspaper is now on fire! You throw the paper to the floor, stamp out the flames with your foot, and look around for an explanation. You're completely bewildered, and no one seems to have noticed what's going on—no one except a young boy at the table across from you who looks to be about 10 years old. He's looking right at you with a mischievous grin on his face, and in his hand, you see he's holding a magnifying glass.

What happened here? Well, evidently, while you were reading the travel section, that cheeky little bugger was using his magnifying glass to focus the sun's rays into a single concentrated point on your newspaper. Until that magnifying glass comes out, your newspaper can sit around in the sunlight all day long and never get any warmer than the air around it. But focus the sun's energy onto one specific point on the page, and suddenly … Smoke! Fire! Panic! Such is the power of *focus*.

Just like that boy brought a concentrated point of focus to your *Daily Herald*, Pam has brought laser-sharp focus to her freelance business. She is focused on serving companies in the nutraceutical industry, and this focus means her business-generating activities are far more efficient and effective. So let me ask you a question that may make you uncomfortable: in your freelance business, what is your area of focus?

If you can't answer that question, you're not alone. A lot of working freelancers can't either. Why? Because the truth is, you can actually launch your freelance business, find clients, perform work, and earn money *without* really having a sharp focus on a particular market. But sooner or later, this lack of focus will trip you up.

The Importance of Focus

In my early years as a freelancer, there was nothing focused about my business. I did copywriting work for pretty much anyone and everyone. I managed to earn a decent income, but after a couple years, I began to get rather frustrated. I was generating enough work to pay the bills, but my freelance business wasn't really taking off. I hadn't given much thought to bringing focus to my business.

Here are some of the things that begin to happen when you plod along without focus:

- You have to spend a lot of time verbally explaining to clients the type of work you do. In my case, clients continually asked me, "What *kind* of copywriting do you do?"

- Marketing is tough. Identifying potential clients and promoting your services to them in a targeted and efficient manner becomes virtually impossible.

- Without an efficient ongoing marketing effort, you experience peaks and valleys in your income and find it harder to reach the level of income you desire.

- You can start to feel pretty agitated, frustrated, and even desperate. This isn't good, because it creates a situation where you have to take on *any* work that comes your way.

- The quality of the clients you do attract is all over the map. Some are cheapskates, some take forever to pay, and some take up so much of your time they drive your effective hourly rate down the toilet.

- "Everyone" is a prospect—which isn't as appealing as it sounds! When "everyone" is a prospect, it means you haven't defined your ideal client. You waste a lot of time talking to prospects who aren't a good fit for you, and it becomes harder to know how to elevate the quality of your clientele.

Each one of these scenarios feels lousy. I know because I experienced them all in my early years as a freelance copywriter. Eventually, however, I began to bring some focus to my business, and when I did, things really turned around.

Focus is what helped me go from barely paying the bills to busting through the six-figure income barrier. Focus is what allows Pam Magnuson to easily identify the companies and trade shows that are likely to be lucrative sources of business for her. And focus can take *you* from good to great.

That's why so many life coaches and human potential experts emphasize the importance of getting "clear" when it comes to setting goals. When you can clearly define what it is you want, your mind is free to focus on achieving that goal. So if focus is so important, how do you bring more of it to your freelance business? One simple way is to follow what I call the *Discover, Identify, and Position* Technique, or the DIP Technique for short. The DIP technique requires that you ...

1. Discover what you have to offer.

2. Identify the market you'll serve.

3. Position yourself in the market.

If you've never taken the time to discover, identify, and position, chances are you've experienced the feeling that something's missing in your freelance business, something you can't quite put your finger on. You keep waiting for things to click, but they never quite do because you're deficient in one or more of these three areas. But give them each the attention they deserve, and your freelance business will really start to gel. This chapter shows you how to make this happen.

Before you proceed, let me point out that this chapter can be helpful for you regardless of whether you're already a freelancer or whether you're still considering becoming one. However, I'm assuming you've already determined the *kind* of freelance work you want to do. So if you haven't yet decided whether you want to become a freelance photographer or a freelance copywriter, some of these techniques will be harder to carry out. Bringing a sharper focus to your business can only happen after you're past that critical first decision point.

Discover What You Have to Offer

So what exactly *do* you have to offer? What's so special about you? What do you bring to the table? These questions aren't meant to sound hostile; rather, I pose them because these are the exact questions that run through your prospects' minds when they're evaluating whether or not to use your services. Either you know how to answer these questions or you don't.

If these questions make you uncomfortable, it means you haven't yet taken the time to sit down and discover what you really have to offer. I know how to answer these questions. So do Steve, Ed, and Pam Magnuson, who you met at the start of this chapter. And here's something I hope you find encouraging: you, too, know how to answer these questions because the answers already lie within you!

It's true. Answering these questions isn't about making up something that sounds good. It's about taking a good, long look at your own experience, skills, and talents and discovering the unique value you can bring to the marketplace. It's time to discover how to do that.

Detail Your Education and Work History

The fastest path toward a focused freelance practice is to leverage the contacts, knowledge, and experience you've already accumulated in your career and build your business on top of this existing "structure."

For some, this will be easy. Bob Bly (Bly.com), a very well-known and accomplished freelance copywriter, studied engineering in college and first began his career working for industrial engineering companies. When he eventually made the transition to freelancer, he focused on helping engineering and manufacturing companies write marketing materials. For Bob, the move from engineering employee to freelancer for engineering companies was a natural segue.

However, if your own area of expertise isn't as immediately obvious to you, don't fret. All it means is that you need to spend some time looking closely at your talents and skills. Begin by detailing your work history, listing all your past jobs and responsibilities. Write as though you were writing your resumé, and leave no details out. Then examine your work history, looking for common threads you can build on.

Let's say, for example, you were an executive assistant for 11 years. What special skills do you have to offer? Well, for a start, you know how executives think. You know what's important to them, what kind of appointments make it into their calendars, what their intricate day-to-day work schedules look like, and what kind of support they need to do their jobs well.

Because you know a lot about corporate executives, your knowledge would be very useful to companies who *sell* to corporate executives. What's the opportunity for focus here? Well, if you're a freelance copywriter, graphic designer, project manger, or marketing consultant, instead of taking on projects that involve every piece of marketing material under the sun, you could begin to focus on those materials designed to get the attention of *executives*. Specifically, this could be direct-mail packages, sales letters, e-mails, and other materials that target this audience. Voilà! You've just discovered a useful skill set from your past work history and how to leverage that to bring focus to your business.

Until now, you might not have seen the link between your freelance work and your work experience as an executive assistant. And that's the beauty of this discovery process! By detailing your work history and your experience, evidence of your unique value can suddenly emerge before your very eyes.

Explore Your Hobbies, Interests, and Passions

As you work on discovering what it is you have to offer, you should give some consideration to those things you really enjoy doing. Marrying your freelance business with your hobbies, interests, and passions is a wonderful way to make a living.

As a freelancer, it makes little sense to pursue a career unless it's something you enjoy. For example, if you're a graphic designer who has never owned a passport, isn't fond of flying, and has no inclination to see the world, you probably won't enjoy (or have any success at) trying to focus on the travel and tourism industry.

So what do you love? What are your hobbies and interests? How do you like to spend your spare time? What *passions* do you like to pursue? List all these things, and examine them in the same way you examined your education and work history. Look for common links or things that jump out as natural links to your freelance business. This is precisely how Pam Magnuson decided to focus on being a copywriter in the nutraceuticals field. In the 1960s, Pam spent a few years living in the Far East, where she developed an interest in Chinese medicine and the healing properties of herbs. She never became a practicing herbalist, but she has maintained a hobbyist's interest in natural healing methods for many years. Eventually, she married that passion with her interests in pursuing a freelance copywriting career.

Lest you feel that this came "easy" to Pam, it's important to note that when she first entered the world of freelance copywriting, she tried her hand at writing copy for business-to-business companies (companies that sell products to other businesses versus consumers; B2B). She never quite made any real progress in that direction, though. Nothing was clicking for her. It wasn't until she took a good, long look *beyond* her work history, at her hobbies and interests, that she discovered the natural (pun intended) area of focus for her. In other words, although in hindsight the link seems obvious, Pam had to take time out to examine herself and *discover* that link.

Look for Commonalities in Your Current Client/Project Mix

If you've already been freelancing for a while, take the time to make a chart of all the projects you've completed to date (or just over the span of a few recent years, if you've been freelancing for a long time).

List the projects in a chart with these headings:

- Client
- Industry
- Project
- Project Description

Next, simply fill in the chart. (Note: In the Project Description column, describe the project in detail, being sure to state the goal and, if possible, the outcome of the project.)

When the chart is complete, look for commonalities. Begin by looking up and down the Client column. Are there any common themes? Are most of your clients small businesses where the main contact was the entrepreneurial founder? Are most companies professional services companies? Are there are a lot of companies beyond a certain size threshold, whether in terms of number of employees or salary? What about geographic commonalities among your client base?

Next, move on to your analysis of the Industry, Project, and Project Description columns, looking for commonalities.

Several Ways to Focus

Focusing on a market doesn't necessarily mean you must focus on an *industry*. Industry is one of the most common ways to focus, but it's certainly not the only option. For example, some freelancers focus by project type, such as the graphic designer who concentrates on consumer goods package design. This type of work can span many industries. Other freelancers focus on certain client attributes. For example, the freelancer writer who writes promotional materials for luxury goods and services. Again, this work spans several industries.

When I first did this exercise years ago, examining my Project and Client columns played a large role in leading me toward my area of focus. A lot of my clients happened to be technology companies. This common theme, combined with my background, led me to focus my copywriting services on B2B technology companies.

$ Success Story

Let Your Business Evolve

Michael Martine (Remarkablogger.com) is a freelance blog consultant who provides coaching and guidance to entrepreneurs (including freelancers) on how to create and successfully launch a blog. Michael says it's the most rewarding and well-paying work he's ever done. But as he recalls, it wasn't always this way.

"My first foray into self employment was as a freelance web designer, and that business actually failed," Michael says. In fact, Michael abandoned his freelance pursuits altogether for a while until he discovered a market for something he was doing on his own time, for his own enjoyment, and quietly developing a great talent for: blogging.

"In 2007 when I was looking for a way to turn my blog expertise into a business, I started off as a kind of jack-of-all-trades blog designer. I would do everything, including initial consultation, design and technical set up and launching of my client's actual blog," Michael explains. "But I discovered I didn't really enjoy the design and the technical work. For me, the real enjoyment came from coaching and helping clients build their overarching blogging strategy." Michael also realized something important—his clients hungered for his knowledge about how to make a blog successful, including everything from clearly identifying the target audience to identifying keywords.

"It certainly was not my plan from day one to be a blog consultant, but my business evolved in this direction because I listened to what the market was telling me, and I followed my new interest in the strategic side of things. Not only is this more gratifying work, it's also more lucrative. I'm able to charge far more for coaching and consulting than I did for the technical and design work."

For advice on blogging from Michael Martine, visit TheWealthyFreelancer.com/martine.

Identify the Market You Will Serve

Once you've discovered the unique value you can offer, you have to identify the market that's best suited to recognize and pay you for your special talents, skills, or expertise.

Some markets are easy to spot because of their size and pervasiveness in everyday media. When Pam discovered the value of her knowledge of herbs and alternative medicine, she didn't have to look very hard to find the nutraceuticals market. Nutraceuticals is an enormous industry that makes regular use of freelance copywriters, graphic designers, and photographers.

But what if your exploration of your own work history or hobbies and interests leads you to a market that leaves you wondering whether or not it's big enough to support your business?

Imagine for a moment you're a freelance photographer of Egyptian descent living in the United States. Until now, you've done a variety of freelance photography jobs for a mix of clients, including agencies, corporations, and small businesses. You begin to examine your hobbies and interests, recognizing your passion for your Egyptian heritage. You love traveling to your native country, and you have a wide collection of Egyptian art as well as extensive knowledge of the culture. This starts you thinking about focusing on servicing companies that offer Egyptian-related products or services. The idea of combining your passion for your heritage and your career excites you! But … is there enough market potential to make this idea a reality? Can you take photographs of Egyptian-related products and services and earn, say $80,000+ per year?

Don't look at me. I haven't got the foggiest idea. Nor do I know of any one person who would be able to give you a conclusive answer. When the market opportunity is not abundantly clear to you, it's up to *you* to assess its viability.

Is the Market Viable?

Let me ask you a question: Is there a market out there for people who want to learn how to make sweaters and other articles of clothing from their pet's hair? Seriously, what do you think?

If you say, "No," then you're *wrong!* Believe it or not, there is a book currently in print by a large, mainstream publisher titled (and I'm not making this up) *Knitting with Dog Hair!* Heaven only knows the conversation that went on between author, agent, and publisher when the idea for that book was first tabled, but one thing is for certain: the publisher must have been convinced that the demand for information on this topic was big enough to bring this book into the world.

So is the target market *you* wish to pursue viable? Let's go over some questions to help you make that assessment. A market is likely viable when you can answer "Yes" to all, or most, of the following questions.

Do the companies in this market need (i.e., spend money on) the type of service you want to offer? Let's look again at the idea of focusing your freelance photography business on serving companies that market Egyptian-related products and services. What types of companies come to mind that fit this description? Here are a few ...

- Importers/exporters of Egyptian goods
- Egyptian travel/tourism industry companies (These could include adventure and eco travel companies and travel magazine publishers.)
- Companies specializing in executive relocation services to and from Egypt
- Egyptian-to-English translation services

Spend some time on the Internet, and you might discover a plethora of each of these types of companies. You'd also discover that the first two types of companies in particular clearly use photographs in all their marketing materials, including websites, catalogs, brochures, and direct-mail materials. So clearly it appears that importers/exporters of Egyptian goods and Egyptian travel/tourism industry companies spend money on photography.

Just for contrast, let's look for a moment at the cement industry. This is a huge, multibillion-dollar global industry. However, you'd be hard-pressed to find many cement companies that use freelance photographers on a regular basis. Why? Because cement companies tend to sell their product (cement) by establishing relationships with local contracting companies and sealing the deal with a handshake. Brochures, websites, and catalogs with colorful pictures of the product really don't come into play in this industry. The size of a market is no guarantee that sufficient demand exists within that market for your particular services.

Are there enough companies doing this type of work to provide you with ample business? You'll want to be able to identify an industry or industry category with 200 to 400 or more companies who might give you work. How many importers/exporters of Egyptian goods can you find? How many tourism companies can you locate that focus specifically on Egyptian travel?

Questions, Questions

From here on, this chapter will present you with more questions than answers. The purpose here is to guide you in your own search for market viability. Emphasis on the words *your own search!*

You can ask people you respect for their opinion on the viability of any industry or industry segment; however, the question of whether or not your market is viable isn't something any one person can necessarily tell you with absolute certainty. For example, one well-known copywriter I know told me there's no market for a copywriter to make a living by writing marketing materials for law firms. I also know of another copywriter who's making a living doing exactly that! Seems the latter copywriter did enough research to find a viable market.

Do prospects gather together in person or online? Are there industry conferences, trade shows, associations, or other groups that service the market you're considering? Are there online destinations, such as forums and blogs, that attract a lot of discussion or commentary about issues related to your services? (If you can identify places where prospects "hang out," you've got an opportunity to establish a name for yourself by hanging out there, too, and adding value to the discussions.)

Can you easily identify a "buyer" within your target companies? My brother is an independent consultant who helps companies build and sustain financial protocols. CFOs and controllers buy his services—not Human Resource directors, not marketing managers, and not IT directors. Consequently, it's easier for him to find prospects by focusing his marketing efforts on CFOs, controllers, and no one else.

Who are the people within your target companies who can buy your services? Are these people easily identifiable? If you don't know, it doesn't mean they don't exist; it just means you have to find them.

Is this prospect group being marketed to already? Are there trade magazines, journals, periodicals, or other publications produced specifically for the audience you're going after? If so, the advertisers in this industry think this market is viable, at least for their service offering. How many of these publications (and advertisers) can you identify? This will give you an idea of the size of the market.

Are there other competitors within this market? Finding competitors (fellow freelancers) who specialize in serving this market is actually a good thing. It means there's enough of a market to sustain a population of freelancers.

How's it coming so far? If you ask yourself these questions and come up with dead ends, or if you have difficulty finding answers after a few solid hours of searching around on the Internet, chances are it's going to be a very tough market to pursue. If you can't even find these companies, how will you be able to identify the names of people *within them* whom you can call on?

You Might Need to Broaden Your Focus

If, after your research, you conclude there just don't seem to be many travel companies that focus on the Egyptian market, that's okay. Just broaden your focus a little. If you expand your focus to travel and tourism companies in general, then bingo! You can easily identify thousands of companies to serve. Adventure travel companies, travel magazines and publishers, cruise ship companies, eco travel companies, ... the list is endless.

Yes, you've broadened the scope of your focus, but make no mistake: you've brought tremendous focus to your business nonetheless. By targeting companies in the *travel* industry, you've eliminated chasing after companies in countless other industries and diluting your marketing efforts.

Position Yourself in Your Market

When you've identified the market you'll serve, the next step is to position yourself as the go-to resource in that market. Now before you begin to panic, allow me to tell you something, which I hope will have you breathing an enormous sigh of relief: *you don't have to be the best.*

There are 947 hockey players in the NHL. Only one of them is the "best" player. The other 946 are not. And yet they *all* still get to play professional hockey at the premier level. They all earn a very high income doing what they love.

I'm not the best B2B copywriter in the world. I've heard both of my co-authors in this book say exactly the same thing. (Did you know we are all competitors in the same market?) Yet all three of us earn high incomes doing what we love.

You don't have to be the best in your industry to be a shining success. Likewise, you don't have to be the "most well known," either.

In my industry, two copywriters are very well known for writing white papers. One is Michael Stelzner, and the other is Gordon Graham. Both bill themselves as *the* place to go when you need a top-notch white paper written. Both Michael and Gordon are excellent writers. Both are very capable. Both are very busy. Which one is "better"? I don't know. Which one is "more well known"? Well, if they're both running thriving freelance businesses, each getting offered more work than they can handle, it doesn't really matter, does it? They're both well known enough!

Whichever one is the best (as if that could ever be proven or measured) is immaterial. Even if you could rank number one and number two, it wouldn't matter; they're both wildly successful freelancers!

So free yourself of this misconception that you have to be *the* best, *the* guru, *the* one and only go-to resource on the planet for service *X*. What's important is not that you *are* the go-to person, but that you *position* yourself as the go-to person. There's a big difference here, and it's important that you don't feel anxious over this. All you need to do is take the value you bring and articulate it in a way that positions you favorably in the eyes of your target prospects.

I'm not saying this lets you off the hook of knowing your stuff. And I'm certainly not saying you should claim to be a subject matter expert if you aren't. But if you have skills, knowledge, and competencies in a certain area, then you can legitimately position yourself as the obvious choice among service providers in your field without feeling as though you need to be the best.

Your Unique Selling Proposition (USP)

I hesitated in titling this section as I did because the words *unique selling proposition* tend to strike fear in the hearts of all who don't have one. That's the problem with business buzzwords like *USP*. People get so hung up and anxious over them and make them out to be far more complicated than they are. We won't do that here.

There's a common "official" definition for USP you can look up online if you like, but for our purposes, we'll work with a much simpler definition coined by Ed Gandia. When Ed counsels freelancers on creating a USP, he tells them that positioning really comes down to being able to answer these three questions:

1. What do you do?

2. For whom do you do it?

3. What makes you different?

If you can answer those questions, you have your USP. Let's look again at Pam Magnuson so you can see how she might answer each of Ed's questions and arrive at her USP:

Question	Pam's Answer
1. What do you do?	"I'm a freelance copywriter …"
2. For whom do you do it?	"… who writes copy for nutraceutical and alternative health companies."
3. What makes you different?	"My knowledge of herbal, Chinese, and alternative medicine began over 40 years ago when I started learning about natural healing methods while living in the Far East. This knowledge, combined with a history of marketing experience, makes me the best choice."

Pam's answers sound like a pretty compelling USP. Because Pam has a knockout USP, does this mean she has the nutraceuticals market sewn up? Of course not! For one thing, the market is way too big for just one copywriter to serve, but more to the point, lots of other individuals with unique skill sets can position themselves as the go-to expert in this nutraceutical industry because of the unique value *they* might bring.

How about a nurse, for example? Or someone with a biology degree? Or someone who worked in a health-food store for seven years, actually explaining and selling natural products to customers? Or for that matter, a customer service representative who worked for a major alternative health supplements company? What about someone who has a history of health problems and has been successfully using alternative health products for years to manage her symptoms? Each of these people can develop his or her own unique answer to Ed's question number 3, what makes you different?

Your answer to question 3 doesn't have to be unique to the extent that it makes you the *only* choice in the market. That's virtually impossible, and not at all the goal, yet many freelancers think this way when they set about creating a USP. What's important is that your answer makes you sound different *enough* to distinctly identify you in the market. That's it!

Let's take a look at all of Ed's questions again, so you can see which of the preceding sections in this chapter can help you develop your answers to each question:

Question	Section in This Chapter That Helps You Develop Your Answer
1. What do you do?	(Here, just state the type of freelance work you do.)
2. For whom do you do it?	"Identify the Market You Will Serve"
3. What makes you different?	"Discover What You Have to Offer"

Recap: Discover, Identify, Position (DIP) Technique

Do you see how answering these three questions is a nice way to articulate the results of your DIP Technique exercises? By completing the exercises in the "Discover What You Have to Offer" and "Identify the Market You Will Serve" sections, you will be able to formulate answers to Ed's questions. That takes care of the Discover and Identify sections of the DIP Technique.

With your answers formulated, you have, in essence, created your USP. Read your answers to the three questions concurrently, just like you read Pam's answers earlier, and you have your USP. That takes care of Position, the third and final component of the DIP Technique. You can always go back and polish your answers so they flow together nicely, resulting in a well-articulated USP.

With your USP created, you now know where to focus your marketing efforts, and you've articulated the essence of your positioning message. You can now exert the same focused effort Pam does when she decides to attend a trade show, or launch a marketing campaign, or speak to a prospect on the phone. In every circumstance, she knows what she has to offer, she knows who to approach, she knows what to say, and she knows what her website must look like in order to position herself as an expert. She's brought focus to her freelance business and is reaping the rewards. And now you can, too.

Wealthy Takeaways

- When you bring focus to your business, your business-generating activities become far more efficient and effective.

- Once you know the *kind* of freelance work you want to do, use the Discover, Identify, Position (DIP) Technique to help you bring more focus to your business.

- Many freelancers focus on serving clients in a certain industry, but you can also focus in other ways, such as by project type or client attributes.

- Discover what you have to offer by examining your work history, hobbies, interests, and passions, looking for the value you can bring to the market.

- If you've been freelancing for a while, examine your freelance project work to date for potential areas of focus.

- It's up to you to assess the viability of a market. Use the questions in this chapter to guide you in this assessment.

- Forget about being "the best." You don't have to be the best or most well-known freelancer in your industry in order to be successful.

- Creating a unique selling proposition (USP) doesn't have to be a complicated or anxiety-ridden task. It's simply a matter of answering three questions: What do you do? For whom do you do it? and What makes you different?

- Having a USP helps you focus your marketing efforts and better position yourself.

Secret 9: Boost Your Productivity—Without Perspiration!

Steve Slaunwhite

When I hung out my shingle as a freelancer about a gazillion years ago, it didn't take me long to realize that the more I was able to get done, the more money I would make. I needed to earn a good income. And I certainly didn't want to have to get a "real" job again. Ugh! So I made a determined effort to adhere to personal productivity techniques that would put my nose to the grindstone and keep it there … no matter how much it bled! I read all the classic time-management books and followed the advice diligently. I bought into the idea that every minute of the day needed to be filled—no, packed solid—with productive work.

My family quickly learned not to interrupt my draconian work schedule. I remember actually growling at my young daughter one day when she had the audacity to creak open my home office door to show me something. She quickly left in tears. As it turned out, she just wanted to give me a drawing she had made for my office wall.

Being a creative, carefree soul by nature, I yearned to go for a midday jog every once in a while, occasionally take my laptop and work at a favorite café, or surprise my daughter by picking her up from school and treating her (okay, and me, too) to an ice cream. But the uncompromising inner drill sergeant I had created would keep my butt firmly planted in my office chair and my fingers tapping double-time on the keyboard.

Was I productive? Yes. Was I miserable? Oh, yes.

After a while—a much longer "while" than I care to admit to—I realized that this wasn't the work-lifestyle I had originally envisioned for my business. The reason I wanted to become a freelancer in the first place was to have a comfortable home office, work on projects that fascinated and inspired me, spend extra time with my family, and yes, have the freedom to join the league of laptops at Starbucks once or twice a week.

To me, that idyllic vision was a big part of what it meant be a *wealthy freelancer.* Yet somewhere along the way, it got beaten down into something resembling a galley slave in an ancient Roman ship, rowing pitifully while the drummer beats faster and faster. I was getting a lot done, but I wasn't having fun!

That's when I decided that enough is enough. There must be some way to be productive and still have the kind of workday I've always dreamed of having. So I went on a quest to find productivity strategies that actually make sense for me and, as it turned out, for many other freelance professionals as well.

What I discovered surprised me. Yes, you can be productive—very, very productive—and yet not feel so tightly scheduled and pressured that you're perpetually miserable. You can take a midday jog, have lunch with your spouse, or go to your son's afternoon basketball game. All that and still get done what you need to get done.

Beware. Many of the "wealthy" productivity ideas I'm about to share with you may seem unconventional. Because they are! But I encourage you to give one or two of these ideas a try, at least for a week or two. I think you'll be surprised at how much more productive you become and how much less stressed you feel. So let's get started with the first technique for productivity without perspiration.

Get Your &%@# to Work!

People with "real" jobs have an advantage over us freelancers—they *have* to go to work! No matter how late they stayed up the night before or how difficult it was to pack the kids off to school in the morning, somehow, some way, they have to drag their butt to the workplace on time. If they don't, someone—perhaps their boss—is going to notice!

But things are different when you're self-employed. There's no punch clock button to hit nor boss to give you a cold look if you stumble into work late. You can happily linger in your pajamas, sipping coffee and reading the paper, for hours. "Gee, I really should get started on that client project," you say to yourself while checking your watch. "Well, maybe after one more cup of java!"

Wealthy Words

50 percent of success is just showing up.

—Woody Allen

That's a problem! Because, in my experience, the number-one reason why freelancers don't get things done—and as a result, often live in a near continuous state of deadline dread—is that they simply don't go to work. They leave things loose. When they have a client project on the go, they allocate it to "sometime this morning" or "right after lunch." There are no firm "office hours." No set schedule.

Big mistake. You *must* have a schedule. That means knowing that at 10 A.M., or whatever time you've determined, you have an appointment with Project X. You'll show up for work at that time, jump into that project with both feet, and work at it diligently until the schedule says to stop.

If you don't have a schedule, it's way too easy to procrastinate. It's also way too easy to leave project work until the deadline comes crashing around the corner, forcing you into a frenzied scramble to get the job done. (Isn't that fun!) Scheduling also helps you plan your work so you can give yourself the time a project requires. There's nothing more frightening—at least to a freelancer—than leaving a project until the last minute, only to realize that it's going to take you many more hours to complete than you had originally anticipated.

Now the good news is, as a freelancer, you can make your own schedule. You can plan your project work in time slots that fit perfectly with your lifestyle, preferences, and workload. You can build in flexibility that allows you to spend time with your kids, play a round of driveway basketball, or walk your dog.

I'm an early bird so I prefer to start at 7 A.M. In fact, I'm so disciplined about showing up to work (via a 20-second commute from the breakfast table to my home office) that I actually feel uncomfortable, even agitated, if I'm late for some reason. I typically work on projects and tasks until 11 A.M. and then either go for a jog or take some work with me to a local café.

 Wealthy Tools

Google Calendar (Google.com/calendar) is a great tool for scheduling your work. You can customize it in a variety of ways and, because it's online, access it anywhere you find an Internet connection. You can also print it, save it on your computer, or sync it with other calendar programs like Outlook and iCal. And the best part is, it's free.

My friend Jan, a graphic designer, has a young child. So she schedules her work in chunks throughout the day to balance parenting and freelancing (a common high-wire act these days). According to Jan, "I schedule three work sessions each day. One hour in the morning while Emily is taking her nap. Another hour just after lunch. And then, when my husband gets home, a third hour just before dinner."

Jan is very productive and gets a lot of work done. Yet she's been able to strike the ideal work-life balance without making a sacrifice on either side. How? She made a schedule and stuck to it. If she had been loosey-goosey with her schedule and just tried to squeeze in client work wherever she could throughout the day, she wouldn't have been nearly as successful.

So never be ambiguous about when you'll go to work and for how long. If you catch yourself saying, "I'll sketch out ideas for that logo design later this afternoon," stop, get out your schedule, and block out the time you need. Then when that time arrives, go to work! You'll get more done with a lot less stress.

Get Organized—the Low-Tech Way

Where did I put that project file? Oh, yes, there it is. Shoved under that stack of papers on my bookshelf. Hey, didn't I take some notes about yesterday's client meeting? Where did I put those? Oh, there they are. But there's a note missing. Wait a minute, it's in my jacket pocket downstairs. …

Sound a little familiar? I admit, it is to me. As a freelancer, disorganization can cost you time and dollars and make things stressful. Hardly the wealthy freelancer way!

And I'm certainly not perfect. Even though I have a great system for managing my projects and tasks, I still slip up every once in a while. Just this morning, I spent several minutes looking for a file on my way-too-cluttered computer screen desktop! I felt like I was playing a game of Where's Waldo?

When it comes to keeping things organized, as a freelancer, you're basically concerned with two things:

- Projects
- Tasks

Projects are those activities that typically take longer than 20 minutes to complete. For example, writing a brochure for a client is a project. So is putting together a podcast, designing a website, or doing your taxes. As a freelancer, you may have two or three projects on the go at any given time, like a couple paying projects from clients and perhaps an in-house project such as updating your website.

A task, by contrast, is any activity that takes less than 20 minutes to complete. It's a traditional to-do item. Over the course of a day, several tasks might need your attention (or in some cases, scream for it) such as paying a bill, returning a phone call, sending an e-mail, or ordering a new toner cartridge for the printer.

Have you ever had a task fall through the cracks then scramble to get it done? Or misplaced important information you need to finish a project and wasted precious minutes or even hours trying to find it? Few things will torpedo your productivity more than disorganization.

Over the years I've experimented with many systems for keeping track of projects and tasks. I've tried software programs, online to-do lists, project management binders—you name it. What ultimately worked best for me?

Some file folders, a stack of 3×5 index cards, and a wall-mounted cork board! Yep, I know that's about as low-tech as it gets, but the system works. Let me walk you through it, starting with how I handle the start of a new project:

1. I pull out a file folder and label it with the project name. That's where I'm going to put all the printed project information. I use an accordion-style legal-size file folder because it holds a lot of stuff and prevents papers from falling out the sides.

2. I make a corresponding computer folder—using the same project name, of course—to hold electronic project information such as documents and e-mails.

3. I write the project name and any key dates, such as the deadline, on an index card and pin it to the cork board adjacent to my desk. (The cork board gives me an at-a-glance view of what needs to get done: projects on the left, tasks on the right.)

That's it! When I "go to work" each morning, I simply look at my cork board, decide which project I want (or need) to work on, pull out the corresponding file folder, and open the corresponding computer folder. Everything I need to hit the ground running on that project is now at my fingertips. I'm working productively in about 15 seconds!

I have a similar system for completing tasks. If there's a phone call I need to return, for example, and I can't do that right away, I simply …

1. Pick up an index card from the stack I keep on my desk.

2. Jot down the task: "Call Michael back to discuss the design changes for the new website."

3. Pin the index card to the cork board.

When I have a few moments, usually while I'm taking a break from working on a project, I just look at the cork board, pick a task, and as comedian Larry the Cable Guy is famous for saying, "Get 'er done!"

My cork board of projects and tasks helps me gain a big picture of what needs to get done and ensures nothing, especially tasks, falls though the cracks. And it sure feels good to take down an index card and toss it in the recycle bin when a project or task is done!

The 50-Minute Focus

Now that you understand the importance of scheduling your work and you have a simple way to organize your projects and tasks, how do you get all those activities done on time? Well, the fact is, you already know the secret to doubling your productivity. You've done it before. And you can do it again and again.

Here's what I mean: say you're at a client meeting discussing a potential project. He's going over the creative brief with you. You're asking questions and taking notes. You're being careful to ensure you understand everything and making a good impression. Typical client meeting stuff. Now in the middle of that meeting, you're not suddenly going to open your laptop and check your mail, make a quick phone call to a friend and chat about plans for the weekend, or pull out your grocery list and add a few items. That would be ludicrous. The client would think you're a wacky creative. (You might be, but you don't want the client to think that!) No, you would give that client meeting your full attention. For those 50 minutes or so, you would let few things, if any, distract you. You'd be "on."

Now think about the last time you did some work on a client project. Were you "on" for 50 minutes, totally focused and absorbed in the work, not allowing yourself to get distracted in any way? Or did you find yourself occasionally answering the phone, checking e-mail, grabbing a coffee, throwing some laundry in the dryer, or playing a quick game of spider solitaire on your computer?

You could easily double your productivity by doing what you already know how to do: remaining totally focused on one thing and one thing only—the project—for just 50 minutes. This technique is called the 50-minute focus. Here's how it works:

1. Get a timer with an alarm. I use the timer on my watch, but you can buy one at an electronics store for just a few dollars.

2. Select the project you want to work on, preferably one where you really need to make some serious progress.

3. Set the timer for 50 minutes.

4. During those 50 minutes, be totally focused on that project, just as you would be at an important client meeting. Don't check e-mail. Don't take a break. Don't let your mind wander to the BBQ plans you have for the weekend. Be totally immersed.

5. When the timer goes off, the "meeting" is over. Completely unplug from the project for 20 minutes. During that time, you can take a break or get a few tasks done.

After 20 minutes, assuming you still plan on working, do another 50-minute focus.

The 50-minute focus technique was developed by my friend, marketing whiz Dean Jackson. The first time I tried it, I was surprised by two things:

• How challenging it is to truly focus on a project, uninterrupted, for 50 minutes.

• How much I was able to get done on a project in that short period of time.

And I'm not the only one. Remember Jan, the freelancing mom I told you about earlier? She divides her workday into three 50-minute focus sessions. "It took me a few days before I could focus that long on a project without distracting myself by checking my email or thinking about what to make for dinner. It was as if I had to exercise my 50-minute focus muscle and make it strong. But once I did, I was amazed by how much more productive I became. Interestingly, the work became more enjoyable, too."

My experience has been similar. Every 50-minute focus I do gives me a quantum leap toward a project finish line. I also like the built-in incentive—that 20-minute break!

Fifty-minute focus sessions are like blocks of superproductive time you can squeeze in anywhere, anytime. I find this technique particularly helpful when I'm tired, under deadline pressure, or just feel unmotivated for some reason. If I'd rather clean my cat's litter box with a toothbrush than work on a particular client project, I simply decide to do a 50-minute focus. I tell myself, "Hey, that's less than an hour. I can do that." Once I get absorbed in the project, my lack of motivation often disappears.

In fact, with just a few exceptions, most of my days are a series of 50-minute focuses and 20-minute breaks. During the breaks, I chip away at the tasks I have pinned (as index cards) to the cork board on my office wall, grab a coffee, or step outside for some fresh air.

Wealthy Tip

You can fit a 50-minute focus into even the most erratic of schedules. Waiting for your daughter to finish her dance practice? Pull out your laptop and do a 50-minute focus! Have a pressing deadline that's difficult to meet? Do a 50-minute focus in the evening. Just put the baby down for a nap? You've got 50 minutes. Do a focus! See what I mean?

Don't Ignore the Muse

You're going to hate me for saying this because it adds a layer of complexity to what I just taught you about working on projects. But there will be times when you need to dispense with the 50-minute focus technique. When? When the muse strikes you.

The muse is a term from Greek mythology that refers to a goddess who inspires artists, writers, and other creative people. In practical terms, the muse is that strange and wonderful creative energy that sometimes takes hold of you while you're working on a project. For whatever reason—you never know for sure—the work suddenly becomes effortless. You're in the flow, and great ideas just pour out of you. If you're a writer, the words fly onto the page. If you're a designer, just the right layout and concepts seem to appear out of nowhere.

I remember working on a copywriting project a couple months ago, a new website for a client. I don't know what it was. Maybe the fascinating subject matter, or the good news (completely unrelated) that I had received that morning, or the buoyant mood I happened to be in. Who knows? But whatever it was, the words just seemed to tumble out of me and onto the screen in just the right ways. I wrote and wrote and wrote at twice the rate I normally do. I was having fun. I didn't want to stop! And when the 50-minute timer on my watch went off, I didn't.

Nor should you. When the muse strikes and you feel energized and "in the groove" with a particular project, go with it. Forget the 50-minute focus. Just feel blessed that the muse has visited for a while and keep working until she goes away. There's no way to predict when the muse will strike and how long she'll linger. Just know that as a freelancer—a writer, designer, programmer, consultant, or whatever—you're going to get that boost of creative energy every once in a while and you'd be a fool to ignore it. Then when the muse fades, take a break. If she doesn't return, simply go back to doing a 50-minute focus.

Take Time to Incubate

Before I sat down to write this chapter, I made some notes about the topics I wanted to cover. I planned out the stories and examples I wanted to use to reinforce the points I was going to make and mapped out my general approach to the subject matter. This is typical planning stuff. And you probably do something similar for the types of projects you handle as a freelancer. But then I did something you may not do. I stuck my notes in the project file folder and didn't look at them again for a couple days. Why didn't I just get started on the next step in the process—writing the darned thing—right away? Because I knew I would get this chapter done a lot faster if I gave it time to incubate.

I know what you're thinking. "Take time off from a project to get it done *sooner?*" But giving a project some incubation time—especially between natural steps in the process such as planning and writing or writing and polishing—makes the work go much smoother and faster.

Of course, you know this already. Think of the last time you got stuck on a project. You're working on a new computer program for a client and, no matter how much you rack your brain, you just can't seem to make any progress. So you take a break, perhaps out of frustration, and go work on something else. Or take a walk. Or sleep on it. Then when you return to the project again, what happens? Voilà! Things just seem to flow again. That's incubation at work.

Let It Incubate

Graphic designer David Holden often gets stuck when working on his designs and illustrations. But it never worries him. "I just write 'Incubate this' and move on. I know my mind will chug away at the problem. When I get back to it, the solution will come to me."

Marketing consultant Marcia Yudkin is a master of using incubation to work more productively. In her booklet *No More Writer's Block!* she describes being able to write a press release in about 45 minutes when most other professionals take at least two hours or more. "I gather all the information I need," she says, "then wait a day or two [incubation] until I feel like the press release is itching to come out of me. And that's when I write it, quickly and easily."

I'm not going to get into the science of how incubation works here. (As if I understood it!) Just know that when you take a physical break from a project, some part of your brain is still working on it. Your subconscious is churning away: generating new ideas, trying out different approaches to the problem, asking new questions, dreaming up inventive new approaches.

Do I hear someone balking, "I don't have time to stick a project in a drawer for a couple days. I have tight deadlines to meet!" Well, if you have tight deadlines to meet, you need incubation more than ever. Think about it. Which would you rather do? Struggle with a project for six hours straight until you stumble, exhausted, to the finish line? Or spend a couple hours reviewing and absorbing the information, then taking a break for a few hours, then finishing the piece in another hour or two, feeling refreshed and energized? Ah …. I'd choose number two.

And by the way, incubation doesn't have to take days or even hours. Sometimes all that's required is a walk around the block.

Push Your Motivation Buttons

Imagine you're having a tough day. Things aren't going well. You're feeling drained and unmotivated. It's hard to paint a smile on your face. And when you do, it looks more like a grimace.

Of course, we all have days like these from time to time. The problem is, as a freelancer, feeling unmotivated can seriously affect your ability to do all the things you need to do that day. It's a productivity killer. You may not feel like starting work on that new client project (you know, the one that's due in just a few days), or making those follow-up calls, or getting those pitch letters in the mail, or updating your website.

That's one of the challenges of being self-employed. When you feel unmotivated, often there's no one else around to give you a lift. No colleagues to commiserate with. No boss to kick your you-know-what. You're on your own.

So what do you do when you're down in the dumps? According to Steve Chandler, author of *100 Ways to Motivate Yourself: Change Your Life Forever* (Career Press, 2004), we all have personal motivation "on" buttons we can push at any time. We just have to know where those buttons are—and have them at our fingertips when we need them the most.

Do you feel inspired when you read a favorite newsletter or blog? Or upbeat when you hear a certain song on the radio? Or less stressed when you sip tea at a favorite café? Or energized when you listen to a particular coach or speaker on a CD recording? "Make it a personal commitment to notice everything that pushes your buttons," says Chandler. "Make a note of everything that inspires you." Once you do, you'll have a repertoire of ways to feel motivated anytime you want to.

For example, if you're working on a particularly tough client project and you're feeling, well—let's say less than enthusiastic—plug in a CD of your favorite music, pat your dog, or pick up the phone and chat with a close friend. The point is to figure out what motivates you and then learn how to quickly turn on that button when you need it the most. I get a lift from reading inspiring passages from certain books, so I keep these within arm's reach. I also have a few close colleagues I speak to (okay, whine to) by phone from time to time.

What are *your* motivation buttons? If you don't know, find them. You can probably come up with a dozen ways to give yourself a boost anytime you need it. And as freelancers, we often need it. A lot.

Don't Go It Alone

I've been focusing so much on working faster and smarter in this chapter that I almost forgot the most effective productivity booster of them all: getting someone else to do it! Ask yourself if it's really necessary, or even wise, for you to …

- Proofread your own materials before sending them to the client?
- Do the "mechanicals" after you've already finished the main creative work on a graphic design project?
- Do your own bookkeeping?
- Chase down sources to arrange interviews?
- Research topics using the Internet?
- Stuff envelopes for your self-promotion direct-mail campaign?
- Package and ship things to clients or customers?
- Do something that requires a skill you just don't have, such as web design or ad writing?

That last point really resonates with me. I remember struggling for days trying to figure out how to create a blog using WordPress software. Finally, I got smart and hired a freelance WordPress designer who was able to get the job done in less than a day and for just $200. When I think of all the billable hours I wasted, I shudder. The client work I could have done instead would have earned me at least $1,500!

Most freelance professionals are classic do-it-yourselfers. I know I was for many, many years. I did just about everything in my freelance business, from bookkeeping to administrative paperwork to stuffing envelopes. I was a bit of a lone wolf and didn't really want others involved in my business. And frankly, I needed to keep my costs down.

That approach worked for a while. But as my freelance practice grew, all those tasks increasingly became a burden. Paperwork, bookkeeping, making appointments, and so on began to bite into my schedule like a ravaging hyena, which meant I was spending less time working with clients and earning income.

Eventually, I decided to bite the bullet and get some help. So I hired a virtual assistant (VA). A virtual assistant is a type of freelancer, just like us. Usually working from a home office (just like us), he or she provides a range of administrative services to clients. I originally hired my VA, Karen, just to do some proofreading and a teleclass transcription. But when I realized how much time she saved me, I quickly began counting on her for many other tasks as well. Karen took a huge administrative load off my shoulders and, almost overnight, I had all this extra time freed up for client work and other projects I wanted to focus on. My productivity soared.

Wealthy Tools

Here are some great organizations that can help you find a virtual assistant: International Virtual Assistants Association (IVAA.org), Canadian Virtual Assistant Connection (CVAC.ca), and Society of Virtual Assistants (SocietyOfVirtualAssistants.co.uk).

These days, I never do a new activity without asking myself, "Can someone else do this for me? Possibly better and faster?" If my answer is yes, then I farm it out to a VA. In fact, in addition to Karen, my main VA, I also work with other VAs for such specialized tasks as podcast editing and bookkeeping.

How much does a VA cost? They typically charge a project fee, such as $5 per page to check a document for typos, or an hourly rate, usually in the $25- to $50-per-hour range.

I know what you're thinking: "I don't have the money to hire a VA!" I can understand that. But are you sure you can't afford it, or is it really because you just don't want to spend the money? If it's the former, then at least plan to hire a VA when your freelance business becomes busier and more profitable. If it's the latter, consider that when you invest in a VA, what you're getting back in return is a freelancer's most valuable commodity: time. You can use that time to cut back on your working hours (while getting the same amount of billable work done) or get more client projects finished and make more money. Either way, you're significantly increasing your productivity by using a VA.

Try it. Hire a VA for just one project, such as proofreading or following up with clients. Once you do, you'll never look back!

Wealthy Takeaways

- You don't have to keep your nose to the grindstone until it bleeds to be productive. You can use many techniques to get things done and still have the lifestyle you want.

- Schedule your working hours, even if you're part-time. Record on a calendar or schedule when you're going to start work on a particular client project and for how long. Then when that time arrives, get to work!

- Organize your projects and tasks using a simple system of index cards and file folders.

- Use the 50-minute focus technique to double your productivity during project work. Focus intently on a project for 50 minutes without interruption and then unplug and take a 20-minute break.

- Don't ignore the muse. When you get a burst of creative energy, go with it! And enjoy the ride.

- Build incubation time into your project schedule. Incubation can shave hours off the time it would normally take to get a project done.

- Discover what motivates and energizes you. That could be as simple as a hot cup of lemon tea or a midday jog.

- Consider hiring a virtual assistant to handle administrative tasks and other chores so you can focus more time on project work and building your business.

Secret 10: Construct Your Own Work-Life Reality

Pete Savage

Several years ago, while backpacking my way along Australia's east coast, I decided one day to take some surfing lessons in the rolling Pacific waters that lap the country's shoreline. I spent most of that morning attempting to follow instructions and stand upright on an uncooperative surfboard. For hours, small ocean waves would rise invitingly beneath my surfboard, swell to just the right size, and roll majestically toward the shoreline without me on them. Time and again, in my attempts to stand up on the board, the ocean would toss, flip, heave, and dump me off. Being pummeled by wave after wave, I *felt* like an uncoordinated oaf. The reality, however, was that in every one of my failed attempts to stand up on the board, I was always just *inches* away from achieving a state of complete and total balance.

I know this because I actually did manage to stand up on that board and surf a wave, not once, but twice—and for *at least* 30 seconds each time!

Fast forward to 2004. Sitting in my home office, and feeling over-whelmed at the amount of work on my plate, I decided to buckle down and … clean my office. Lucky for me, I also listened to an audiobook, *Ready for Anything: 52 Productivity Principles for Work and Life* (Viking, 2003) by productivity expert David Allen. As I moved around my office, half listening to the audiobook while avoiding the real work that lay in front of me, Allen said something that made my ears perk up:

> "The difference between riding a wave and being pummeled by it is smaller than you think."

Instantly, my mind raced back to the warm coastal waters of Byron Bay and my 30-second stints as "surfer dude" atop those cresting waves. I thought about what I had just heard Allen say. And he was right.

On those two successful surfs, in those moments when I had gained my balance and actually surfed, it was because of *minor*, incremental adjustments to my body position. The distribution of my body weight among my feet, the rotation of my hips, the position of my head—when each of these things was off, even slightly, by a mere inch or two, I'd be dumped into the water. But when all these things were moved to where they should be, by way of a minor—not grandiose—movement of the spine ... balance! The *incremental* difference in my posture made a *quantum* difference in my results. As Allen puts it, the difference between riding my wave and being pummeled by the wave was smaller than I thought.

That's where a lot of us are when it comes to work-life balance. Somehow, we've come to believe that this state of harmony between our work and our personal lives is some elusive, far-away utopia. Wrong!

You are, right now, inches—*not miles*—away from enjoying work-life balance. It's not in some far-off distant land. It's as close to you as your feet, hips, and head.

Correcting Limiting Beliefs About Work-Life Balance

If you're really so close to enjoying a harmonious work-life balance, why does it continue to allude you? And what can you do about it? As with many challenges you might face, the path to resolution appears only when you realize you have an incorrect *perception* of the problem.

In society today, there are two pervasive beliefs surrounding work-life balance, and they do us much harm:

1.   Work-life balance is something to be *pursued*.

2.   *Balance* means "equal."

If you desire more balance in your life but have yet to consistently experience it, these two limiting beliefs may be holding you back. Let's acknowledge them and then abolish them, so we can go forward with some strategies to help you create and enjoy your own work-life reality.

Limiting Belief #1: Work-Life Balance Is Something to Be Pursued

Work-life balance is no more a pursuit than is walking to your refrigerator to grab a jug of orange juice. Just as you can enjoy a glass of OJ anytime you like, so, too, can you enjoy balance in your everyday life, starting right now.

The problem with seeing work-life balance as a *pursuit* is that this automatically puts a certain amount of perceived distance between the life you lead right now and some mythical, harmonious one, way off in the future, that is balanced. If you perceive your own search for balance as a quest, it will remain one. And you don't want that. Quests take ages to fulfill!

So right now, stop telling yourself that you're *pursuing* work-life balance. Correcting this next limiting belief will help you do that.

Limiting Belief #2: *Balance* Means "Equal"

There's a problem with using the word *balance* to describe that state of harmony where work and personal life coexist without one depleting the other. The word *balance* connotes "equal." And that causes us to think, if only subconsciously, that for our work and personal lives to be in "balance," we must divide our waking hours equally between work and leisure. For most of us, that's not only absurd, it's impossible.

So if not 50-50, what's the right balance between work and leisure? The right split is up to you to decide, but first, try this one-minute exercise that's guaranteed to give you a new appreciation for what the word *balance* really means:

1. Stand up with your legs shoulder-width apart.

2. Keeping both feet on the ground, lean a little toward the right, without falling over.

3. Lean a little bit farther right, again without falling over.

4. Now stop and hold it right there ….

Notice the distribution of your body weight. I'm just guessing, but perhaps 80 percent of your body weight is being supported by your right foot and 20 percent by your left. An 80-20 weight distribution is certainly not equal, and yet, you haven't lost your balance at all, have you?

You don't suddenly lose your balance when your body weight shifts from one foot to the other. Balance can still be maintained even if your weight is distributed in an 80-20 ratio! *That* is balance! Now if you think of your right foot as your working time and your left foot as your leisure time, you'll notice something encouraging: to enjoy balance between your work life and your personal life, you don't have to spend equal time in work and leisure activities. Not even close! You can work hard, you can even work a lot of hours, and you can *still* enjoy balance in your life.

The strategies in this chapter show the hardworking freelancer how to enjoy this state of balance with increasing regularity. Now that you know what *balance* really means, all you need to do is give some thought to what a balanced lifestyle looks like for you.

What Does *Balance* Mean to You?

To affect the quality of the day, that is the highest of arts.

—Henry David Thoreau

I can't imagine Thoreau was thinking of freelancers exclusively, or at all for that matter, when he penned those words. And yet, I think his poetic quip is most applicable for today's freelance professional.

Freelancers have tremendous freedom to create their own reality when it comes to work-life balance. Consider this: if you work in an office located 90 minutes by car from your home, it's pretty hard to flip your laptop shut at noon and indulge in a 1-hour workout on the mountain bike trails behind your house. Or spend 30 minutes in your garden planting a few veggies or blooms.

We freelancers don't have to build a life around a corporate work schedule imposed on us by others. Instead, because we set our own schedules and we often work from home, we can create a work-life reality that fits our own unique circumstances!

When my son approached the terrible twos, he had difficulty napping in the afternoons. It seemed the only times he would fall asleep was when he was in motion—either in his car seat or in the bicycle seat attached to my mountain bike.

No problem, I'm a freelancer. For months, virtually every afternoon, I would stop work at 1:30 P.M. and enjoy my afternoon bike ride for two. I'd pedal all over the place, through the neighborhoods and parks that surround my house, to coax my little guy to sleep. Sometimes he'd conk out within 10 minutes; other times it took more than 40. It didn't matter! To me, I had allowed an hour in my day for this critical ritual. Often, my wife, who was pregnant with our little girl at the time, would use this downtime as a window to catch a nap herself.

For our circumstances, this hour of personal time worked wonders for the whole family. I got some fresh air, a little exercise, and a mental break from work. And everyone else in the house who needed a nap got one!

This worked for me because I kept pretty rigid "office hours" throughout the rest of the day so I could really take advantage of this one-hour hiatus in the middle of every day. But maybe rigid office hours don't appeal to you. They certainly aren't mandatory when you're a freelancer. Who's looking over your shoulder to be sure you're punched in by 8:30 A.M.? Nobody!

Michael Klassen (MikeKlassen.com), a freelance graphic designer, completely eschews the notion that work life and home life must be separated:

> For me, it's more of an easy flow between the things that I
> do whether it's working or spending time with my family. I
> might move back and forth between the two multiple times a
> day. That kind of goes against the usual advice of having fixed
> hours for your working time at home, and not returning to
> your work once you're done for the day.
>
> But that's part of the joy of freelancing … moving between work
> and personal life as needed and on your own terms, not putting
> things into fixed hours or a set schedule. I'm not a designer for
> X number of hours a day and a husband/parent for another set
> of hours a day … I'm all those things all the time and I focus on
> each aspect of what I need, or want, to do as appropriate.

For freelancers who prefer their work and personal lives to be separated by a solid, not dotted, line, Michael's boundary-hopping attitude may make them queasy. But it works for him! "This saved me from chasing after some undefined goal of work-life balance," Michael says.

The point is that you must give some thought to the kind of work-life reality that will work for *you*. In the following sections, I share with you three ways to do just that.

Recall Your Ideal Day

Remember the ideal day exercise you did in Secret 1? Look at it again. Did you really paint a complete picture of what you want your work-life reality to look like? Or did you focus just on the work aspect of the day?

Revisit that exercise, and paint a clear picture of what a *balanced* day looks like for you.

Discover When You Do Your Best Work

My freelance business was in full swing for years before I gave much thought to the idea that I may be more productive and creative at certain times of the day than others. But I did an informal poll on Twitter and found that many freelancers know when they do their best work. (Incidentally, the split between early birds and night owls was roughly 50-50.)

I decided to pay attention to when I work best, and it didn't take long before I realized I'm most productive in the mornings. When I discovered that, I changed my day around to support it. I bumped my workout sessions to afternoons, stopped scheduling morning meetings so I could stay productive and get more writing done, and clustered administrative or routine tasks toward the end of the day, when my energy and creativity wanes.

To discover when you do your best work, just observe how you feel at different times of the day. Try it for a week and you'll see when your hot spot is. When you've found it, leverage it! Block out that time so you can do your best work, and fit everything else around it.

Go Away and Think!

Productivity and performance coach Jason Womack (JasonWomackBlog.com) recommends you give your idea of perfect work-life balance the attention it deserves. Jason's advice:

To explore and define what work-life balance means to you, carve out 60 minutes a week so you can go *away* from your work and think *about* your work. Don't just do this once, practice this for five weeks to get a very clear understanding of how your work life and your personal life can exist in harmony.

[$] Success Story

Stay-at-Home Mom Makes Freelance Business Fit

Katie Kelly (KatieKelly.ca) is a great example of a freelancer who makes her work life fit her home life. A freelance graphic designer, Katie describes herself as a full-time mom, part-time freelancer. For her, being a wealthy freelancer means having the flexibility to be the primary caregiver to her two young school-age children, earn a steady income—and stay fit! (Katie maintains a morning running regimen before hitting her home office each day.)

"During the day, I have about a four-hour window to work while the kids are in school," she says. "When the kids are home in the early afternoon, I monitor emails and voice mails. If anything urgent comes in, I can usually take care of it in a matter of minutes while the kids play together. In the evenings I have time to work when everyone is in bed and the house is quiet! For me, it's a very balanced way to make being a mom, a wife and a businesswoman work."

To keep things manageable during the summer when the kids aren't in school, Katie got creative. "My sister-in-law and I regularly babysit for one another. Two days per week I have her kids; two days per week she has mine. This lets me honor my commitment to clients throughout the summer months, but in a way that works for me," she says. Being creative and efficient with how she structures her work-life reality even leaves Katie with time to explore other creative business pursuits. She recently launched *Kate.*, her own line of holiday cards and customized stationery products.

The Jigsaw Puzzle Visual™

Whenever I used to encounter biographies or anecdotes about famous people who achieved great things in business while maintaining healthy, balanced, even model, relationships with their loved ones, I was always left with burning questions like, "How did this person accomplish so much?" And "How did he or she find the time to lead such a successful, happy, balanced life?"

In recent years, as more and more opportunities have come my way while greater demands have been made on my time, I've figured out the secret: busy, accomplished people "find the time" to do worthwhile and exciting things not by constantly adding to their list of commitments, but by constantly evaluating those commitments and making decisions. They add, delete, modify, and reprioritize what's on their plates in response to the changing circumstances and opportunities that show up in their lives.

What's more, they don't struggle to make these decisions because they live a simple truth. It's one we all know, but many of us fail to recognize it:

We have a finite amount of time in which to do anything.

There are only 24 hours in a day. You can't fit 40, 30, or even 24.5 hours of activity into any 24-hour period. Although we all know this, most of us spend our entire working lives trying to defy it! And freelancers are among the worst offenders. We cram project after project into our schedule. We work late, we get up early, and we let work bleed into our nights and weekends and overrule our other commitments. (Perhaps it's because we have so much control over how we use our time that we also think we can control the *amount* of time we have!)

But when you accept—I mean *really* accept—that you're working with a finite amount of time, you enter a whole new world of possibility in terms of what you can achieve in life, and you're much better equipped to do so in a healthy and balanced manner.

When I finally accepted this truth, I was able to make far better use of my finite amount of time. Now I'm able to get more done, have more fun, and experience far less stress along the way. What made all the difference? I began to visualize the total "capacity" of my work life (that is, my finite amount of time) as a jigsaw puzzle.

Control Your Workload with the Jigsaw Puzzle Visual™

Picture in your mind a completed jigsaw puzzle. For now, the number of pieces doesn't matter. Now let's say this jigsaw puzzle represents your workload. Each piece of the puzzle represents one of the projects you currently have on your plate. By "projects," I mean the major categories into which your individual tasks or "to-dos" are grouped.

For simplicity, say there are six projects in total, labeled as follows:

1. My direct-mail campaign

2. My blog launch

3. Current client projects

4. Write *TWF* book proposal

5. Commercial real estate opportunity

6. My next buzz piece

So six projects on your plate equal six pieces in your jigsaw puzzle. That would mean your jigsaw puzzle looks like this:

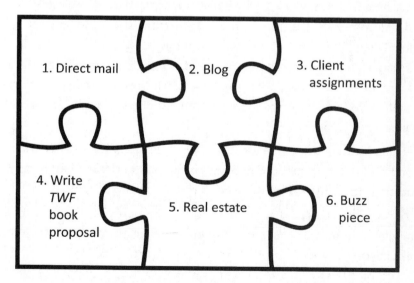

These six projects are fictional, but items 4 and 5 were real puzzle pieces in my own jigsaw puzzle last year. Take a look at item 4, "Write *TWF* book proposal." About a year ago, the book you're reading right now was nothing more than a well-researched idea. The project on my plate at the time was to write a book proposal for *The Wealthy Freelancer* and send it to publishers. Lo and behold, soon after the proposal was finished and sent, it was accepted. What did this mean for me? It meant *The Wealthy Freelancer* book idea went from idea to reality virtually overnight, and I instantly found myself committed to co-authoring this book with Steve and Ed!

Writing the book proposal required no more than a few hours of my time each week. But suddenly I had a book deal on my plate, and writing the actual book was about to require several hours of focused work each day!

Prior to using this Jigsaw Puzzle Visual™, I would have just looked at my list of projects, re-labeled project 4 to read "Write the book!" and left it at that. *Wrong!* You can't just re-label an item on your project list and go on your merry way. You have to consider the extra time this new project is going to require. But that's the problem when you're working with a list rather than a visual tool like the Jigsaw Puzzle Visual™: each new project just becomes another item on the list. You lose sight of that all-important truth:

We have a finite amount of time in which to do anything.

After all, we are working with a fixed capacity, so when project 4 changed from writing the book proposal to writing the actual book, it suddenly required more time, which meant puzzle piece 4 had to take up more space on my jigsaw puzzle. And because the jigsaw puzzle represents my capacity, which is fixed, the overall size of the jigsaw puzzle is finite, too. Therefore, for item 4 to expand in size, another puzzle piece had to shrink or disappear altogether.

This realization, and the use of the Jigsaw Puzzle Visual™, has made all the difference for me in terms of how I control my workload by prioritizing, allocating, and using that most precious resource—time.

Now here comes the hard part: honoring this newly accepted truth that your time is limited. It's not enough to know this truth. When a puzzle piece swells in size, *you have to shrink or delete another puzzle piece!*

As a result of getting the book deal, I decided to bump item 5, the commercial real estate opportunity, off my list of commitments. Was it uncomfortable to do this? Yes! I had to call my friend in this project and tell him I wasn't able to move forward. (We were in the very early preplanning stage of the project, so by no means was I leaving him high and dry!) Was he disappointed? A little bit, but he understood that writing this book was a passion and a priority for me. Once I told him, I was instantly freed of the anxiety over when and how I would be able to fit that project item into my schedule. (Less stress!) And he was freed to explore the venture on his own or find another interested, committed party.

My re-jigged jigsaw puzzle looked like this:

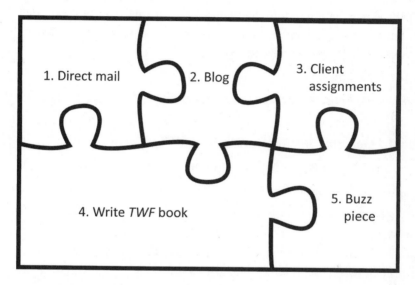

Is there any way I could I have kept the commercial real estate deal going? Yes, there is one way. To make it work, I could have cheated and added to my work capacity by "borrowing" some time from my personal life. What would this require? Sacrificing a few hours every night, and on weekends, to move the project forward. I could burn the midnight oil. I could eat into other things like playtime with my kids, my Friday-night movie ritual with my wife, my early-morning meditation, exercise, and sleep. Wow. What fun. What a life.

I hope I've illustrated the point. In reality, it's your choice if and when you spill into your personal life to achieve your work goals. You might choose to do so once in a while for short spells. Sometimes I do. But by keeping this Jigsaw Puzzle Visual™ in mind, I know that when I do this, I'm working slightly beyond capacity, and that it's not advisable to do that over the long term.

Just like in the balance exercise earlier in this chapter, it's okay to lean a little harder on your right foot from time to time. You can even take your left foot right off the ground for a little while if need be. Just be sure to put it back down as soon as possible. If you don't, eventually your right leg will cramp up and you'll come crashing down.

Ⓒ Wealthy Words

If you're overcommitted and under a lot of stress, you've got a much better chance of becoming sick, tired or just plain crabby, which won't benefit you or anyone else.

—MayoClinic.com

How to Use the Jigsaw Puzzle Visual™

Putting the Jigsaw Puzzle Visual™ into practice is easy to do, and you'll quickly get the hang of it—and reap the benefits!

Getting started is as simple as listing all the major and minor projects you have on the go. Then on a separate sheet of paper, jot down each item from your list, locating them randomly around the page. You want some distance between each item as you write it down, as though you were placing clumps of cookie dough on a cooking sheet. (I usually use a very large sheet of paper from my kids' scrapbook pad so I can get lots of space between my projects.)

When all your projects are written down, create your jigsaw puzzle pieces by drawing borders between one project and the next. You can draw fancy lines that look like proper interlocking jigsaw puzzle pieces if you want to, but drawing straight lines, like I do, works just fine.

When each project is contained within its own puzzle piece, look at the jigsaw puzzle you've just created. Ask yourself if you really have time to make progress on every single puzzle piece. Is each project critical enough to be taking up a piece of the puzzle? You might be able to edit out some projects.

Now re-draw the puzzle with pieces that roughly represent the time allocation required for each item.

Keep this puzzle posted in your office, and look at it each day to be sure it still accurately reflects the projects you work on. This now becomes your master "list" of projects on your plate. As projects come and go, and swell and shrink in size, redraw your puzzle piece. Expect to redraw it once a week—sometimes more frequently.

Laying out your projects visually like this, and making each project into a puzzle piece, helps reinforce that you are working with a finite amount of time. Whereas before you might have easily just added a new project to your list of projects, I'll bet you now see that it's a bit difficult to just add another project in there without shrinking or deleting another puzzle piece.

Strategies to Support Your Healthy Work-Life Balance

Now that you have a new perception of work-life balance, you may suddenly begin to experience this state of balance more consistently. Embrace it and enjoy it! And most importantly, make it a permanent addition to your life. Let's review a few of the best strategies you can use to support your ideal work-life vision over the long term.

Get Each Project Moving Right Away

If you get a project with a due date that's far away, the temptation is to put off starting that project for a while. Don't!

As soon as you're given an assignment, get right into your regular start-up routine. Print all your reference material, create a folder on your computer, start a physical file folder, and do some initial work. There's nothing worse than starting a project late and then having to rush to complete it. That's a surefire way to eat up your personal time.

Outsource and Grow Rich

If you want to be a wealthy freelancer, it's time to give up chores that take up too much of your precious time. This includes shoveling the driveway, mowing the lawn, and cleaning the bathrooms. You simply cannot afford to do these things when you work for yourself. Your time is money.

This can be hard to get your head around if your upbringing was anything like mine. I'm the proud son of hardworking, middle-class immigrant parents who lived through World War II. If your parents were frugal like mine were, you probably have deep-rooted beliefs that it's frivolous—even scandalous—to pay someone to do work around the house you can do yourself. You must rid yourself of this belief.

Come on, be honest. If you spend three hours cleaning the eaves troughs, what have you got, really? Clean eaves troughs. Whoopee. But after those three hours, is your business, or your bank account, any further ahead? Certainly not. Are you any happier or less stressed? Probably not as happy or stress-free as you would have been had you met your best friend for coffee, gone for a massage, attended a yoga class, or read a great novel while lying in your chaise lounge.

Pay someone else to do the things you hate doing, and spend the time you gain back making money or doing something you enjoy.

Train Clients to Respect Your Time

This great strategy comes from freelance graphic designer Ben Hagon (HagonDesign.com), and it's especially helpful when you're moonlighting. Says Ben:

> Never send emails to clients outside non-business hours. As soon as you do that, you set the perception that you're a hungry freelancer, someone who works all hours of the day and night and is at the client's beck and call. This actually trains clients to *expect* round the clock response. What's more, they'll think nothing of calling you on Friday with an assignment that they want done by Monday.

While moonlighting as a freelancer, Ben always waited until mid-morning to send design work to clients that he'd done the night before. He credits this disciplined strategy with allowing him to hold down a job as creative director at a design firm, doing freelance design at night, and being an involved family man. "As a result, my freelance clients never contacted me during non-business hours, which means the time I set aside to spend with wife and kids was never interrupted."

Wind Down Before Bed

Who among us hasn't lain in bed, exhausted and wanting desperately to fall asleep, while work-related thoughts raced around our minds, sometimes for hours?

Not getting quality sleep throws everything out of whack. Even if you routinely work at night, you should take at least half an hour, and ideally more, to do a relaxing nonwork activity that quiets your mind before you go to sleep. Meditation, light yoga, reading fiction, or just relaxing with an herbal tea are great prebed rituals that can help your mind and body shut down and slip more easily into a peaceful, rejuvenating slumber.

A Wealthy Freelancer Is a Healthy Freelancer!

Although you should expect to work long hours in your start-up phase, don't kill yourself. There's no honor in working yourself so hard it makes you miserable, strains your relationships, or makes you physically ill.

No one who has ever experienced true burnout ever looks back fondly at the experience. Unfortunately, I know many freelancers who have been there, including me. You *must* allocate time into your schedule for regular exercise and some relaxation, or you will surely burn your poor self out.

Yoga, running, meditation, hitting the gym—whatever it is you find energizing and rewarding, do not sacrifice it! Make time to do it frequently so you stay balanced.

One of the people I approached to interview for this chapter made no bones about the fact that I had suggested an interview time that conflicted with his morning workout. I so admired his commitment to staying balanced! We picked an alternate time, and everyone was happy.

⦿ Wealthy Words

Everyone should treat themselves to daily relaxation. You deserve it (and need it).

—Dr. Joe Vitale

Handle Technology with Care

I love BlackBerries and iPhones. They're wonderful tools for staying in touch. They're also very, very dangerous. For a long time, I allowed my BlackBerry to creep into my personal time which, for me, is my evenings with my wife and kids. I was always quite good about not *responding* to e-mails after I had left my home office, but whenever I saw that flashing red "You've got mail!" light on my BlackBerry, I would always open it up and read it. The trouble was, if I read an e-mail at 7 P.M., it would be on my mind for hours, and this prevented me from detaching from work after a long day and being fully mentally present with my family. Even if I didn't physically reply to any e-mails until the next day, I found myself beginning to craft replies in my mind all evening!

After letting this problem go on for too long, one day I just decided to take the "drastic" step of cancelling the data plan on my phone, meaning I stopped paying for the service that delivered the e-mails to the phone itself. Presto. My evenings have been a delight ever since.

I suppose if I were really brave I would have gotten rid of the BlackBerry altogether. However, I find having the device itself a tremendous convenience in my personal life. My wife and I phone or text one another over details about who's picking up the kids, etc.

The point here is that I eliminated the technology that was hindering my personal life, and I retained and use the technology that helps it. I'm not telling you to cancel your data plan or trash your cell phone. All I'm saying is, take a good, hard look at your use of technology like BlackBerries and iPhones and ask yourself this one question: "Is this technology supporting or upsetting my work-life balance?" If so, take steps to make the technology work for you, not against you.

Harmony at Home: Getting Along with Your Loved Ones

Work-at-home freelancers who are married or live with a partner face an additional double-sided challenge: your home space and your office space are under the same roof, and any violation of the work-life balance tends to impact your co-habitant. ("What do you mean you have to work all weekend? My parents are coming!")

I could have spent this chapter telling you, the freelancer, how to manage this delicate, two-pronged dilemma, but let me do you a favor instead. Just pass this book to your spouse or wife and direct him or her to the following Open Letter to Spouses and Partners of Freelancers. Go ahead—it's addressed to them anyway. (I'm not kidding about this. Before this book was published, several freelancers shared this letter with their partners, and many reported that it actually improved the harmony in the home!)

An Open Letter to Spouses and Partners of Freelancers

Dear Significant Other,

You have the hardest job of all. Living with a freelance professional who works from home ain't easy. We know that, and in the interest of peace and harmony at home, please allow us to make a few special requests ...

Let us off the hook for past commitments. I know, we promised to build a deck, refinish the antique dining room table, and shingle the roof, but that was *before* we launched the business, and it's unlikely we'll have time to follow through on some or all of these things. Which of these are noncritical at this point in our life? Can we cancel or postpone them for now? Or pay someone else to do them?

Forgive if we forget. If you tell us something while we're working, or in passing, we're likely to forget. If you say "Annie has ballet this Saturday at 2 o'clock," she may very likely be late, or miss it altogether, and have to run laps at the start of next week's class when you take her. (This forgetfulness is much worse if we are male.)

Let's start a family calendar (a paper or online version) where all those details are recorded, so we can keep track of things that are important to us both in our business and personal lives.

Help us protect our time. We creative/entrepreneurial types are not always the most disciplined people in the world, and we tend to get distracted easily. (Oh, you've noticed?) Please help us guard our time by resisting the urge to interrupt us when we're hard at work. Even if you just pop into our office to tell us something quickly, this can be enough to send us off track for the next half-hour! Before we know it, we're checking e-mail when we should be back to the task at hand, or we're following you out into the kitchen to continue the conversation and make coffee. Staying focused and disciplined when you work from home is *hard!* So unless the house is on fire, let's talk at dinner.

Be prepared for peaks and valleys in our cash flow. If we freelancers go a few weeks without much work, sooner or later we'll feel it in the bank account. Try not to worry. If you honestly believe we're working hard to make the business work, have faith that the ups and downs will smooth out.

Also, realize that we're really at the mercy of whenever our clients get around to paying us. Some will be prompt; others will take their sweet time. It drives us crazy, too! But sometimes it's beyond our control.

Help us relax. We've a lot on our minds! We're constantly thinking about clients, our workload, how to market ourselves, how to get more and better work, and millions of other things about our business.

At the end of the day, or week, it can be hard to let go, wind down, and leave the business behind. But we want to! So let's actually *schedule* some relaxing or romantic time together each week. We'll go out to dinner, we'll take a long walk, or we'll just sit together on the couch and watch a movie. (Sans laptop.)

Oh, and, if we haven't said it lately ... we love you. And we're so grateful you put up with us.

Sincerely,

Pete Savage, on behalf of your significant other

Wealthy Takeaways

- You are likely already much closer to enjoying a state of work-life balance than you think.

- Work-life balance is not something you pursue. If you perceive your own search for balance as a quest, it will remain one.

- To enjoy balance between your work life and your personal life, you don't have to spend equal time in work and leisure activities. You can work hard and still enjoy balance in your life.

- Freelancers do not have to build a life around a corporate work schedule imposed by others. Instead, you can create a work-life reality that fits your own unique circumstances.

- Before you can enjoy a harmonious work-life balance, you must first think about and define the kind of work-life reality that will work for you.

- You're working with a finite amount of time. When you accept this, you can make better decisions about how you will spend your time. This will help you enjoy less stress and improved performance.

- Use the Jigsaw Puzzle Visual™ to help you take control of your workload and enjoy a more harmonious work-life balance.

- A variety of strategies can help you enjoy a better work-life balance now and over the long term. Familiarize yourself with them and implement the ones that most appeal to you.

- If you live with a partner, share with him or her the Open Letter to Spouses and Partners of Freelancers at the end of this chapter. It will help your partner understand how to support, tolerate, and even forgive you!

Secret 11: Create Alternative Streams of Income

Steve Slaunwhite

As a freelancer, there's a practical limit to how much money you can make plying your trade in the traditional way. Even if you're well established in your particular category and command top rates for your freelance services, your income is restricted to the hours you're able to spend on client work. When you're not writing, designing, creating, advising, or whatever it is you do for your clients, you're not earning income.

That's not necessarily a bad thing. After all, if your average hourly rate is $75 per hour (based on being a project pricer, of course, as recommended in Secret 7), and you're able to keep yourself booked solid with client work, you'd be earning about $80,000 per year. Not bad!

But what if you want to earn more? Or make that same amount of money but work fewer hours so you can spend more time with your family, hobbies, and other interests? Can you make money as a freelancer without having to punch the clock?

The good news is, you can raise the freelance income ceiling and even shatter it altogether. And it doesn't involve doing anything outside your area of professional interest. (No, you don't have to sell your DVD collection on eBay!) In fact, all the alternative income strategies discussed in this chapter are a natural extension of your current freelance business. They capitalize on what you already know and do well and, in most cases, are more about picking up money you're unintentionally leaving on the table rather than starting a new enterprise.

Understanding Active vs. Passive Income

But before we go any farther, you first need to understand two important concepts:

- Active income
- Passive income

Active income is income earned only when you're actually working. Passive income, on the other hand, can come in anytime—even while you're sleeping.

For example, imagine you're a kid with a lemonade stand. Every hot Saturday afternoon, you sell your cool beverage to appreciative neighbors for 10¢ a cup. You work hard and efficiently for those 2 or 3 hours and pocket a few well-earned bucks. But when it's time to close down your operation because Mom says "Come in for dinner!" the dimes stop rolling in. That's active income. You make money only when you're working.

Now being a smart, young entrepreneur, say you also write and publish a little recipe booklet on how to brew your famous lemonade and convince the local convenience store to stock copies of it for sale. Assuming the booklet sells well, you'd be making money even while you're playing in the park with your friends or attending school. That's passive income. You don't have to "show up for work" to earn it.

As I said earlier, active income limits you. There are only so many hours in the week. (And toiling away on client projects until you achieve workaholic status—just to make more money—is definitely not the wealthy freelancer way!) However, like that enterprising kid, you can increase your income potential significantly, without adding much more to your workload, by cultivating passive, or at least *near*-passive, income streams. In fact, the most successful freelancers I know have done this, adding 10 to 50 percent to their incomes—and in some cases, much, much more!

Let's take a look at how you can accomplish the same thing.

Pay Attention to What You're Already Doing for Free

Here's a strategy that actually involves active income, but I've included it here because it's such an effective way to increase your revenues without increasing your work hours. It involves looking closely at those little—and sometimes not-so-little—extras you do for clients for free. Those freebies could potentially be converted into services your clients would be happy to pay you for.

Free-to-Shining-Fee Strategy

I discovered this "Free-to-Shining-Fee Strategy," almost by accident, just a few years ago. At the time, I was doing a booming business writing case studies (a kind of product success story). This type of project requires someone to interview a client's customer to flesh out the story and get some good testimonials to use in the piece. Sometimes the client would handle this and just send me the recording or transcript. Other times, I would do the interview myself. Regardless, I always charged the same fee for the project.

Then one day I realized that doing that customer interview was additional work I was essentially doing for free. I decided to package that activity as a separate consulting service. My plan was this: my fee to write a case study would still be $1,250, but if the client wanted me to handle the customer interview as well, that would cost an additional $500.

Frankly, I was a little nervous about introducing this separate consulting service, based on something most freelance corporate writers still did at no charge. But to my pleasant surprise, clients were fine with it. In fact, many appreciated and valued my "Success Story and Testimonial Development" service—as I now called it—simply because I made it distinct, gave it a name, clearly communicated its value to clients, and charged accordingly.

Overall, my average income from case study work increased by about 25 percent. And I didn't have to work additional hours to earn it!

What's Your Free-to-Shining-Fee Strategy?

Take a close look at the things you do for free for clients and ask yourself, "Is this something I could charge a separate fee for?" You might be surprised, like I was, that clients will be more than willing to do so. One thing for sure, you won't know until you try.

At this point, you might be thinking that my case study example is a special case and there's nothing you're doing for clients now that can be realistically developed as a separate for-a-fee service. Think again. Here are just a few examples of freelancers who have used the Free-to-Shining-Fee Strategy to increase their incomes:

- A graphic designer who now charges a "quality assurance" fee to attend press runs and check that everything is correct.

- A PR writer who now gets a separate consulting fee to submit press releases to media-release companies and monitor results.

- A grant writer who has developed a separate consulting service that involves finding prospective grant programs for her nonprofit clients. (That service, which she used to do for free, now represents the majority of her income!)

- A portrait photographer who now charges a fee for his formerly free service of organizing digital photos into online albums that make it easier for his clients to view and enjoy.

- A freelance corporate trainer who used to provide training binders to participants for free and now charges clients a separate per-person charge for these materials.

- A web marketing strategist who specializes in search engine optimization who used to research keywords for free but now charges for that service.

In all these cases, the freelancer was originally doing the work at no charge. What happened when a price tag was suddenly applied to the service? It was met with little, if any, resistance from clients.

The trick is to package the service in such a way that clients understand the full value and don't see it as just an expensive add-on. For my Success Story and Testimonial Development service, my package includes the customer interview, an MP3 recording, a transcript, a short synopsis of the success story, and a list of customer quotes that can be used as testimonials. To most clients, the $500 price tag is a deal!

Wealthy Words

When I started writing sales copy for companies in the technology and medical industries, I used to spend a lot of time developing the key marketing messages—especially for first-time clients. Then I created a service called "Key Message Platform" and sold it as a separate consulting program. Not only were clients willing to pay for this service when they hired me to write their sales copy, some companies even purchased it separately!

—Casey Demchak, copywriter and marketing podcaster

So look closely at those little extras you do for clients. Yes, I'm sure they appreciate them. But chances are, you're not going to lose any goodwill by converting some of those freebies into attractive service packages you can—and perhaps should—charge a professional fee for.

Do You Really Have to Do All the Work Yourself?

Here's an income-boosting strategy I learned from my dentist. When I visit his office for my twice-yearly appointment, the dental assistant typically spends about a half-hour scraping and cleaning my teeth. Lots of fun. Then my dentist comes in and does a checkup, which usually lasts no more than 10 minutes. After one of these appointments, while I was signing the insurance form at the front desk, I noticed how the fees were broken down: $45 for the cleaning; $105 for the checkup. My dentist obviously knew where he added the most value and made the most money. He focused on the consultations and hired other people to do the rest.

As a freelance professional, it's smart to think of your business the same way my dentist does. Figure out where you add the most value on the project work you do and then hire an employee, virtual assistant, or another freelancer to handle the other aspects of the job. If you do, your project income will go up substantially.

It's Okay to Get Help

I admit, for years I was resistant to bringing in others to help with client projects. Like most freelancers, I did—and in some ways felt I should do—

everything myself. Then one day, I got a job to write a massive travel website. The deadline was crazy. So I decided, almost reluctantly, to hire another freelancer—an experienced travel writer—to help. She wrote all the travelogue stuff—"On Day 2, you'll enjoy a delicious breakfast against the breathtaking backdrop of the Kilimanjaro mountains ..."—and I wrote the sales-oriented messages—"Book today and get 15 percent off ...." I also supervised and edited her work to ensure the overall quality of the website copy was up to my, and my client's, standards.

I got that job done a lot faster than I would have normally—actually way ahead of schedule, which was nice!—and I made a lot more money considering the hours I put into the project, even after factoring in what I paid the travel writer. Did the client mind me working with someone else? Not at all. As long as I was directing the overall website copywriting, he was fine with it.

So ask yourself if there are aspects of the project work you do for clients that could be done faster, better, and/or more cheaply by someone else. If you're a PR consultant, perhaps a good virtual assistant could make those follow-up calls to editors. If you're a technical writer, wouldn't it make sense to get a freelance editor to proofread your documents rather than you spending hours on that tedious chore? The idea is to focus on your "sweet spots"—those activities clients are *really* hiring you to do and you do very, very well—and get others to take care of the rest.

Break It Down

As a freelancer, it's easy to get caught up in the thinking that a project is just one "thing" you have to do for a client and that *only you* can do that one thing. However, with few exceptions, most freelance projects require a series of activities, and you don't necessarily have to be involved in them all—just the important ones where your hands-on attention matters most.

For example, say you're a freelance blog ghostwriter. If you were to break down a typical project into a series of steps, it might look something like this:

1. Decide on a blog post topic.

2. Do the research.

3. Write the blog post.

4. Source a royalty-free artwork image to go with the post.

5. Submit the piece to the client for his or her review.

6. Make requested revisions, if any.

7. Proofread the post to ensure it's error-free.

8. Send it to the client's web master for posting.

Now really, do you have to handle all these steps personally? Your client isn't paying you top dollar for your proofreading expertise or ability to search a database for artwork images, is he? Although he needs the whole project done, what your client wants most from *you* is your talent for crafting an effective blog post that gains the attention of his target audience. If you think of the project in that way, you could just do steps 1, 3, and 6 and hire a good virtual assistant or another freelancer to handle the other steps. If you did that, projects would get done faster and you'd probably earn a lot more money. And as an additional benefit, you would likely enjoy the work more because you're focusing on what you do best, and probably enjoy doing most.

I know several freelance professionals who use this strategy to boost their project incomes. A graphic designer friend of mine focuses only on creating the initial drawing—what she calls the "artist's comprehensive." Once that's approved by her client, she passes it on to other trusted free-lancers to do the detailed design work under her direction. According to her, when she switched from "I do it all" to "I do only those things where I add the most value," her income doubled.

Even bringing in help for a seemingly minor aspect of a project can make a big difference. A newsletter writer I know used to do all her own proof-reading. Once she farmed out that job to a freelance editor, however, she was able to shave an hour off her project time. That doesn't sound like much, but when you consider that she handles about four newsletter projects per week, that's an extra two days of productive time she gained per month.

Bottom line: you don't have to go it alone when doing client work. Figure out what you do best (and enjoy doing) and then find other people to handle the other steps required to complete the project. You'll get more project work done faster—and probably better—while increasing your income.

Create Information Products and Sell Them on Your Website

Remember the booklet that young lemonade entrepreneur created and sold at the local convenience store? That isn't just a cute story. That's a great passive-income strategy and one many freelance professionals have used to dramatically increase their incomes. In no time in history has it been easier to create a profitable e-book, special report, audio program, how-to guide, or other type of "information product." And the good news is, you can sell it simply and cost-effectively right from your website.

That's what Michael Katz (www.MichaelKatz.com) does. A highly successful freelance professional specializing in e-newsletters, Michael gets thousands of people visiting his website each month seeking his advice and services. For any number of reasons, he can't take on everyone as a client. Either his schedule is full or they can't afford him. So he offers an alternative, a "store" section on his website where visitors can purchase his book on e-newsletters, a complete e-newsletter creation system, or a range of how-to audio programs on topics related to creating and using e-newsletters.

Visitors to Michael's website who, for whatever reason, could not hire his services would have walked away empty-handed. But by offering these people his expertise in other formats, Michael can still accommodate them—at least to a degree. I'm not sure how much extra income Michael earns from his information products, but I'm sure it's more than a drop in the bucket. Those buyers would have just gone elsewhere to get the information and help they needed. If Michael didn't offer them his expertise in the form of information products, it would be like being a fishing guide and not renting rods and reels!

What Can *You* Offer?

As a freelance professional there's no doubt you have tips, ideas, best practices, and good old-fashioned wisdom you could share in an e-book or audio program. Think about it. You're already driving people to your website as you promote your freelance services. Why not take advantage of their interest in what you do by offering comparable information products?

Wealthy Tools

An information product not only creates a new revenue stream, it also attracts more clients for your traditional freelance services. Karen Zapp, a fund-raising consultant, has recently begun publishing short how-to booklets on various fund-raising topics as part of a series she calls *Zapp Guides*. Not only is she now making more money through booklet sales, she is also attracting more clients because they see her as the expert. After all, she "wrote the book"—or in Karen's case, the booklets!

There are all kinds of ideas you could explore:

- Are you a graphic designer with experience creating company annual reports? How about a booklet called *The Annual Report Planning Guide?*

- Are you a freelance editor with a track record of proofreading documents and identifying 99.9 percent of the mistakes? How about a tip sheet called *The Practically Perfect Proofreader's Guide to Finding Every Error?*

- Do you specialize in creating websites that sell? How about a one-hour audio program where you interview another expert in that field?

- Do you have a knack for getting trade magazine editors to run materials from product press releases? How about an e-book called *9 Surefire Ways to Get Trade Editors to Cover Your Product Launch?*

- Are you a fund-raising consultant? How about a short booklet called *The Anatomy of a Successful Fund-Raising Letter?* (Actually that *is* a booklet, by my friend Alan Sharpe.)

How do you decide on a topic? Think about the kind of problems and challenges a client is facing when she's looking for your type of services. Then make a list of topics that address those needs. If you're a PR writer specializing in effective press releases, for example, you can expect that your clients will be interested in topics related to getting publicity for their products. And who better to get that information from than the PR practitioner they trust—you?

The Basics of Info-Preneuring

The topic of developing and selling an information product is an information product in itself! There's a lot of ground to cover. I give you the basics here, but to learn more, I suggest you get a copy of *The Complete Idiot's Guide to Starting a Web-Based Business* (Alpha Books, 2009). It includes chapters on creating information products, setting up an online payment system, promotion and sales, and much more. (Full disclosure: I wrote that book!)

Let's go over the basic steps to creating a profitable, good-selling information product. First, select a topic you suspect your target audience would be interested in and willing to pay for. That topic, of course, should be related to your business in some way!

Then decide on the format for your information product. That could be an e-book, special report, how-to guide, audio recording, tip sheet, home study course, checklist, planning guide—the list is almost endless. Be sure your product can be published electronically so you can sell it as a digital download. (You can always invest in getting a physical version done once you know for sure your product will sell.)

Get your information product created. The big three elements of this process are writing, design, and production. If you're creating an e-book, for example, you'll need to get it written, get the cover and page layouts done, and then publish it as a PDF.

Set the price for your information product. A short e-book or audio recording can sell for $19 to $97, depending on how scarce and valuable the information is to buyers. A longer how-to guide or course can sell for hundreds of dollars. Check out what information products comparable to yours are selling for on the Internet.

Set up a method of accepting payments on your website. Many options are available. I suggest you start with PayPal, which is the most well known and affordable. PayPal offers online merchants (that's you!) a free "shopping cart" that places a customizable "buy now" button on your website. When your customers click on the button, PayPal handles the entire transaction for you and deposits your money into your PayPal account. GoogleCheckout. com offers a similar service.

Promote your information product. The best way to do that is to announce its availability to everyone in your contact network, including prospects and those subscribed to your newsletter and blog feeds. Be sure it's prominently featured on your website, too.

By the way, your information product doesn't have to be a book-length tome. My friend Alan Sharpe, whom I mentioned earlier, started by creating a series of very short guides—some fewer than 10 pages—that he sold on his website for $10 each. It wasn't long before he was generating a good monthly income in sales.

Information Product in Less Than a Day

An audio recording is perhaps the quickest and easiest type of information product to produce. My former coaching client Nicky Jameson created one by having me interview her on her area of expertise: writing for social media. We used a teleconference line that had recording capabilities. We were done in about an hour, and after doing some minor sound editing, Nicky was able to offer her new "audio program" for sale on her website.

I think every freelancer should try his or her hand at creating at least one information product. Even if it doesn't sell well, it can still do what authorship does best: build your reputation as a skilled and knowledgeable professional in your field. And if it does sell well, your information product can add hundreds, or even thousands, of dollars to your income each month— income that's mostly passive. I can tell you from experience, it's sure nice to boot the computer in the morning and find out you've made a few sales while you were sleeping!

Sign Up for Some Good Affiliate Programs

Early in my freelance career, I was contacted by the owner of a list management company (a company that rents mailing lists for direct-mail campaigns).

He said, "Steve, I noticed that you've been recommending us to your clients. We really appreciate that. Why don't you sign up for our affiliate programs so the next time one of your clients needs a mailing list, we can pay you a commission?" I'm all for making extra money, so I said, "Sure."

Frankly, I didn't expect much. I thought perhaps I'd earn a few extra dollars to fund my Friday lunch excursions to Starbucks. Imagine my surprise when, a couple months later, I received a commission check for $1,600—for doing nothing more than what I was doing anyway, recommending a good company.

What's an Affiliate Program?

An affiliate program is simply a program many companies offer that pays you a commission for referring your clients, prospects, and website visitors to their products and services.

Say you're a freelance speechwriter. You probably get asked for advice and recommendations all the time on giving a speech, using presentation technology, easing the speaking jitters, and more. Sign up for Amazon's affiliate program (which they call their "Associates Program"), and you can create a list of recommended books on your website. Then when you suggest one of these books to a prospect or client, or even when a casual website visitor comes across it, you'll receive a commission from any purchases made as a result.

Affiliate programs are yet another way to generate more passive income from an activity you're probably doing anyway. Here are the basics for taking advantage of this strategy:

- Review the products and services you're currently recommending to prospects, clients, and other contacts.
- Visit the websites of these companies and find out about their affiliate programs. (Look for a link called "affiliate program," "associate program," "partner program," "earn cash," or something similar.)
- Carefully review how each company's affiliate program works.
- If an affiliate program seems like a good fit, sign up.

- Once you're accepted into the program, you receive access to "affiliate links" and banner ads that contain special tracking codes that keep track of your referrals and sales.

- Place these links or ads in appropriate places on your website, such as a "recommended resources" page.

- You can also actively recommend an affiliate product or service by sending the link by e-mail. "Hey John, here's a great book on preparing for a speech I often recommend to clients …."

- At the end of each payment period, which is usually monthly or quarterly, you'll receive a commission payment for the sales your website and recommendations have generated.

The great thing about an affiliate program is that it is perhaps the most passive form of income available to you as a freelancer. It requires very little time and virtually no cost to get started. And once you've set up the banners or links on your website, there really isn't much else to do but what you're already doing anyway—recommending resources to your prospects, clients, and other contacts.

Don't Go Affiliate Crazy

Affiliate programs can be lucrative, and it's tempting to want to fill your website with links and banners. But ask yourself how would something look to potential clients who are visiting your website to learn more about your professional services? Adding a few good recommended products and services is fine. Just don't overdo it.

Affiliate programs can give your income a significant boost. I know one technical communications consultant who claims that more than 15 percent of her income comes from affiliate commissions. She joined the affiliate programs of all her suppliers, including a printer, a technical drawing service, a proofreading company, and Amazon.

Take a look at the affiliate programs associated with the products and services you frequently recommend. You're recommending these companies anyway, and they're benefiting financially from your referrals. Why not get a small piece of that action?

Where to Find an Affiliate Program

The best place to start when looking for affiliate programs to join is with the companies you already know.

Another good source is *affiliate program directories*. These websites compile information on affiliate programs companies offer and organize that information into product and industry categories. If you're a web designer, for example, you can go to AffiliateScout.com, click on the Web Services category, and find hundreds of affiliate programs.

Here are some other popular directories:

AffiliateSeeking.com

ClicksLink.com

JamaAffiliates.com

AffiliateOnline.net

WhichAffiliate.com

AffiliateRanker.com

Top-Affiliate.com

Be sure to also check out Google AdSense (Google.com/AdSense), Yahoo's Apt! program (Publisher.Yahoo.com), and other similar programs many of the major search engines offer. They work a little differently from traditional affiliate programs, but the end result is the same. You earn income by recommending products and services associated with what you do.

Teach Others What You Know

When catalog marketing expert Suzanne Quigley launched her freelance business, she expected to spend the majority of her time writing effective product descriptions for her clients. After all, she was essentially a freelance writer. Imagine her surprise when, while prospecting for new business, a company invited her to spend a day at their location and teach what she knows to their marketing staff.

"I had never done a seminar on writing catalog copy before," Suzanne remembers, "but I obviously know a lot about the topic." She spent a week developing the seminar, which involved breaking the topic down into short lessons—or "modules," as they're called in the corporate training field—creating the slides, and rehearsing. When the day came to do the seminar, it went off without a hitch and the company was impressed.

Unexpectedly, Suzanne developed a new income stream: teaching what she knows to others.

The Benefits of Teaching

Teaching, of course, is not passive. You definitely have to show up for work to earn the money! However, it is a smart *active* income strategy that can build your business in a number of ways.

First of all, you can usually book seminars and other teaching gigs weeks, and often months, in advance. That gives you a greater sense of security in knowing there's guaranteed work coming up. The problem with most traditional freelance projects is that they're usually jobs that need to be completed within a few weeks. So with few exceptions, you're never booked much beyond the next month or two. You hope there'll be more work coming in after that, but you really don't know for sure. With seminars and other speaking gigs in your future, you do.

Secondly, you can often get paid more to teach what you know how to do than actually doing it! For my corporate training program, *Writing That Sells*, one-day seminar I present to corporate marketing staff, I get $3,500 plus expenses. Some of my friends in the training industry insist I should be charging a lot more.

And finally, leading seminars attracts more clients for your regular freelance services. Clients think, correctly I believe, that if you teach what you do, you're probably also very *good* at what you do. I know a fund-raising consultant who gives seminars throughout North America. Most of his clients come from his audiences. "It's like getting paid to market my services," he says.

From a work-life standpoint, I like the change of pace that comes from the occasional seminars and other speaking I do. No matter what category you happen to be in—writing, design, consulting—freelance project work can be a grind when you're doing it day in and day out. Getting out of the office to do a 1-hour "lunch and learn" session with a group of people at a local company can be refreshing.

Booking Gigs as a Teacher

So how do you make this teaching-what-you-know strategy work for you? You could start by listing seminars on the Services page of your website and other promotional materials. Let your prospects, clients, and the rest of the world know you do them. If you don't, you may never get asked.

Or create a "one-sheet" of your seminar. In the speaking industry, this is simply an overview of your presentation and includes such pertinent details as the title, topic, description, length, and your bio. Be prepared to send this to potential clients when asked.

You could also send an e-mail or letter to your clients, prospects, and other contacts letting them know about your seminar.

Check out the professional publications and associations in your field or those of your clients. Do they offer teleclasses, webinars, seminars, and other professional development events for their readers or members? If so, contact them and ask if you can be a speaker.

Finally, try sending a letter to clients and prospects in your area and ask if you can come in to do a "lunch and learn" on your topic. This is exactly what that term implies: a short presentation you do during a lunch. These types of presentations usually don't pay a lot, often just $500 or even less, but they're a great way to get your feet wet.

For a good example of how to let prospects and clients know you're available to teach, visit the website of my friend and fellow copywriter Jonathan Kranz at kranzcom.com.

Keep in mind that unless your goal is to become a professional seminar leader, you don't want to spend a whole lot of time and money promoting your speaking services. After all, your *freelance* services are your bread and butter. However, if you do a few simple things to let others know that you do teach, those opportunities will certainly come your way.

Wealthy Takeaways

- Your traditional freelance service isn't the only way you can earn income. In fact, exploiting alternative active and passive income streams can dramatically increase your earnings.

- Take a close look at those little extras you typically do for clients for free. Can any of those be packaged in a service you can charge a fee for?

- You don't have to do every aspect of a project yourself. Focus on what you do best and enjoy doing, and outsource the rest to other professionals.

- Consider creating information products around your area of expertise and offering them for sale on your website.

- Make a list of the products and services you most often recommend to your clients. Check if those companies offer an affiliate program. If they do, sign up.

- Offer to do seminars and other forms of teaching on what you do.

Secret 12: Live and Work in the Wealthy Triangle™

Ed Gandia

> "Money isn't everything, but it will solve or alleviate roughly 9 out of every 10 problems in life."

My dad shared that bit of wisdom with me when I was just 13. As an adult, I now realize how right he was. But money is also a complex and sticky subject. So in this chapter, we're going to peel that onion one layer at a time. We'll take a broader look at money and finances from a freelancer's point of view. And we'll discuss the role money plays in designing and funding the lifestyle you truly want and turning your most important goals and dreams into reality.

Our journey begins in Silicon Valley ....

A Tale of Two Achievers

Mike and Joe worked together as software engineers for a rapidly growing technology company in Silicon Valley. Besides being co-workers, they were good friends. One day, Joe decided to leave the company and strike out on his own. A few months earlier, he had freelanced on the side for a noncompeting software company. He really enjoyed the project, and the experience made him realize how big a demand there was for his specific skills. Most of all, Joe wanted his time back. He had two young kids whom he rarely saw during the week because of the long hours he kept at work. So the idea of creating his own schedule was extremely appealing.

However, by the beginning of his second year as a freelance software developer, Joe was still earning 20 percent less than he did as an employee. And because he no longer had employer-provided benefits, his net income (after he paid for health insurance and had no paid vacations) was considerably lower. So even though Joe liked working for a variety of clients, enjoyed the challenge of learning new skills, and loved being able to spend time with his family every day, he wished he could earn about 20 or 30 percent more. That would enable him to take better and longer family vacations and have more time to do volunteer work through his church, something he was passionate about.

Mike, on the other hand, stayed with his growing employer. And a few months after Joe left, he even got a promotion to vice president of development. Within a year of his promotion, Mike's income nearly tripled. He and his wife bought a bigger house, traded up their cars, bought a vacation home on a lake, and put their two kids in private school. Financially, Mike was set. But he wasn't all that happy. He traveled virtually every week and worked 15-hour days, even on weekends. He rarely saw his kids or made any of their ball games—and his marriage was crumbling.

One day, Mike and Joe ran into each other. It had been a while since their last conversation, so they spent some time catching up. "I enjoy what I do, and I love the flexibility," Joe eventually told Mike. "But the money is just not there yet. We often struggle to pay our bills with what I'm bringing in. It must be nice to be in your shoes and not have to worry about these things."

Mike stared into his drink for a few seconds and then replied, "Well, Joe, let me tell you. Yes, I'm earning more than I ever dreamed of. We have a beautiful house, a gorgeous vacation home on the lake, and all the toys I ever wanted. But I would give it all up to have the time and flexibility you have! I never see my kids, and my marriage is a mess. And I'm in a situation that's not so easy to walk away from. You, my friend, are the true success here—not me."

The Time-Income Curve and the Wealthy Triangle™

Whether you're an employee, business owner, or freelance professional, one of the biggest struggles you're likely to face is the trade-off between time and money. As Mike eventually realized, in most cases, the more you earn, the less free time you tend to have. And the more free time you have, the less you tend to earn.

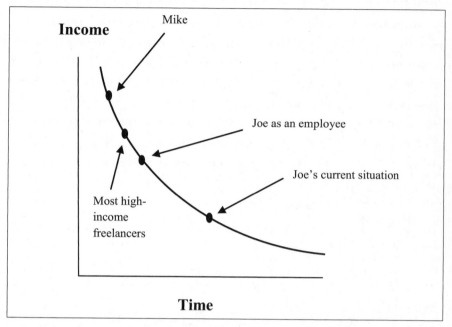

Generally, an inverse relationship exists between the level of income you earn as a freelancer and the amount of free time you have available.

By going out on his own, Joe was able to get back some of his free time, which he desperately wanted. However, he did so by sacrificing a big chunk of his income. Conversely, Mike got on the corporate fast track and nearly tripled his income. Yet this robbed him of the little free time he did have, causing great damage to his relationship with his wife and kids.

Joe's point on the time-income curve is representative of where many freelancers find themselves. They have a great deal of time and freedom, but their income is not where they'd like it to be. Mike is at the opposite end of the curve. He has a very high income but almost no free time.

You'll also notice a third point on the curve. This is where many high-income freelancers find themselves, especially if they experience great success shortly after launching their businesses. The money is great! But they have to put in 60 hours a week, leaving them little time and freedom to pursue other interests. Steve, Pete, and I have all been there, and believe us when we say that it's not all it's cracked up to be!

But here's the big question: does this inverse relationship between time and money hold true every time? In other words, are we forced to make a choice between the income we earn and the free time and flexibility we have?

Fortunately, there is a way out of this cycle. And the principles and ideas we've shared with you in this book, when you apply them, will help you find a more appropriate space *outside* of this curve—the perfect balance among income, time, and flexibility. For many of you, that point will lie somewhere to the right of the curve and in the upper portion of the graph. This is a point where you can earn an executive-level income while enjoying the freedom and flexibility few executives have. This area is called the Wealthy Triangle™, and it's where you, my freelancing friend, must strive to be.

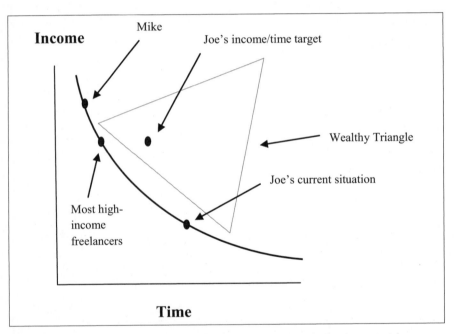

By moving into the Wealthy Triangle™, freelancers can enjoy a higher income without a proportionate increase in the amount of time required to get to that level.

What You Give Up—and What You Get Instead

Besides showing the time-income conundrum, the story of Joe and Mike also brings up the question of what we *really* give up when we go from employee to freelancer. Let's not fool ourselves. When you quit your day job to become a freelancer, you give up a number of valuable benefits most full-time employees enjoy. You often walk away from great medical benefits. You give up paid vacations and maybe even an employer-subsidized retirement plan.

These sacrifices are very real. You'd be foolish not to take them all into consideration. But you also have to be careful here. Corporate benefits and financially rewarding career advancement, as our friend Mike eventually found out, can also rob you of time and freedom no amount of money can buy.

On the other hand, freelancing enables you to set the strategic direction for your business. You get to pick the clients you work with and the projects you take on. You set your own schedule, make all the decisions, and keep all the profits. But for wealthy freelancers, the solo opportunity is about much more than this! That's because working and living in the Wealthy Triangle™ also enables you to create the lifestyle you want *and* make your dreams a reality.

To put it another way (and borrowing a quote from entrepreneur and motivational speaker Jim Rohn), *wealthy freelancers don't just make a living. They design a fulfilling and meaningful life.*

Joe may not have the same level of income and material wealth Mike enjoys. But by going out on his own, at least he was able to meet his top priorities: more time with his family and more meaningful and rewarding work. The missing piece was a high-enough income to cover his bills, pay for nicer family vacations, and enable him to do a greater amount of volunteering at his church. He was willing to give up some of his free time to get to this level, *but only if every unit of freedom he gave up would pay off significantly in the way of increased income.*

In fact, if you look at the preceding figure, you'll note that Joe's new target (which lies in the Wealthy Triangle™) represents a significant increase in income without a proportionate increase in the amount of time required to get there.

Using the strategies and techniques we've shared throughout this book, Joe can successfully move into the Wealthy Triangle™. And so can you. But before you do so, you must first lay a strong financial foundation.

Laying a Solid Financial Foundation

Before you can build the kind of career that allows you to fund your desired lifestyle, you need to build a solid foundation on which that career can grow and thrive. Specifically, you need a certain amount of money to establish and maintain your freelance business through the inevitable first-year ups and downs. You also need enough savings to cover emergencies and other unexpected expenses. You need to create and start funding a retirement savings account. And you need a certain level of insurance coverage to protect you from events that could wipe out or severely impact your finances.

That might sound overwhelming, but it's actually pretty straightforward once you break it down. So let's look at each of these elements individually.

How Much Savings Do You Need?

Aside from the inability to land enough clients and projects, inadequate cash reserves is the biggest reason why freelancers are forced to abandon self-employment and re-enter the workforce. It takes time to build a business. So if you don't have enough savings to help supplement your income until you get on your feet, the well will dry up. Before we get into actual figures, let's talk about what kind of savings you need. Doing so will help you better determine the amount appropriate for you.

Rather than coming up with an arbitrary figure, take the recommendation of Veronica Dostal, an accredited financial counselor and financial coach who regularly works with the self-employed. She suggests that you think along the lines of three different savings buckets and work backward. For instance, the most obvious type of savings you'll need is the true *emergency fund*. These savings are intended to cover things such as medical emergencies, unplanned (and expensive) home repairs, or the occasional $1,500 auto repair bill.

New freelancers also need *reserves to cover income shortfalls* that arise during the first year or two in business, before the work is steady and predictable. But even established freelancers should set aside some funds to cover slower months.

Finally, there are expenses that are more predictable but still outside your regular budget—things such as property taxes, back-to-school clothing for the kids, and preventative maintenance for your car. These aren't true emergencies, but they are expenses that may be difficult to fund from your monthly cash flow, so you should create a *cyclical set-aside* to fund them.

All these savings buckets can go into one main savings account. But track the amounts in each bucket so you know what you have set aside in each and can better determine which one, if any, may need additional funding as your situation changes. Once you have your savings buckets set up, you can start thinking about how much you actually need in each. Most financial advisers suggest keeping three to six months of total living expenses in your emergency fund. However, because your income as a freelancer can vary month to month, especially when you're getting started, I strongly suggest you shoot for at least six months of living expenses (not income but actual living expenses), which you can split between your emergency fund and your income-shortfall reserves.

How Much Insurance Do You Need?

If money were no object, you could conceivably insure yourself against just about any calamity. But as a freelancer, you want to drastically reduce the risk of financial ruin, not necessarily eliminate *all* risks you may face. With that in mind, here are the four types of insurance policies you'll want to consider:

- Health
- Long-term disability
- Life
- Liability

Health insurance. Regardless of your age or current state of health, you're putting yourself and your family at great risk if you don't have health insurance. With today's high medical costs, just one trip to the hospital can wipe you out financially. Unfortunately, it's not always easy to get coverage as a solo professional. In the United States, health insurance is tied to your employer, so if you decide to go out on your own, your choices are somewhat limited. And if your spouse isn't employed or doesn't have access to health insurance benefits through his or her employer, your only option may be to seek individual coverage.

In many cases, individual coverage costs more (both in terms of monthly premiums and out-of-pocket costs) than does comparable coverage through an employer. But what many freelancers fail to realize is that the objective is *not necessarily* to obtain the same level of coverage you may have had as an employee. The objective is to get access to quality care—even if you have to pay slightly higher premiums than you were paying as an employee—while also covering your risk of catastrophic medical events.

Additionally, in the United States, health savings accounts (HSAs) make higher out-of-pocket medical expenses much more affordable by allowing you to pay for them with after-tax dollars. And in some cases, you may be able to deduct the cost of your premiums as a business expense, further reducing your overall burden. Also, organizations such as the Freelancer's Union (FreelancersUnion.org) offer group-rate health insurance to independent workers in a number of states.

A great place to start your search is with a good insurance broker. These professionals have already invested the time to learn all the options. They know the ins and outs of the business. They know the pitfalls. Better yet, you don't usually pay extra to buy the policy from a broker (brokers are paid a commission by the insurance company), which means that their advice is free!

Whatever your situation, don't give up on your goal to become a full-time freelancer just because you believe you're not insurable or adequate coverage will be out of your reach. Seek the advice of a professional. There may very well be a workable option for you.

Long-term disability insurance. Long-term disability (LTD) insurance is designed to replace a portion of your income should you not be able to work because of a disability. Statistically, your chance of sustaining a serious injury in your 30s or 40s is much higher than your chance of dying. Yet surprisingly, 60 percent of working adults in the United States do not have disability insurance, according to the Health Insurance Association of America.

Your ability to generate an income is one of your most important assets, especially if you're the sole breadwinner or even a contributor to your family's total income. You need to protect that asset, and that's what LTD insurance is designed to do. Let me warn you, though: LTD insurance is not cheap. But considering the risks of not having a policy, the expense is often justifiable. Talk to your broker about the best options for your specific situation. And be sure to shop around.

Life insurance. The final type of policy you may want to consider is life insurance, which is designed to help replace lost income in the event of your premature death. Now if you're single and have few obligations, you may not need life insurance. But if you have a spouse and children who depend on your income, life insurance is a lot more important, unless you're already financially independent and your assets could support your family in the event you were no longer in the picture.

You may want to consider a policy for your spouse, even if he or she does not generate an income. My wife is currently a stay-at-home mom. She doesn't generate an income, but we bought a term policy for her a few years ago. In the event of her premature death, I would still need to work full-time, and that would require me to hire someone to take care of our son while he's not in school on weekday afternoons and summer vacations, for example. Child-care costs money—money I don't currently budget for. So that's where her policy would come in.

Many people put off the life insurance issue because they don't want to think about their or their spouse's death. Yes, it's downright depressing to think about death and the emotional impact it would have on your family. But it's even sadder to see a family struggle as a result of a parent's passing. I've seen it firsthand, and it's not a position you want to be in. So get in touch with a good insurance broker or agent and review the best options for your situation.

Professional liability insurance. Also called errors and omissions insurance, professional liability insurance coverage protects you from allegations of poor decisions or bad advice. Now before you panic, you should know that most freelancers won't need such coverage. Not only is it overkill in many cases, it's also very expensive. Plus, the exact definition of "wrongful act" (the event that would trigger coverage) varies from policy to policy, so you need to be careful about what's excluded from coverage and how much the policy will pay out in the event of a lawsuit. You could end up paying for something that doesn't cover your biggest risks.

Consult with an attorney who knows your business well or who at least works with many self-employed professionals in fields similar to yours. Find out what the risks are and what type of policy—if any—would make sense for you. If you determine it's worth buying some degree of coverage, have your attorney review the quotes you receive and help you make the best decision.

How Much Retirement Savings Do You Need?

These days, a growing number of workers are opting to work beyond age 65. Some are doing this because they want to, others because they *have to*. The stock market correction of 2008 put a huge dent on retirement savings for millions of workers who were on the verge of retirement, forcing them to stay on the job or find other ways to supplement their retirement income.

At the same time, many people are now challenging the whole idea of retirement. They're exploring other alternatives that are better aligned with their goals and values. For instance, in his best-selling book, *The 4-Hour Workweek: Escape 9–5, Live Anywhere, and Join the New Rich* (Crown, 2007), Timothy Ferriss introduced the concept of "mini-retirements"—the idea that instead of saving it all for the end, we should redistribute our retirement savings throughout our lives and use them to take mini-retirements of one to six months every year.

I agree with much of Ferriss's reasoning on why the traditional view of retirement may need revising. However, whether you subscribe to the traditional model or are inclined to follow a more unorthodox mini-retirement lifestyle, you still need to create a nest egg to fund your plan. Even if you're not currently sure which direction you'll take, it's a good idea to start saving now, if you haven't already. At a minimum, a sizable retirement savings account buys you freedom and flexibility—especially later in life, when you may not have the patience or desire to put up with other people's crap!

What Does Living in the Wealthy Triangle™ Mean to You?

As we've discussed throughout this book, freelancing is one of the few career paths that enables you to earn an executive-level income while also having the time and flexibility to do, have, and enjoy more of what you really want. That's life in the Wealthy Triangle™.

But what does life in the Wealthy Triangle™ specifically mean to *you?* What would you like to have, do, see, or experience? What hobbies or passions do you want to pursue? What places do you want to visit and experience? What moves you outside of your work? What kind of legacy do you want to leave behind?

Let's explore some of the possibilities.

Spend More Time with Loved Ones

For many freelancers, the real payoff of freelancing is the ability to spend more time with their loved ones—something that's often difficult to do when you hold a demanding corporate job. For Margie Yansura, owner of Wordsmith Communications, a public relations consulting business in West Palm Beach, Florida, that's precisely what drove her to seek a more flexible working environment.

Margie's decision to start her own solo business came after one of her young children experienced a near-drowning in a neighbor's pool at a neighborhood block party. "My daughter was fine, but I wasn't," says Margie. "I decided I wanted to have more flexible work hours so I could be closer to my children as they grew up." After nearly 20 years in business, Margie enjoys a comfortable six-figure income. She has also received a number of awards for her business accomplishments. And most importantly, she has been able to be very active in her children's lives—both at home and in their extracurricular activities in school.

"I love the flexibility my solo business provides," she says. "My children are all grown now. But while they were home, I was able to make it all work. I've set up media interviews while taking 20 of my daughter's friends on a trip to Miami, while on vacation in New York City, and while tending to other family matters. It's been a perfect fit for me."

Care for a Loved One

Other times, it's not a child but an ill parent or spouse who forces some professionals to seek greater flexibility in their schedules. That's precisely what happened to Yolander Prinzel (www.YolanderPrinzel.com), a freelance writer who left a steady and secure job at a major financial services firm after her husband's heart attack made both her and her husband reevaluate their priorities.

"My husband is 19 years older than I am," says Yolander. "Because of our age difference and heart disease standing between us, I needed to find a way to spend more time with him *now*." Although Yolander's freelance income is still erratic, freelancing gives Yolander the time and flexibility she needs while supporting her and her husband financially.

"Even before his heart attack, my husband always encouraged me to take risks and become the woman that I wanted to be," Yolander says. "He has been integral to my success, and I'm so happy to be able to be there for him now."

Live a More Exciting Life

A freelance career can also be a great platform for experiencing life to the fullest. And for Marina Martin, a freelance business efficiency consultant (www.TheTypeAWay.com), fun and excitement are a top priority. Marina has set a personal goal to drink a Guinness beer in every country in the world, a feat she chronicles in her blog, Guinness Globetrotter (www. GuinnessGlobetrotter.com). Not surprisingly, Marina loves to travel, and her freelance practice enables her to do much of her work from anywhere in the world. In 2008 alone, she spent a total of 185 days away from home, including a two-month stint in Germany.

"This lifestyle would never have been possible if I weren't a freelancer," she says. "Independent professionals are infinitely more able to drop every-thing to do something fun than is someone with a demanding 9-to-5 job. In fact, I use this 'get up and go' concept to encourage my clients to look at being more organized as a way of being freer instead of being tied down."

Similarly, for freelance graphic designer Jenny Leonard (www.Razviti. com and www.whereisjenny.com), freelancing is about having the freedom to pursue long-held dreams. At age 18, Jenny wrote a list of things she wanted to accomplish in life—everything from traveling to exotic places to learning new languages and doing volunteer work. Since launching her freelance practice in 2003, she has put quite a dent on her list.

In 2006, she took six weeks off to travel to Vanuatu to volunteer for Project MARC, an organization that helps bring sustainable health care to indigenous people. And more recently, she took a five-month backpacking trip through South America, working only for a few select clients via her laptop and the occasional Internet connection. During this trip, Jenny swam with sea lions in the Galapagos, found the Lost City in Colombia, ate guinea pig (a Peruvian delicacy), hang-glided over Rio de Janeiro, climbed into a glacier, caught and ate piranha, rode a bicycle down the world's most danger-ous road, and had the adventure of a lifetime.

"Freelancing has allowed me to realize some of my wildest dreams," says Jenny. And in terms of how she's able to balance client work with a busy adventure schedule, she says, "I carefully choose my clients to fit within the culture of my life, and I work with them through long-term relationships."

Pursue Other Passions

Some people choose the freelance path so they can have more time to follow an artistic pursuit. Lisa Bell, a freelance public relations and marketing consultant, decided to go solo in 2001 so she could have more time to spend with her young son and to realize her dream of becoming a professional singer (www.LisaBellMusic.com). Thanks to the ability to alter her schedule, Lisa can sing on a regular basis at nightclubs, large festivals, and corporate events. She's also able to more easily fit in rehearsals, recording sessions, and even the occasional out-of-town singing gig.

For Phil Bundy (www.PhilBundy.com), who has a golf-marketing freelance practice, it was his toddler Charlie who inspired him to take full advantage of his freelance freedom. An avid golfer, Phil launched a quest in early 2009 to play on the PGA Golf Tour, and as of this writing, he has already won two small mini-tour events. According to Phil, his efforts are not about winning major championships but about learning the answer to the question "Can I make it on the Tour?" He also felt compelled to set a positive example for his young son to always pursue his dreams.

Says Phil, "If I were sitting in a cubicle and not self-employed, I would never have the opportunity to pursue this personal dream."

Enable the Dreams of a Loved One

A few years ago, when I was just getting my freelance business off the ground, my wife decided to go back to school to pursue a nursing degree. A long-time corporate professional, she had always dreamed of working in health care. So after leaving her corporate job to stay at home with our newborn son, she realized this was her chance to retool. Her goal was to be a registered nurse by the time our son entered the first grade. And I'm happy to report that she's almost there. In fact, this past May, she graduated from nursing school and is currently studying for her board exams. If everything goes as planned, she'll start working within weeks of our son entering the first grade.

Fortunately, my freelance career provided the flexibility we both needed to help make my wife's goal a reality. I was able to take our son to school and pick him up and stay with him in the afternoons and on weekends when my wife was in class or at the library studying. Spending this time with my son is not only a joy for me, but it allowed my wife to pursue her dream.

Improve Your Physical and Emotional Health

Thousands of people quit their jobs every year because their jobs made them sick—literally! Long-term job-related stress and anxiety can lead to major health troubles such as heart disease and high blood pressure, forcing workers to reexamine their priorities and find better alternatives.

That's where June Cramer found herself a few years ago. After having three miscarriages, June decided to quit her stressful 60-hour-a-week job to start freelancing as a writer and corporate communications professional. A year later, her son was born. "He's ten years old now and the joy of my life," she says. "I never have regretted going the freelance route, and I know that if I had stayed at my old corporate job, I probably wouldn't be a mom right now."

Buy Your Dream _____

A freelance income can also help fund purchases or enable a lifestyle that may not have been possible before. A bigger home. Nicer and more reliable cars. Or maybe a boat, a vacation home on the beach, or something that brings meaning and pleasure to your life.

As a result of working as a freelancer, Kathy Goughenour (www. LeadBoosterClub.com and www.ExpertVATraining.com) has been able to fulfill her and her husband's dream of living in a rustic cabin overlooking a beautiful Ozark stream in Missouri's Mark Twain National Forest. "Our cabin is about 50 miles from the nearest town with a Wal-Mart," explains Kathy. "We have no cell phone service and I have to use satellite Internet. My husband and I have always wanted to live out here, but there were no good jobs in the area. The Internet and the ability to freelance from home have now made it a reality. We have a great life out here!"

Set an Example

Some of the biggest and most rewarding benefits of freelancing are often completely unexpected. For freelance copywriter Kara Gray (www. NewHorizonConsult.com), one of the most positive aspects of being a freelancer is also one she never thought about until very recently.

"My six-year-old daughter is beginning to realize the possibilities of being an entrepreneur and serving as 'your own boss' (although I tell her that my clients are actually my bosses)," she explains. "She's come to recognize that 'traditional' employment isn't the only option, and that's very cool. I'm proud of the example I'm setting for her. That's something I didn't expect would happen when I first went out on my own."

Make a Difference in the World

After spending many years as an advertising creative director and writer, Joan Daidone left a high-profile job after a bout with double pneumonia and a growing impatience with corporate politics. Her goal: to be able to support herself as a freelance writer in order to devote more of her time to two lifelong passions—art and philanthropy. One of these is a nonprofit organization called Niños del Lago (www.ninosdellago.org), which provides inspiration, hope, and joyful experiences to children in Guatemala. The other is a contemporary art gallery (www.elisatucciart.com) founded by Joan and her business partner, Lisa Cooper, dedicated to changing the world through art.

Says Joan, "Although these two years have been difficult financially, in spite of the hardships, they have also been some of the most rewarding years of my life, and I wouldn't have been able to make an impact on these organizations had I not gone out on my own."

Wealthy Takeaways

- Whether you're an employee, business owner, or freelance professional, one of the biggest struggles you're likely to face is the trade-off between time and money.

- Wealthy freelancers know how to break away from this cycle by applying the strategies we discuss throughout this book. Doing so enables them to live in the Wealthy Triangle™—a point where you earn an executive-level income while enjoying the freedom and flexibility few executives have.

- Before you can move into the Wealthy Triangle™, you need to build a solid foundation on which that career can grow and thrive. This foundation requires having adequate savings, appropriate levels of insurance, and a retirement account that can fund your view of retirement.

- Wealthy freelancers don't just make a living; they design a fulfilling and meaningful life. Take time to ask yourself what life in the Wealthy Triangle™ means to *you*. Then set your goals and build a business based on that vision.

Where Do You Go from Here?

Steve Slaunwhite, Ed Gandia, and Pete Savage

There's no denying that the wealthy freelancing journey will present you with challenges, difficulties, and tough decisions. And while it's certainly not the easiest path, we believe (and we suspect you do, too) that it *is* the most rewarding one. Few careers enable you to continually choose the people you work with, the projects you work on, the income you earn, and the lifestyle you enjoy, all at the same time! And fewer still allow you to adjust each of these variables as your needs and interests evolve. Of course, there's also the satisfaction of seeing your plans, strategies, and hard work pay off—the satisfaction of generating a great income by delivering great value to your clients, not from a paycheck that may not truly reflect your individual contributions.

But there's something else. Wealthy freelancing, if you allow it, can help you experience life in full stereo and vivid Technicolor. There's something about being able to decide what you work on, whom you work with, where you go, and how you'll get there that will bring out the very best in you. It will make you come alive and help you attract more of what you want—at times, almost without effort. As you commit further to your dream of freelancing, you'll notice that people, places, and opportunities seem to suddenly align themselves in your favor.

We're not the first to offer this advice. In fact, the great German thinker and writer Goethe best described what's in store for you once you take bold action toward your dream:

> Whatever you can do, or dream you can do, begin it.
> Boldness has genius, power, and magic in it. Begin it now.

So hold fast to your vision of becoming a wealthy freelancer. Give it everything you've got, and expect good things to unfold. As you do, your whole life will become clearer, richer, and more exciting. It's the difference between seeing the movie *The Matrix* on an iPod and seeing it on a giant IMAX movie screen … in 3-D!

Fortunately, anyone can reach this level of fulfillment in his or her freelance career. All you need is the right mindset, the right strategies (which we've shared with you in this book), and the right level of action and determination.

But where do you start? How much should you do? How do you successfully implement these ideas? It's all up to you. However, if you're excited about the possibilities of wealthy freelancing, we suggest you get started *now*, while the excitement is high and you're motivated to take those first few steps. What follows is a simple framework (and a bit of inspiration) for putting the ideas in this book into action.

Determine the Size and Nature of the Gap

Start by analyzing the current state of your freelance business. What types of projects are you working on? What kind of clients are you working with? What income level are you earning? What kind of lifestyle are you enjoying? Go back to the "Wealthy Freelancer Worksheet" you filled out in the first chapter, the one where you detailed the types of projects, clients, income, and lifestyle you want. How does your current state compare to where you want to be? How big is the gap between your current state and your ideal state? Give that some thought.

Don't get discouraged if the gap seems huge. Instead, draw excitement from the fact that you alone are in control of bridging that gap. Not your manager, not some bureaucrat, not some sort of exploratory committee. Yes, you may have some work to do, but take comfort in knowing that most of the secrets to helping you narrow that gap are contained in this book.

Put Your Plan into Action

As we suggested in the first chapter, rather than letting the ideas in this book overwhelm you, pick a few strategies you'd like to implement over the next few weeks and create a simple action plan for putting them into play. But don't just stop there. After you've drafted your plan, *write down three simple and quick steps you can take in the next three days to help implement the first item on your list.*

Following this advice is crucial if you wish to move quickly toward your wealthy lifestyle; so get your pen handy and identify those three things now! Pick something you could do immediately, something you can do tomorrow, and something you can do the day after. These tasks shouldn't take you long to accomplish, and they should be tasks that will give you quick wins, even if they're small, psychological victories.

For instance, if the first idea you want to implement is to revisit your goals and set bigger and better ones, maybe your first task is to sit down with your spouse or significant other this evening and talk openly about where you want to be 1, 3, 5, and 10 years from now. On day two, based on that conversation, you could carve out 30 minutes to write down both your long-term and short-term goals. And on day three, you could spend an hour breaking down each of your one-year goals into monthly milestones and weekly action items. Frankly, it doesn't really matter what three tasks you pick for this exercise, as long as they help you implement one of the secrets—and as long as you commit to doing them as if your life depended on their accomplishment.

Don't underestimate the effect these baby steps will have on your psyche. Taking even the smallest action will get you on the right path and will start building the momentum you need to keep yourself focused.

Think "Ready, Fire, Aim"

According to Michael Masterson, author of the bestselling book *Ready, Fire, Aim: Zero to $100 Million in No Time Flat* (Wiley, 2008), most people spend too much time trying to get things just right before they take action. In other words, they practice a "ready, aim, fire" philosophy. Masterson says, "The nothing-less-than-perfect attitude has been the theme of many success stories, but it is exactly the wrong notion to have in your head when it's time to launch a new product or business. When the time is right, you must fire. If you spend another moment aiming, the opportunity to hit your target may pass you by."

So if you're just now launching your freelance business, don't wait to start prospecting until you have a logo, business cards, a great-looking website, and an impressive portfolio. Instead, tap into your network to find businesses you can help, even if you do it for a highly discounted fee. If you're already an established freelancer, don't let perfection get in the way of action. Go back through this book and make a list of all the ideas you want to implement. Prioritize them, draft a simple plan for putting them into practice, and then take action!

Remember: it doesn't matter where you get started. Just get started somewhere ... now!

Don't Put Your Goal on a Pedestal

Every worthwhile goal we've reached became far easier to attain when we stopped thinking about the goal's "grandness."

For instance, as a sales professional, Ed started landing big software deals only after he downplayed the difficulty and skill necessary to be successful at it. He also resigned from his job to become a full-time freelancer, but only after he realized that doing so was just the last step in a well-executed plan.

When Steve wanted to achieve his dream of writing a book, at first it seemed overwhelming. Who was he to think he could be a successful author? It was only when he focused on the first step—learning how to create a winning book proposal—that he eventually had a breakthrough. Today he has six books to his credit and counting.

When Pete wanted to step up the caliber of his clientele and start doing freelance work for large, well-known corporations, he put his fears aside and took massive action by building a self-promotion strategy from scratch. That campaign—a direct-mail package that he wrote, printed, and then manually assembled on his dining room table—landed him a lucrative retainer contract with the largest corporation in Canada!

The moral here: don't put your goal of wealthy freelancing on a pedestal. Think of it as completely achievable, as natural and mundane a goal as saying you'll wake up at 6 A.M. tomorrow. When you take away the goal's "grandness," you take away its power over you. And once you're no longer standing in the dark shadow of the gargantuan goal that once towered before you, you can begin taking action to accomplish it.

Be Tenacious

The biggest reason freelancers fail to develop a wealthy business is not a lack of opportunity, it's giving up too soon. Too many aspiring freelancers get discouraged at the first sign of rejection and decide that maybe the opportunity is not real. And a staggering number of experienced freelancers, jaded after years of grinding it out the old-fashioned way, conclude that this level of performance is reserved for a few lucky souls.

Nothing could be further from the truth. The ideas and advice contained in this book come directly from the trenches. Each of us has used these ideas and strategies to develop wealthy freelance businesses in a relatively short period of time—and so have thousands of our coaching students, newsletter subscribers, and readers of our blog, TheWealthyFreelancer.com.

Interestingly, each of us came from very different circumstances and faced very different challenges when we each decided we wanted to change the way we made a living. Ed had become disillusioned with the exhausting treadmill of direct sales. He wanted to take charge of his future so he could be home with his young family and have more control over his career. But Ed didn't want to sacrifice his six-figure income or his family's financial future in the process. Therefore, he developed a methodical action plan to go from successful salesperson to successful freelancer, a process that took 27 months of hard work to complete.

Pete, on the other hand, was pushed "backward and blindfolded" into the world of freelancing when he was fired from his job at a boutique marketing agency. For Pete, there was no time for self-pity at the loss of his job. Instead, he began mentally plotting his move to become a freelance copywriter *during his dismissal interview!* That was on a Friday. By Monday morning, Pete had landed his first freelance gig.

And Steve, well, he just plain hated being an employee. He admired his father, who had been successfully self-employed all his life. Steve wanted to do the same, so he combined his writing, teaching, and marketing skills to make that happen.

It's All Worth It!

At the end of the day, is it worth it? Is pursuing a wealthy freelance business worth the trouble, pain, effort, and inevitable disappointments along the way? Absolutely it is! And it's worth it no matter where you are in your career or what wealthy freelancing means to you. In fact, the challenges you will face in the pursuit of a wealthy freelance business are not that much greater than those you will encounter if you opt for the status quo.

But the rewards from wealthy freelancing are so much sweeter!

Famous motivational speaker Jim Rohn once said, "We must all suffer from one of two pains: the pain of discipline or the pain of regret. Discipline weighs ounces, regret weighs tons."

Pay the price. Endure the pain of discipline. You'll be a better person for it. You'll inspire others. And you'll live in peace knowing you truly made the most of your talents and your time while on this Earth.

Are you prepared for what's to come? You bet you are! You've just read the book, now go live the life. And be sure to savor the moment when it comes, that moment when you realize that The Wealthy Freelancer … is *you*.

And then please share your wealthy freelancing story with us. Visit our blog at www.TheWealthyFreelancer.com/success.

Opportunities and Obstacles to Becoming a Wealthy Freelancer

Steve Slaunwhite, Ed Gandia, and Pete Savage

The 12 secrets we've covered in this book feature more than 50 great ideas that will help you attract the projects, clients, income, and lifestyle you want. But on the road to wealthy freelancing, there are some special opportunities, along with a few nasty obstacles, that you're bound to run into and that will have either a positive or negative impact on your business. It all depends on how you deal with them. In this appendix, we take a closer look at the most common "Double O's" and provide you with tips and strategies on making the best of these situations.

Our advice comes from the school of hard knocks. In our own freelance businesses, we've had to deal with everything you'll read about in the following pages! And we know only too well the mistakes that can be made.

Think of this appendix as a kind of freelancer's emergency room. When you come across an opportunity or obstacle and you're not sure what to do, check these pages for some helpful advice.

A Piece of the Action—Is It Worth Considering?

As a freelance professional, there's no doubt you'll run into situations where a client wants you to work for a percentage of sales or profits or some other results-based compensation model rather than a traditional project fee. You'll encounter this more with entrepreneurial business owners than with larger corporate clients. It's often referred to as a *contingency fee arrangement*.

Should you consider such a deal? After all, you could earn more for the project than you would have otherwise. Perhaps a lot more. On the other hand, you could end up suffering the freelancing equivalent of losing your shirt—working long hours on a project and receiving no money in return.

Here's a typical example of what you might hear: "Dave, we want you to create an e-mail campaign for us that promotes our new Product X. We'll pay you 15 percent of all sales your campaign generates."

When you get an offer like that from a client, it's a little like being on the game show *Deal or No Deal*. You're being asked to trade a suitcase that has a guaranteed project fee inside for one that may contain a lot more—or a lot less—money. It's a risk. And you can win or lose.

In our experience, most of these types of offers are *not* good ones for freelance professionals. They often come from business owners who don't have the money to hire you (that's why they're offering you a contingency deal instead) or, worse, are trying to rip you off. However, there are some circumstances when such a deal can be a good opportunity for you. One of us recently freelanced for a seminar producer on a commission basis and earned many times the income he would have normally.

So how do you decide: deal or no deal?

Your first step is to gain a *realistic* understanding of what the income potential is for you. If the client is launching a brand-new type of product no one has heard of, to an industry that doesn't know his company, and the whole thing is being done on a shoestring budget, then, frankly, success is a long shot. You might as well go to a casino so you can at least enjoy a margarita while you're losing your money.

However, if your client is well known in the industry, has an excellent track record of success, and is reputable, then his offer to work for a piece of the action might just be worth your serious consideration.

Bottom line, use common sense when making your decision. Ideally, you want to work in this manner with a client you already know, at least by reputation. If you're toiling away on a contingency fee basis for a stranger, you're taking your chances. If you don't know the client, at least ask for references.

Don't let a client sway you with his big dreams of sales, profits, and success. It's fine that a client is enthusiastic about his business; in fact, that's a good sign. But for you, a contingency fee arrangement is a serious business decision requiring a cool head. Ask yourself these questions: Do you like this client? Does he seem reputable, honest, and reliable? Do you really want to work with him in this way? If there is any nagging doubt, say no.

If your fees for the project are going to be contingent on sales, clicks, conversions, downloads, or something else that's trackable, ask to have access to the reports. The most reliable reports are those that come from an outside source, such as the client's online payment processor.

Avoid a deal where your commission is calculated on profits. There's just too many ways profits can be calculated, and you might find that after the client has applied every arcane expense against the revenues, there's little left over. Instead, ask for a percentage of something clearly trackable and beyond dispute, such as sales.

Also ask for a nonrefundable advance payment before you start the project. A 50 percent deposit against your expected commissions or other form of contingency payment isn't unreasonable. If a client is confident about the mutual success of the deal, he won't have a problem with your request. If he balks, it's a red flag.

And don't forget to get everything in writing. You want a no-wiggle-room agreement as to exactly how and when you'll get paid, your access to sales figures and other reports, and precisely what you're required to do on the project.

Dealing With Endless Reviews and Revisions

There's a funny variation of a Norman Martin children's song we heard employees singing at a design firm recently. "This is the job that never ends! It just goes on and on, my friend! We took on this stupid project, not knowing what it was. And now we keep revising it, forever, just because! This is the job that never ends …."

When a project drags on and on, with seemingly endless requests from the client for revisions, it's not only stressful but also eats into your income. You're held back from moving on to other paying work. How do wealthy freelancers deal with this? We have some ideas.

First, spell out in your quotations, proposals, and agreements how many rounds of revisions are included in the project fee. And put a time limit on revision requests. The policy of many freelance writers and copywriters, for example, is to accept revision requests up to 30 days after submitting the draft.

Clearly define in your quotations, proposals, and agreements exactly what a revision is. Otherwise, a client might think a major change in the direction or scope of a project is just a revision—and one you should do for free. It's perfectly okay to charge a separate fee for revisions that aren't covered in your original quotation. Just be sure to communicate this policy to the client.

When going over revision requests with the client, ask if these are the *final* revision requests. If not, explain that you prefer to receive all such requests at one time rather than piecemeal. This will go a long way in preventing revisions from dragging on.

When you do receive a revision request, send the client an e-mail confirming exactly what you will be revising and changing.

Find out in advance who will be reviewing your work. Do you have just one person to please? Or a committee? If the "review committee" is large, factor this in when quoting the job.

Finally, when submitting your work, include a note that explains how you would like to receive your revision requests and your policy regarding them. Freelance copywriter and Internet marketing strategist Bob Bly includes this cover note with the copy he submits to clients:

> Please keep in mind that this is a preliminary draft. As you read, you may find extraneous information you want to delete, or think of missing information you want to add. You may want to change the organization of the piece, or make wording changes to heads and body copy. Please do so without hesitation, marking your comments directly on this manuscript. That will give us the best draft possible. At this point, you can make as many changes as you want, without cost or delay of any kind. *Note:* If we do not hear back from you within 30 days, we assume there are no changes and you approve the copy as-is.

When the Client Says "Your Work Sucks"

> "I just reviewed the draft you sent me and I have concerns. Please call me immediately."

Now there's a voicemail message no freelancer wants to hear! Few things are more distressing than a client who is less than pleased with your copy, design, illustration, script, video, report, or other freelance work. You're going to take it personally, at least to some degree. Everyone does.

But before you do anything, take a deep breath. You may even want to take a walk around the block or make yourself a cup of tea. You don't want to let your emotions guide how you're going to handle this.

When you do call the client, your goal is not to seem defensive or even disappointed. What you want is for him or her to feel reassured that a prompt revision or other change—done by you, of course—will make it all better. Our 6-step strategy will help you do just that:

1. Don't be defensive.

2. Explain your approach.

3. Ask for specifics.

4. Confirm the requested changes.

5. Set a deadline.

6. Complete the revisions exactly as directed.

(This strategy uses freelance copywriting as an example but can be easily adapted to any kind of freelance work.)

Don't Be Defensive

You want feedback, not combat. Listen carefully to the client and try to determine what went wrong. Be open to criticism, suggestions, and new ideas. Don't act angry or defensive, even if you disagree. Be the consummate professional.

Explain Your Approach

Sometimes the client doesn't understand why you wrote something the way you did. You may need to explain your strategy or justify a particular element.

Steve once wrote a direct-mail sale letter for the owner of a very small company. When the client saw that Steve had used a P.S. in the copy, he balked. "Hey. Is this really necessary?" But once Steve explained that a postscript in a sale letter almost always gets noticed and read—and is therefore an ideal place to put an important key message—the client agreed to keep it in.

Ask for Specifics

Never accept vague feedback like, "Paragraph three just doesn't work for me." Nail down specifics. Ask your client such questions as …

- Are all the facts correct?
- Am I missing anything?
- Is there any extraneous information I should delete?
- Are there any awkward passages or transitions?
- Did I explain all the features and benefits clearly and persuasively?
- Does the style, tone, and vocabulary fit the target audience?

Don't guess. Know what needs to be fixed *before* you revise the copy.

Confirm the Requested Changes

Once you've gone through the copy and clarified the areas that need revision, confirm those details with the client. Be sure you're both in agreement as to exactly what you'll be improving or changing. There should be no surprises when you submit your new draft.

Set a Deadline

Never say, "I'll turn this revision around in a couple days." Always confirm exactly when you'll complete and submit the revised draft.

An exact date-and-time deadline is very reassuring to a client. "I'll complete this revision this week and will e-mail the new draft to you on Thursday by 1 P.M. Does that work for you?"

Complete the Revisions Exactly as Directed

When revising the copy, you may be tempted to explore new angles or try new ideas. Don't. Complete the revisions exactly as requested. If you have a great idea, present it separately.

This 6-step strategy works; it really does. As one freelancer told us, "I've had clients go from being unhappy with the copy to praising my writing skills and offering me more work—all during the same phone call!—simply because I followed these steps."

So the next time you receive the dreaded "We need to talk" phone call or e-mail, you know what to do. Keep your chin up. Follow the steps. Act professional. Then get to work on those revisions.

Who's Your Ideal Client? (and Why It Matters)

Making good decisions about which clients and projects you pursue and which ones you turn down all starts with what we call the "ideal client profile," which is simply a description of the type of client you would love to have more of.

Imagine you own an Airstream recreational vehicle. You're planning a road trip from New York to San Francisco, and you have room for up to six friends. Wouldn't you limit your invitations to people whose company you truly enjoy? Of course you would. Well, it's no different when you're a freelancer.

Let's take Ed as an example. As a copywriter, his ideal client is a midsize to large software company. His primary contact can make copy decisions on her own without consulting with a review committee. She values Ed as a key member of her team, so his fees are not an issue, especially considering the unique perspective he brings to the table as an experienced marketer and sales professional. Finally, Ed's ideal client has a steady stream of work for him. She doesn't come to him with just a one-time need.

Of course, this doesn't mean Ed automatically turns down opportunities that don't meet every single one of his criteria. What it means is that he carefully qualifies every potential client and project based on a list of criteria that make sense to him. Factors you may want to consider in your decision can include these:

- The added prestige to be gained from working with this client (if any)
- The desirability of the project in question
- Where you currently are in your career
- How much capacity you currently have
- The project's turnaround time
- The perceived difficulty of working with the client
- Whether or not the client is willing to pay your fee
- The client's apparent ability to pay on time
- How difficult it may be to secure the business
- How badly you need the work

These aren't the only factors to consider, but they're some of the most important.

But what if you're just getting started in your freelance business? In that case, you need to consider both short- and long-term objectives when making these decisions. Just be sure that as your business grows, you draft a clear description of the types of clients and projects that are right for *you* and use that as your guide.

Remember, it's a long ride from New York to San Francisco. Be careful who you take with you.

The 75 Percent Solution to More Efficient Prospecting

As a freelancer, one of your most valuable resources is your time. So as a general rule, you should try to spend as much of your day as possible on billable work while reducing the time you spend on nonbillable activities. One way to do this is to ensure that your prospecting efforts, website, key messages, and other materials do an excellent job of helping prospects self-qualify (that is, helping them determine whether they should call you). This helps reduce the time you spend talking to (and putting proposals together for) low-quality prospects.

Think of the effort it takes to convert a prospect into a client as the distance between two points. Before the prospect even knows you exist, he's at point A. As he finds out about you and your services, he moves closer to point B, which is the point where you actually land the work.

To be a wealthy freelancer, your long-term goal should be to have your marketing materials and website produce only prospects who are at least 75 percent "sold" on hiring you before they even make their first contact. In other words, prospects who are three-quarters of the way to point B. These are prospects who already understand the true value of a freelancer in your field and who realize that a high-caliber professional doesn't come cheaply.

Granted, there's no scientific way to measure whether a prospect is actually 75 percent sold. The point is that you want to get to a place in your career where your reputation and/or your marketing materials and messages do most of the heavy lifting for you. So if someone is roughly three-quarters of the way to hiring you, it means you have only 25 percent of the way left to go. That means you can use the initial contact to start a meaningful dialogue, not to sell the person on the value of hiring a freelancer or explaining why he should even consider you. Over time, this enables you to spend less time "selling" and more time working on client projects.

How can you tell if a prospect is mostly sold on hiring you? Pay particular attention to important signals. For instance, a close match to your ideal client profile (discussed earlier in this appendix) is a telling sign. Also, consider the prospect's source. On average, a prospect who comes to you via a client referral, a referral from someone you know well, one of your direct-mail campaigns, or an industry association you're involved with is probably better matched than, say, someone who found you via a Google search (which means that he's probably talking to three or four other freelancers).

This attitude may come across as elitist, but it's really not. In fact, this approach actually helps your prospects just as much as it helps you. People don't want to waste time talking to a service provider who can't help them or who they can't afford.

So what can you do to help prospects self-qualify? Here are a few ideas:

- Be sure your marketing materials (including your website) are written for prospects who already understand the value of hiring a freelance professional in your field. Again, don't try to sell the value of your profession. Enough prospects will "get it" to avoid wasting time on those who don't.

- Take a stand. Be clear about the type of work you do and *don't* do, as well as the type of clients you work with.

- Be explicit about what makes you different. Don't try to be everything to everyone.

- Consider developing a specialty and communicating why you're the obvious choice for that type of work or for that industry.

- Add credibility elements to support your claims. This could be in the way of samples, testimonials, client lists, success stories, awards, and so on.

How to Avoid the "Getting Paid" Nightmare

Aside from picking good clients, there are simple things you can do as a freelancer to increase the chances of getting paid on time, every time.

First, always put it down on paper. At the end of the day, a simple written contract trumps a verbal agreement should things go wrong. Period. You may not need anything fancy. But be sure the basics are there—scope of work, deadlines, payment terms, and so on. At a minimum, having a written agreement sets the tone for the type of business you operate. Seek legal counsel on these matters. Your attorney will tell you what you need to include in your agreement and what factors you should consider. It will be money well spent.

Next, get a deposit from new clients. With all new clients, the three of us always insist on a deposit of 30 to 50 percent of the total project value *before* starting work. You should, too. Asking for a deposit is a common industry practice. Your client should understand this and be willing to pay it. If you get resistance, that should be a red flag that this client may carry more risk than you want.

Tie final payment to submission of *initial* draft or comp. Your payment terms should clearly state that final payment is due within a specified period after submission of your initial draft, comp, or sample, not the final version. In other words, your payment shouldn't be delayed just because the client is taking longer than usual to review your submission. This is a very reasonable request, and we can't overemphasize its importance.

Be flexible, but limit your exposure. If you have a steady, high-volume client, he or she may prefer a simpler invoicing structure. One approach that can work well in these situations is to invoice twice a month (on the 15th and 30th) for all work submitted over the prior 15-day period. That keeps the client from getting 10 different invoices from you every month. And it limits your exposure to only two weeks' worth of work.

Use a "kill fee" provision. Should the client terminate the project midstream for whatever reason (budget constraints, change of direction, new priorities), you need to be protected. No reasonable client would expect you to eat those hours. So make it clear in your written agreement that a "kill fee" will apply should the project be cancelled or put on hold before you submit a draft. That fee should be based on the total number of hours you've put in and a predetermined hourly rate.

Follow up every time a payment is late. Make it a habit of following up on every invoice that's more than three to five days overdue. Don't be shy. In most cases, past-due invoices are the result of an oversight, not an unwillingness to pay. This is especially true for larger companies, where things can fall through the cracks more easily. Good clients understand that your livelihood depends on getting paid on time. They won't mind your follow-up. And they'll respect you for your diligence.

The Real Value of Tracking Your Time

Even if you quote most of your work as a flat project fee, you should still track your time. Why? Because you'll develop better pricing intelligence. Knowing how much time you spend on projects enables you to adjust your project fees as you learn what it takes to get the job done right. It also helps you see which types of projects and clients are profitable and which are not.

You'll also develop more accurate scheduling. When you know the average time a certain type of project will take, scheduling becomes a lot easier. You don't have to guess. You can just plug an average into your schedule and add a few extra hours as a cushion. That means you're not always scrambling to get the work done. And you're not turning down work because you've overestimated your current workload.

You'll also gain clearer visibility into your monthly billable time. If you haven't tracked your time before, you'll be shocked when you start doing it—shocked at how little billable time you actually have every week. When Ed started freelancing, he used to think that 90 percent of his time was spent on billable work. But it was closer to 65 percent when he ran the numbers. By facing reality first, he was able to dig deeper into the causes and find opportunities to increase that percentage.

You'll achieve greater discipline. There's something about knowing you're "on the clock" that makes most of us work more efficiently. Plus, when you track your time, your goal is to end up with an accurate time estimate for every project, which means you'll be less likely to surf the web, read the news, watch TV, or check your stocks when you should be working.

In terms of time-tracking tools, there are a few good ones out there. Steve and Ed use TraxTime (www.traxtime.com). It's not the best tool for report generation, but it works just like a punch clock, so it's super easy to use. Mac users have other options. We keep hearing that On The Job from Stunt Software (www.stuntsoftware.com/OnTheJob) is a great option—and not too expensive at $24.95. It doesn't really matter what you use. Just stick with something that works for you, and learn how to use it strategically to improve your business.

How to "Fire" a Client Gracefully

Why would you fire a client? For any number of reasons. As your freelance business grows, not all clients will be able to keep up with your rate increases or wait for their projects to be fit into your schedule. You'll also encounter clients whom you simply don't enjoy working with, but whom you put up with because you need the work.

Whatever the reason for firing a client, you want to do the firing with professionalism and integrity. Here's how:

1. Be honest. Give them an honest reason why you're moving on. Not only is it the courteous and professional thing to do, it also helps your contact communicate the reason to others. "We can't use Joe for graphic design services anymore because ...."

2. Be clear. Do not waver in the language you use. Make it absolutely clear that you won't be servicing them anymore.

3. Be professional. If you can, offer to connect them with another free-lancer. At the very least, thank them for their business in the past.

4. Temper emotional language. This is a business decision, so watch how much emotion you inject. It's okay to be human, but if you're too emotional ("I'm really, really sorry ..."), you'll actually make it sound personal, causing the client to have a personal reaction to being fired.

Can you fire a client via e-mail? Absolutely. In fact, you should, so there's a record of you severing the ties. Should you also phone the client? That's a judgment call you can make, based on the degree to which you want your relationship to hold up after you part ways.

Although you should always try to end relationships on good terms, real-ize that once in a while a client may take offense. If a client reacts negatively despite your best efforts to sever the ties amicably, there's nothing you can do about that. There's no need to feel bad or guilty and, more to the point, you absolutely shouldn't try to make the client feel better. Besides, you'll likely find that the client who reacts negatively is the one whom you didn't particularly like to begin with.

Remember the "Set Standards and Prosper" section you read about in Secret 1? Always measure clients against your standards and know that those clients who don't measure up will eventually either leave of their own accord or ultimately be fired by you. When the time is right, fire these clients and make room for better ones!

Don't Be Afraid to Say "Yes"

There will come a time when you get a call from a client asking you to do a project you've never done before. If the project sounds interesting, say "Yes!"

Don't let fear stop you from what could be a great learning experience, a well-paying assignment, and perhaps even your first step toward becoming an expert in that particular project type!

Many clients, upon contacting you, will be ready to hand you the project as soon as you say yes. This is what happened to Steve. A client once called him to ask if he'd be interested in writing an annual report. Steve said yes and got the job. After he hung up the phone, Steve began the frantic process of researching annual reports and figuring out how to write them! This was the beginning of several annual report projects for Steve over the years—projects he never would have gotten had he been too afraid to say yes to that first opportunity.

Sometimes, however, you'll find you actually have to sell the client on your ability to complete the project if you've never done it before. This is exactly what happened to Pete the first time a client asked him to write a case study. The client began by asking, "We need to produce some case studies. Have you written any before?" He hadn't! But he wanted the project, so he offered this honest, and persuasive, reply:

> I must admit I've never written a case study before. However, I've written all kinds of press releases and newsletter articles. And the process for writing a case study is exactly the same. It comes down to researching the scenario and asking the right questions to draw the story out of the interviewee. Then as the writer, it's up to me to write the story in a compelling and engaging style. So far, each time I've gone through this process, the end result has been in the form of a press release or a newsletter article, but I could just as easily create a case study for you.

Although he'd never written one before, Pete's response convinced the client he was up to the job. Since then, Pete's become an expert in writing case studies—an expertise that came from being willing to say yes when asked to do a project that was new to him.

We usually get the most satisfaction, and growth, by having the courage to do those things that initially scare us. Say yes to new projects, and watch your freelance business grow.

Avoid the Client Who Makes Big Promises

> "Can you give me a price break on this first project? Trust me, we have a ton more work to send you in the future."

When you hear a client say this, your answer should be a polite "No." This is an empty promise. Most every freelancer who has agreed to this scenario has a story about how he or she agreed to a reduced fee (or even agreed to work for free!) because of some loose "understanding" that more work would come their way. Unfortunately, all these stories have the same ending—the boatload of promised work never comes!

Resolve now that you will not reduce your fee for the promise of future work. It's better to say no to the proposition and spend the time you would have spent working on the project (poorly paid time anyway) looking for clients who will pay your fees.

Prevent Freelance Burnout Before It Happens

Burnout is a very real and common problem among freelancers. It happens for one reason: you take on too much work. Although no one who has ever suffered from burnout likes the experience, lots of freelancers experience it more than once. Let's look at some things you can do to prevent it.

Start by reassessing your work-scheduling process. On any given day, you should have an idea how full your schedule is and when—that is, on what exact date—you can take on new work. Doing so is much easier than it sounds. For each of the projects on your plate, estimate how long, in hours, they will take to complete. Map these project hours onto a calendar, based on how many hours per day you have for billable project work. (Activities like checking e-mail, entering receipts, and marketing your business are not billable project work hours.) For example, if you know you tend to work productively for, more or less, 6 hours per day, and you have projects totaling 40 hours on deck, that means you can't begin another project for seven work days.

Of course, you *can* agree to take on work before those seven days roll around. If a terrific new client calls you with a mouthwatering rush job and you want to take it on, go for it. Just know that by doing so you're going to be pushing yourself to your creative and even physical limits. It's wise to schedule a day or two off for respite when the crazy stretch comes to an end.

⟨⟩ Wealthy Tip

For more help in managing your workload, see the Jigsaw Puzzle Visual™ explained in Secret 10.

It also helps to find better-quality clients—those who pay well and send work your way regularly versus once in a while. One of the best ways to prevent burnout is to be constantly increasing the quality of your client base. By finding better-quality clients, you can work less and earn more. What's more, over time, you can become quite knowledgeable about their business. This accumulated knowledge will cut down on the amount of time you need to spend learning the basics about the company or industry. You'll spend less time working on projects for clients with whom you're already oriented and up to speed, as opposed to constantly engaging and learning about new clients.

Finally, developing multiple sources of income also helps. Secret 11 shows you how to develop alternative sources of income so you can earn money by doing things that don't require you to bill for your time.

Don't Get Too Comfortable!

As a freelancer, when you're making decent money and feeling little pressure, it becomes too easy and enjoyable to "go with the flow." With all the bills paid up, and no immediate need to bring in more business, you can become undisciplined. Maybe you start to sleep in an extra hour or two. You lose focus. You spend a little more time each day surfing around on Facebook, e-mailing friends, and generally wasting time.

Tony Robbins calls being comfortable the "death rattle" for your personal finances! Why? Because there's no outside pressure to work harder and make more money. When you have enough money to experience a certain level of comfort, you tend to get lazy. You don't pick up the phone and call clients. You don't send out sales letters, and you stop thinking about creative ways to find new business.

Money in the bank and a few happy clients can be the death rattle for freelancers because these things give us a false sense of security. But remember, the defining characteristic of freelance work is that it's *project based*. And all projects come to an end, so you must keep up your search for new projects by *consistently* marketing your services.

Most freelancers are strapped into the feast-and-famine roller coaster because they only get out and market themselves when they're desperate for money! But keep marketing even when you're doing well, and you'll find those famine periods become fewer and eventually disappear forever. Step off that roller coaster once and for all, and start living the balanced, wealthy freelancer life you deserve.

Index

B

C

G

N

T

About the Authors

Steve Slaunwhite is a popular marketing coach, award-winning copywriter, speaker, and author of several books and learning programs, including *The Complete Idiot's Guide to Starting a Web-Based Business, The Everything Guide to Writing Copy,* and *Fast Track to Great Clients*. He is the co-founder of TheWealthyFreelancer.com, the foremost blog for freelance professionals, and the creator of ForCopywritersOnly.com, a highly respected resource site for corporate writers and copywriters. A sought-after speaker, Steve leads more than 75 seminars and training sessions each year.

Pete Savage is an award-winning copywriter, marketing consultant, author, speaker, and coach. As co-founder of TheWealthyFreelancer.com, he provides guidance, strategy, and motivation to help freelance professionals achieve their potential. Pete is also the founder and host of UltimateSupperClub.com, an audio interview series focused on success and human potential. Pete lives in Peterborough, Ontario, Canada, with his wife, two children, and Ringo, the family Weimaraner.

Ed Gandia is a successful copywriter, marketing consultant, speaker, coach, and author. An expert on the topic of successfully transitioning from employee to freelancer, he is the co-founder of TheWealthyFreeelancer.com and author of the popular e-book *Stop Wishing and Start Earning: A Low-Risk Plan to Escape 9–5 and Launch a Profitable Copywriting Business*. Ed is a self-proclaimed wine geek and lives with his wife, son, and two dogs in Marietta, Georgia.